ADVANCE PRAISE FOR
Teaching Emancipation and Reconstruction, 1861–1876

"Teaching Emancipation and Reconstruction introduces the questions of Reconstruction that have loomed over the era in many educational institutions. The authors promise and deliver on providing the multiple perspectives that students, teachers and historical enthusiast can use to engage with Reconstruction through the eyes of every American then and now."
—Nichelle Pinkney, Social Studies Coordinator and Author of Civil Discourse: Classroom Conversations for Stronger Communities

"The authors aim to move beyond the traditional textbook approach and effectively bridge the gap between the past and the present while ensuring the inclusion of truthful history. This work offers a deeper understanding of the Reconstruction period, providing educators and students with the knowledge to navigate the critical racial progress of that time. As many social studies and history curricula across the country continue to overlook Black History in classrooms, this volume offers the opportunity to reshape the teaching of Emancipation and Reconstruction."
—Michelle Tovar, Ed.D., Director of Education, Buffalo Soldiers National Museum

Teaching Emancipation and Reconstruction, 1861–1876

Caroline R. Pryor, Erik B. Alexander, James M. Mitchell,
Whitney Blankenship, Michael E. Karpyn, and Jenice L. View

General Editors

Vol. 5

Teaching Emancipation and Reconstruction, 1861–1876

Edited by
Matthew R. Campbell

PETER LANG
New York · Berlin · Bruxelles · Chennai · Lausanne · Oxford

Library of Congress Cataloging-in-Publication Data

Names: Campbell, Matthew R. editor.
Title: Teaching emancipation and reconstruction, 1861–1876 / edited by Matthew R. Campbell.
Description: New York : Peter Lang, [2025] | Series: Teaching critical themes in American history, 2576–0718; vol. 5 | Includes bibliographical references and index.
Identifiers: LCCN 2024035579 (print) | LCCN 2024035580 (ebook) | ISBN 9781433184277 (paperback) | ISBN 9783034351799 (pdf) | ISBN 9783034351805 (epub)
Subjects: LCSH: Reconstruction (U.S. history, 1865-1877)–Study and teaching. | Enslaved persons–Emancipation–United States–Study and teaching. | United States–Race relations–History–Study and teaching. | African Americans–History–Study and teaching.
Classification: LCC E668 .T26 2025 (print) | LCC E668 (ebook) | DDC 973.8071–dc23/eng/20241108
LC record available at https://lccn.loc.gov/2024035579
LC ebook record available at https://lccn.loc.gov/2024035580
DOI 10.3726/b22167

Bibliographic information published by the Deutsche Nationalbibliothek.
The German National Library lists this publication in the German National Bibliography; detailed bibliographic data is available on the Internet at http://dnb.d-nb.de.

Cover design by Peter Lang Group AG

ISSN 2576-0718 (print) ISSN 2576-0726 (online)
ISBN 9781433184277 (paperback)
ISBN 9783034351799 (ebook)
ISBN 9783034351805 (epub)
DOI 10.3726/b22167

© 2025 Peter Lang Group AG, Lausanne
Published by Peter Lang Publishing Inc., New York, USA
info@peterlang.com - www.peterlang.com

All rights reserved.
All parts of this publication are protected by copyright.
Any utilization outside the strict limits of the copyright law, without the permission of the publisher, is forbidden and liable to prosecution.
This applies in particular to reproductions, translations, microfilming, and storage and processing in electronic retrieval systems.

This publication has been peer reviewed.

Teaching Emancipation and Reconstruction, 1861–1876
Editor: Matthew R. Campbell

Table of Contents

Preface	ix
About the Book Series Teaching Critical Themes in American History	xi
Acknowledgments	xiii
Introduction: Teaching, Learning, and Historiography Matthew R. Campbell	1
Chapter One: Teaching Emancipation as Racial Progress and Reconstruction Violence as Racist Progress Shannon M. Smith	7
Chapter Two: Dismantling Scarlett O'Hara: How Slaveholding White Women Supported Slavery and Resisted Emancipation Kristen Brill	21
Chapter Three: Jus Post Bellum and the Moral Imperatives of Reconstruction Kent A. McConnell	31
Chapter Four: A Reconstruction Timeline Jenice L. View	69

Chapter Five: Drawing Conclusions: Using Political Cartoons in the Classroom to Analyze Reconstruction Era Images of African Americans   93
Tim Dorsch

Chapter Six: Representations of Reconstruction: Social Transformations and Textbook Portrayals of the Past   115
Adam J. Schmitt and Ashley Towle

Chapter Seven: The Road to the 19th Amendment: Examining the Women's Suffrage Movement during the Reconstruction Era with Historical Empathy Pedagogies   135
Katherine Perrotta

Chapter Eight: Reconstruction's Accomplishment: Black Education and the Rise of the Civil Rights Movement   153
Scott L. Stabler, Justin Sheldon, and Timothy J. McKeeby

Chapter Nine: "There Is No Redemption from Our History": Reconstruction, Memorialization, and Public Memory   173
Mark Pearcy

Chapter Ten: Reconstruction Resources   191
Jenice L. View, Caroline R. Pryor, and Amy Wilkinson

Contributor Biographies   205

Index   209

Preface

This series of volumes began as an introspective on themes often less discussed in public schools, grades 7–12. As the series progressed, the theme of civil rights emerged from the contributors' essays, lesson plans and resources and served to focus the approach to our series. It appeared to us (the editorial team), that we truly are a nation that began our exploration of civil rights much earlier than is typically taught in schools. In part, as John Marshall Harlan chided in his discussion [dissent] from Plessy v. Ferguson (see Thernstom & Ravitch, 1992)—the nation's forging was grounded in civil liberty and codified, albeit imperfectly—in civil rights. It is to this end, the exploration and importance of the historical journey of civil rights that we present the editorial leadership of Matthew Campbell and the authors of this volume.

Caroline R. Pryor, Series Editor, on behalf of the Editorial Team, Erik Alexander, James Mitchell, Whitney Blankenship, Jenice View and Michael Karpyn.

REFERENCE:

Ravitch, D., & Thernstrom, A. (1992). *The Democracy Reader: Classic and Modern Speeches, Essays, Poems, Declarations and Documents on Freedom and Human Rights Worldwide.* New York: HarperPerennial.

About the Book Series Teaching Critical Themes in American History

In working with teachers who had developed lesson plans for our earlier publication on Abraham Lincoln, the theme that we (Pryor & Hansen) most often discussed was the nature and embodiment of civil rights and civil liberties. We learned from teachers who participated in our workshops that the challenges of teaching main events of the Lincoln era were many—however, the larger challenge was how to teach *critical themes* of this era, such as the topic of slavery—and civil liberty. A challenge for these teachers had been how to address critical issues emanating from Lincoln's announcement of the Emancipation Proclamation. What role would newly free slaves have? Would they be citizens? If citizens, what rights would they have (e.g., the right to vote). From this experience, we wondered what content and pedagogical resources teachers might need to more deeply address the critical issues of *all of American history—civil liberties and civil rights.*

These and other questions continued to emerge as we developed the volume topics for this series. Our goal was to provide students a more robust experience when learning about historical events. As the editorial team developed the topic for each volume, we also noticed numerous challenges of teaching topics embedded within each of these themes. Then, as early volume proposals were submitted to us, prospective editors pointed to the lack of attention most school textbooks place on the theme of human need and social response. We drew from this pedagogical challenge the need to describe the political philosophies underlying the American historical narrative, a journey of personal freedom.

BOOK SERIES ORGANIZATION

The series was initially composed of 10 separately titled books examining a different significant problem/critical themes in American history. Having published the first few of these titles, we expanded the series to include additional titles such as Women's History and two volumes on the United States Constitution. Each volume contains disciplinary content in American history, a discussion of disciplinary connectedness linking past and present thematic issues, a discussion of the pedagogical challenges in teaching that content, examples of lesson plans, and resources teachers could use in the classroom. Each volume address the Common Core Standards (CC) adopted by 46 states (http://www.corestandards.org), the C3 Framework (C3.ncss.org) and the National Curriculum Standards (NCS) of the National Council of the Social Studies (ncss.org).

This series provides teachers an examination of critical themes in American history with resources to teach these themes. The resources found in this series are: (a) historical content for exploring critical themes (b) historical context for addressing the themes of civil liberties and rights, (c) examples of how to use national standards to augment lessons, and (d) primary and secondary source material to support the investigation of critical themes in American history.

Moreover, the Peter Lang website provides links to the Series website—which contains a range of teaching resources such as links to primary documents, secondary literature, and projects that the teacher can assign to students.

Acknowledgments

I would like to take this opportunity to thank the Series Editorial Advisory Board for their work, insights, and dedication to teachers, students, and the production of this series. Specifically, I am indebted to Dr. Caroline R. Pryor for all her wisdom and coaching through this process. This project would not be possible without her.

To the team at Peter Lang, Dr. Alison Jefferson, thank you for walking me through this publication and for all the suggestions along the way.

To my colleague whose work are within these pages—it is my immense pleasure to share this space with you. I hope that these ideas resonate with teachers and students in classrooms across our country.

And on a personal note, thank you to my family—Anna, Caden, and Brooklyn—for your support and for giving the time for this project to come together.

Introduction: Teaching, Learning, and Historiography

MATTHEW R. CAMPBELL

Anytime educators mention the problems of teaching Reconstruction it usually comes back to the space where it is taught in the survey of Unites Stated history curriculum. Teachers typically do not have enough time to get to it in the first half of the survey and give it scant attention in the second half of the survey course. While this may just be a problem of semantics and where we divide the survey courses, it has played into the fact that it is a lesser-known era of history than many of the others taught in introductory classes. Reconstruction scholars as well as those who study late nineteenth and early twentieth century race relations or politics agree that the years following the Emancipation Proclamation were formative years in the trajectory of the United States as a country. So, why then, does this era of history not get the proper attention it deserves? The contributors of this volume would collectively agree that there are few resources known to educators and typically teachers do not feel comfortable diving into the subject without proper content knowledge. These authors hope to provide an entry to the subject and spur ideas on where teachers may lead discussions about this import era of history.

Of utmost importance in the study of Reconstruction is understanding that the historical interpretation is always changing. One of the biggest detriments to teacher's understanding of the era is that it has been plagued by the historical memory of the Lost Cause. We must think about what is important to us in the present day to properly analyze how to teach this era. While it is commonplace for teachers to use textbooks to garner information about Reconstruction, doing so only yields a representation of the era that is typically narrow. Many textbooks describe Reconstruction as a failed attempt at connecting the southern states back into the United States. Second to that, they downplay the role that slavery had in the Civil War, completely omit the Lost Cause, and typically gloss over the growth of Jim Crow in the South. This is especially the case with many K-12 standards in the United States. What mattered to historians and teachers fifty or a hundred years ago is not necessarily the same today. As teachers of history, we must think about how Reconstruction came to represent a critical time in the United States. Much of it stems from the country experimenting with Black equality and no system of slavery for the first time in hundreds of years. However, the fight for racial, economic, and political equality took many years as the country fought about how the nation would function in a post-Civil War society. What is important to us now? What is the value of Reconstruction to our overall knowledge of United States history? What parts of Reconstruction are important to the lives of students moving into adulthood? We must ask good questions to probe why Reconstruction is truly a critical theme in American history.

Some of the more recent historiographical work that is useful to a broader understanding of Reconstruction is a 2017 special issue of *The Journal of Civil War Era* collectively entitled "The Future of Reconstruction Studies" which marked the 150-year anniversary since Reconstruction and as well as a reflective article in *The Journal of the Gilded Age and Progressive Era* about Foner's *Reconstruction* titled "Reconstruction at 25" (Harlow, 2017; Staszak et al., 2015). Since the publication of these articles, there have been many more studies to emerge in the historical field, but the arguments put forth in the special issue remain a logical point of trajectory for understanding the status of the field of Reconstruction studies. Tasked with reviewing where this field has come since Foner, they collectively call for an "expansion of the boundaries of the field" in part by viewing the collection of events in broader places, different chronology, alternative lenses, and with the connection to the public at large (Harlow, 2017, p. 4). Given the political and ideological polarization of America in the last few decades, it stands to reason that competing views of Reconstruction may begin to fill conversation when including public perceptions.

The authors of the special issue recognize the magnitude of Foner's *Reconstruction* and that no comprehensive summary of Reconstruction has been published which would replace the work. In addition, they call into question, as do critics of Foner, the periodization of Reconstruction from 1863 to 1877. They argue that it is incorrect to think that Reconstruction somehow ended with the election of 1876 and the withdrawal of Union troops from the South. Likewise, the Emancipation Proclamation did not immediately give rise to Reconstruction as many political and sectional issues existed prior to the shots at Fort Sumter (Harlow, 2017). The very title of this volume is an example of the ways in which we typically go about teaching Reconstruction—confined to the dates 1863–1877. As the authors of this volume will echo, Reconstruction cannot be constrained to 1877 since the effects of the Civil War reached decades past the event. The dates in the title of this volume were given to hopefully periodize the discussion which is what most high school classrooms need help doing. All too often teachers try to relate all historical lessons to the present which can be problematic for a host of reasons—including downplaying historiography and leaning into modern cultural biases.

For novice teachers, it is useful to consider that the study of Reconstruction has gone through many iterations of study. Michael Perman (2003, p. 2) argues that there are three major eras of Reconstruction historiography: the Dunning School, Revisionist, and Post-Revisionist. The Dunning School included mostly scholars of the postwar South who followed William A. Dunning's ideas. He argued that Reconstruction failed because it was hostile to the South and became more of a northern retaliation against the former Confederacy. Radical Republicans in Congress failed to reach across the aisle when it came to post-war law making. This school of thought permeated textbooks and scholarship until the 1950s. When revisionist historians put pen to paper in the mid-twentieth century the narrative flipped. Reconstruction was not successful because of the stubbornness of southern whites. Radical Republicans of the 1870s could not be to blame because their politics should not be viewed as extreme if the goal was to implement a restored and more civil nation. Post-Revisionists broke from this theory and contended that these very Radical Republicans were to blame because they did not take the opportunities afforded to them to pass more legislation aimed at equality for formerly slaved people. Given the heightened racial climate in the post-Civil War era, these Republicans avoided and dismissed potential opportunities for meaningful change such as anti-discrimination laws or protections for Blacks in the South. In essence, both southern and northern whites were complicit in destroying hopes of Reconstruction. All these historiographic views center on blame. Was Reconstruction really a failure? And what would have made it successful? Teachers and students need to look beyond oversimplification when it comes to the process of Reconstruction. Many threads of history loop through Reconstruction as an anchoring or transition point—women's history, Black history, and even environmental history of land use. For students to fully understand the importance of this period we need to break down the many threads to see what truly was being accomplished and to what degree these changes became permanent. Highlighting these smaller histories of the time will help students give greater meaning to Reconstruction.

While this basic historiography gives context to much of the scholarship on Reconstruction, it is by no means exhaustive or even inclusive of the handful of others that are deemed important by historians. Perman argues that Emancipation was the result of the Civil War and that the fate of formerly enslaved people was a central element in the period of Reconstruction. The advantage that freed people had during this period of Reconstruction was far more than other post-emancipation period in other countries. This is evident by Black suffrage, office holding, and education in the years to follow (Perman, 2003, p. 39). Viewing Reconstruction as a failure, as did the previously mentioned schools of thought, discounts the people and events that transpired during this transitional period. When scholars look at the broader societal impact of Reconstruction it highlights its importance to the U.S. history canon. Reconstruction historiography offers some useful baseline information for those that may not be familiar with Reconstruction as a field of study or those who would like to enhance their understanding. It helps teachers make better contextual sense out of the resources that exist on the Civil War, Emancipation, and Reconstruction. The more teachers can gain an understanding of how the field of study has changed, the better they can recognize antiquated conceptions about Reconstruction in the classroom.

It is no doubt that the race relations birthed in the 1880s were brought about by policies of the Reconstruction era as well as some four million freedpersons working to navigate their freedom for the first time. More than knowing why this era of history is important, it is also imperative that we lead students to discover deeper meaning and ask skilled questions about Reconstruction. As educators and historians, we need students to understand the continuity and change that has existed after Reconstruction. In the same vein, to what degree is Reconstruction unique among time and place in U.S. history?

The texts in this volume all ask questions about Reconstruction that allow students to dive deeply into discussion in classrooms. Overall, the authors aim to extend the nuances of the historiography by exploring related disciplines, issues of race, politics, and historical memory. This volume is an attempt to bring the topic of Reconstruction to the forefront of teaching, not to complete the discussion or historiography. The topics covered are insights for investigation and continued research. One major theme is how we view the participants of Reconstruction, the foundation of which is an examination of the difference between progresses of equality and conversely a rise of racism in the nation that help center our teaching. Smith argues that Black southerners took action to emancipate themselves, make their voices heard, and create community against systems that fortified separation and breakdown in their lives. It calls for teachers to rethink the ways in which U.S. history is often taught in a vacuum of racial progress, or in other circumstances as racist progress.

Included in this context are topics related to the narratives of elite slaveholding women and their roles in resistance to Emancipation. Brill's "Dismantling Scarlett O'Hara" offers a diverse collection of primary materials to examine women's roles regarding emancipation in the South. Furthermore, how do students view Reconstruction when considering the reasons for the start and end of the Civil War? McConnell analyzes these ideas in *"Jus Post Bellum,* Reconstruction, and the American Civil War" and how those ideas might change how we study Reconstruction in the classroom.

Another emerging theme found in the text is that of the juxtaposition of political, economic, and social forces during Reconstruction. Typically, students analyze these in isolation as only a portion of the era's events are highlighted. It can be difficult for students to make connections when only given small windows of time to study Reconstruction. View's "Reconstruction Timeline" gives teachers a window into the cause-effect world of economic and political systems present during the years following the Civil War. Political cartoons, a staple teaching tool, do so much for helping students to analyze Reconstruction and the socio-political nuances of the period. As such, Dorsch argues that cartoons are indispensable for teachers in classroom conversations about stereotypes, popular politics, and shifting perspective about African Americans during Reconstruction. Building on pedagogical strategies like political cartoons, Schmitt and Towle discuss textbook portrayals of Reconstruction as a practice for creating more meaningful historiographical context for what students read in their classrooms.

The latter part of this volume discusses Reconstruction in terms of its trajectory into the late nineteenth century and early twentieth century civil rights movements. Perrotta argues that Reconstruction can provide students a lens to use historical empathy. By viewing various perspectives, she highlights issues related to voting rights and the women's suffrage movement during Reconstruction. This era also spurred on the rise of Black education. Stabler, Sheldon, and McKeeby discuss the agency of Blacks after the Civil War and the space they carved out in the educational landscape. Ultimately, Reconstruction planted the seed of success for historically Black colleges as well as the Civil Right Movement. Pearcy shows how Reconstruction represents an inflection point in the country's ability to reconcile with its past. The history of Reconstruction is the product of ongoing debate and shows that we have not dealt with the history of slavery to a full extent. The final chapter of this volume is devoted to resources. Filled with links, it can serve as a foundation for student and teacher research into the world of Reconstruction. While it is not exhaustive, it does try to cover many of the more useful and timely resources that are available.

Whether you agree or disagree with the arguments set forth in the following chapters is not what is most important. This volume's authors bring about many talking points for teachers and students to consider. In keeping with effective pedagogical practices, we want students to explore and debate these ideas as a way of learning this critical point in American history.

REFERENCES:

Harlow, L. E. (2017). Introduction: The future of Reconstruction studies. *The Journal of the Civil War Era, 7*(1), 3–6. doi:10.1353/cwe.2017.0001.

Perman, M. (2003). *Emancipation and Reconstruction* (2nd ed.). Harlan Davidson.

Staszak, l., Masur, K., Williams, H. A., Downs, G. P., Glymph, T., Hahn, S., & Foner, E. (2015). Eric Foner's "Reconstruction" at twenty-five. *The Journal of the Gilded Age and Progressive Era, 14*(1), 13–27. http://www.jstor.org/stable/43903055

CHAPTER ONE

Teaching Emancipation as Racial Progress and Reconstruction Violence as Racist Progress

SHANNON M. SMITH
College of Saint Benedict and Saint John's University

One challenge of teaching about emancipation and Reconstruction following the American Civil War is that it disrupts the narrative of inevitable racial progress that Americans love to tell about our past. One year after the murder of George Floyd and the worldwide calls for racial justice, a Pew Research survey found that nine out of ten Americans say the United States has made progress on "ensuring equal rights for all Americans." However, the public remains deeply divided by race, political partisanship, and age on how much more work needs to be done or whether increased attention to the history of racism and slavery is a good thing. (Pew Research Center, 2021) American citizens often focus on racial progress but fail to acknowledge racist persistence.

Students, parents, politicians, and others cultural commentators often view resistance to racial progress as aberrations by small groups rather than a central feature of US history. But the historian Ibram X. Kendi noted, "As I carefully studied America's racial past...I did not see a *singular* historical force taking steps forward and backward on race. I saw *two* distinct historical forces. I saw a *dual* and *dueling* history of racial progress and the simultaneous progression of racism (2017, p. x)." Rather than considering U.S. history as a story of constant progress with brief moments of backlash, this framework analyzes two competing forces of rac*ial* progress and rac*ist* progress. These two forms of historical change, continually reinvented alongside each other, offer a path for students to celebrate the joys of emancipation while acknowledging the impact of ongoing violence. This is also an opportunity for students to practice talking about race in our current moment of racial reckoning and cultivating empathy for the hopes and fears of all families in the aftermath of the Civil War.

Emancipation and Reconstruction offer many reasons for celebration and ongoing cautions for our own political and social environment. Aligning with the inquiry arc of the NCSS C3 framework, students will frame their inquiry around the question, "How and why in this moment of emancipation do we see both racial progress and racist reinvention?" Students will explore primary sources to learn how formerly enslaved people envisioned their lives and worked to secure their families' futures. At the same time many White people used violence and reinvented institutions to maintain their economic and social power. As they investigate these questions about the past, students can consider how remnants of both rac*ial* progress and rac*ist* progress of the Reconstruction era continue to manifest in today's society. Furthermore, students can reflect on how their understanding of the past can guide their informed action and civic participation to create the world that they want to live in today.

RACIAL PROGRESS AND HOPE

As Black people freed themselves by crossing Union lines and the US Army enforced emancipation during and following the Civil War, formerly enslaved people expressed their hopes for what freedom meant and how they would live. The world was turned upside down in a moment of immense possibility. Who would get to remake society and define citizenship and freedom? Black people saw an opportunity for racial progress in which they would be recognized as American citizens with full political and social participation and could use their skills and energy to contribute to society. They did not want to be defined by their race but understood that it was impossible to escape the long effects of slavery. Black people articulated a version of citizenship that included land ownership, military service, access to education, and personal safety. Studying emancipation is an important occasion to celebrate Black joy and agency as formerly enslaved people tried to reunite their families, forged their own communities, and sought to contribute politically, economically, and socially to an American society in which, they hoped, they would not be hindered by racial animus and the burden of slavery.

Black Ministers

Less than a month after the Union March to the Sea, twenty Black leaders met with General William T. Sherman and Secretary of War Edwin Stanton.

Garrison Frazier spoke on behalf of the Black ministers (Colloquy with Colored Ministers, 1865). Their conversation focused on the public and political roles of formerly enslaved people and how they viewed their relationship to the US government. When asked how Black people might "best assist the Government in maintaining your freedom," Frazier replied that "the way we can best take care of ourselves is to have land…. We want to be placed on land until we are able to buy it and make it our own." Women, children, and old men would use their labor to improve the land, while "the young men should enlist in the service of the Government." They said they would prefer "to live by ourselves, for there is prejudice against us in the South that will take years to get over." Many formerly enslaved people would "make any sacrifice to assist the Government." This primary source emphasizes that Black people supported both the military and economic systems of the federal government. They were not looking for handouts or to overthrow the social order but just wanted the opportunity to reap the benefits of their labor. Formerly enslaved people also saw property ownership and military service as important demonstrations of their citizenship.

Jourdan Anderson

A letter from Jourdan Anderson, a formerly enslaved man from Tennessee, to his former enslaver encapsulates many of the hopes and dreams freedpeople expressed for emancipation. In this letter Anderson declines an invitation to return to Colonel Anderson's plantation as a laborer. He describes the living conditions of his family in Dayton, Ohio, celebrating the ability to move where they wished, his children's access to education, worshiping in Black-controlled churches, and being addressed with respect. The Anderson family had the option to choose their workplace and earn fair wages—one task that the Freedmen's Bureau both assisted and complicated in southern states. Anderson sarcastically states that they might consider returning to work for Colonel Anderson if he pays them back wages for the time they were enslaved. He demands an astronomical sum of $11,680 that would be impossible for the enslaver to pay, especially if he had lost most of his property. "If you fail to pay us for faithful labors in the past," Anderson continues, "we can have little faith in your promises in the future." He offers a warning to former enslavers: "Surely there will be a day of reckoning for those who defraud the laborer of his hire." Jourdan Anderson concludes his letter by demanding safety for his daughters, citing the horrors of slavery visited upon his older children. Anderson's letter pairs well with images such as the 1865 lithograph "Emancipation" by Thomas Nast, which features a well-dressed, multigenerational Black family in a well-furnished home. These sources together allow students to explore the hopes and dreams of Black families while recognizing the restrictions they faced while enslaved.

These sources also provide an opportunity to discuss the reception of a northern audience to letters and images printed in publications such as *Harper's Weekly* and the *New York Tribune*. How might former Union soldiers and their families respond to Jourdan Anderson's demand for fair wages and safety for his family? How would the predominantly White, middle-class readers of *Harper's Weekly* interpret Nast's image at a time when Black families were attempting to secure their own housing and access to schools? Students can ask questions of the sources and try to understand the mindset of people who lived during and after the Civil War while situating their interpretations in the context of the time.

Voting Rights

These primary sources demonstrate that formerly enslaved people wanted what the historian Gregory Downs has called "practical freedom"—the ability to make their own choices and live their lives (Downs, 2015, p. 54). But emancipation required enforcement by the US Army or former enslavers could refuse to release unpaid workers. The desires for education, reaping the benefits of one's own labor, and building a safe home created belonging and participation in society. Formerly enslaved people, especially Black men who had served in the military, knew that gaining the vote was necessary for full political citizenship. Many Black people immediately began organizing to advocate for the right to vote.

In a speech to the Massachusetts Antislavery Society in April 1865, Frederick Douglass argued that without the vote, Black men's "liberty is a mockery" and "he holds his liberty as a privilege, not as a right. He is at the mercy of the mob and has no means of protecting himself." In a country where suffrage was key to political participation, Douglass stated, denying Black men the right to vote was declaring them unfit and branding them with "the stigma of inferiority." Douglass continued, "What I ask for the Negro is not benevolence, not pity, not sympathy, but simply *justice*." That justice required full political participation, which could help secure access to economic and social belonging.

Black leaders organized conventions throughout the country to articulate plans to fight for suffrage and the right to testify in courts. The text of these convention proceedings can be found through the Colored Conventions Project, where teachers may locate convention primary sources from their own states. The Negro Republican Party held its first convention in Lexington, Kentucky, in November 1867. Black political leader William F. Butler echoed Douglass's sentiments that "We ask no man for pity. We only ask you to take your hand off the black man's head and let him grow to manhood." Butler further argued for the need to fight for one's rights: "First we have the cartridge box, now we want the ballot box, and soon we will get the jury box. We went out and fought the battles of our country, and gained our liberties, but we were left without means of protecting ourselves in the employment of that liberty." (Marshall, 2010, p. 47) The right to vote was a necessary pathway to full citizenship in the United States—a right that Black men had earned through their military service.

Analysis of these primary sources helps students understand that emancipated people wanted for their families what most families want—homes, food, personal safety, reliable jobs, and an opportunity to participate as full members of society. Students cultivate empathy and kinship for people with similar human desires and goals. However, the justifications that enslavers had created for race-based slavery did not die with the end of slavery, so African Americans still faced prejudice and violence as White southerners tried to re-establish a social and racial order similar to before the war.

RACIST PROGRESS AND VIOLENCE

Reconstruction violence was a powerful contradiction to the optimism of formerly enslaved people for full social and political citizenship. While similar to the violence that undergirded the system of slavery, postwar violence was not exactly the same. The changing context of emancipation and Black activism required the development of new methods to maintain White supremacy. We often teach about the role of violence in Reconstruction as backlash against the economic progress of Black people and White fears of equality. Applying Kendi's framework to primary sources, we can explore the reinvention of racist ideas by individual employers, legal systems, and state and local agencies in need of labor, as well as the reinvention of violence by the Ku Klux Klan and other paramilitary groups. This helps us understand the motivations of those who used violence to control free Black people's behavior, limit political and economic participation, and claim that formerly enslaved people were not ready for citizenship. White violence led to the forceful overthrow of Reconstruction aims and the reassertion of White power structures from the federal government to the state and local level. However, Black people and White allies consistently used the courts, government, media, public opinion, and armed defense to fight against those who harmed them. Reconstruction sources let us analyze the persistence of racist beliefs, noting that White people who advocated for emancipation and Black voting rights did not necessarily advocate racial equality.

Black Codes

While formerly enslaved people sought to purchase their own land and control their economic future, former enslavers wanted to restore an inexpensive workforce and push out economic competition. These goals prompted the creation of Black codes to govern free Black people, the enforcement of labor contracts through the Freedmen's Bureau, and the use of the Thirteenth Amendment to implement convict leasing and create "slavery by another name" for those accused of crimes (Blackmon, 2008).

The 1865 Mississippi Black Codes were a model for other state laws enacted by White lawmakers who were not yet under federal jurisdiction. Formerly enslaved people had some rights, but they were not allowed to vote, provide testimony against White people, or serve on juries or in state militias. The Black Codes also restricted interracial marriages, where Black people might own or rent property, and their ability to carry weapons. Some laws dictated Black labor practices and were easily manipulated to the benefit of White employers. So-called "vagrancy laws" demanded that Black workers without a yearly labor contract could be arrested and hired to White landowners. These practices, in conjunction with the "loophole" in the Thirteenth Amendment that allowed involuntary servitude for punishment of a crime, created the convict-leasing system that thrived in southern states until well into the twentieth century. Furthermore, the punishments enacted against White people who traded with Black residents helped drive a wedge between poor people who might otherwise have found common cause with each other.

White Northerners were outraged by the blatant disregard for Black rights demonstrated by the Black Codes. Coupled with the increase in vigilante violence by the Ku Klux Klan and other groups, these actions prompted an increase of federal oversight known as Radical Reconstruction (Foner, 1988). Racist violence and the reinvention of racist practices had real political consequences at the federal, state, and local levels.

Ku Klux Klan

Many White men saw violence as the best method for combatting Black social and political gains, restoring a system based on White supremacy, and justifying their actions during the Civil War and after. White vigilante and paramilitary groups, of which the Ku Klux Klan was one of many, enforced social and economic sanctions against any who dared to challenge the system. Secret organizations in the South used all sorts of methods to intimidate those who dared to purchase land, refuse to work for Whites, fight for political or social rights, or defend themselves against White abuses. These vigilante groups typically operated with the knowledge if not full support of White local and state leaders.

Black economic, military, and political activism were the focus of these attacks. These organizations tried to end Republican rule by intimidating or attacking Black and White voters who supported the Republican Party. Black renters and landowners were often forced to abandon their homes, their land, and their crops as they fled to safer places. These so-called "regulators" tried to discourage White employers from hiring Black workers. In a culture where a man's weapons were vital to protecting himself and his family, White raiders often took weapons away to humiliate and emasculate Black men, especially former Union soldiers. The attacks grew worse during winter months when they tried to force Black workers to sign unfair labor contracts. These groups were most active in places where the demographic balance was close, neither overwhelmingly Black nor White, and where the balance of power was most in jeopardy. (Smith, 2021)

Black Testimony 1871

In March of 1871 a committee of six distinguished Black citizens of Frankfort, Kentucky wrote an appeal for federal assistance and sent it to the U.S. Congress. The resolution listed 116 grievances that "organized bands of desperate and lawless men, mainly composed of soldiers of the late rebel armies, armed, disciplined, and disguised," had enacted in the previous two years against the area's Black residents. They stated that "life, liberty, and property are unprotected" because the violent acts of the Ku Klux Klan and paramilitary organizations had "render[ed] insecure the safety of persons and property, overthrowing all those rights…which are expressly guaranteed to us by the Constitution of the United States." The Klan was "spreading terror…by robbing, whipping, ravishing, and killing our people without provocation" and they received no assistance from Kentucky lawmakers. Black citizens called upon the federal government to intervene as "we have been law-abiding citizens, pay our taxes, and in many parts of the State our people have been driven from the polls, refused the right to vote; many have been slaughtered while attempting to vote." Just as Frederick Douglass advocated for Black men to have voting rights as protection, the Klan and White vigilante groups saw Black men's right to vote as a threat to White power. It took the creation of the Department of Justice and federal intervention using the 1871 Ku Klux Klan Act to decrease the power of the organization.

Students can use images from illustrated papers such as *Harper's Weekly* or *Frank Leslie's Illustrated Newspaper* to see Northern critiques of these practices. Frank Bellew's 1872 "Visit of the Ku Klux Klan" demonstrates the threat that vigilante violence played to the hopes and dreams of Black families. Bellew shows armed invaders threatening the peace and prosperity of the comfortable, orderly household. Viewers at the time would see that the Klansmen might destroy the home or even kill the family. Thomas Nast's 1874 drawing "Worse than Slavery" shows that the violence was effective in discouraging Black families from full public participation and social citizenship. The image states, "This is a White Man's Government," which was increasingly true as Southern states were "redeemed" from Republican control and returned to White Democratic control.

While publications such as *Harper's Weekly* might encourage a largely White, middle-class audience to condemn vigilantism in the South, that did not necessarily translate into voter support for federal intervention. In time White support for the ongoing presence of the US Army dwindled. (Downs, 2015)

Results

It is too simple to analyze Reconstruction as either racial progress or backlash—there were both successes and failures in the political process and in African Americans' social advancement. The historian Eric Foner has argued that the Thirteenth, Fourteenth, and Fifteenth Amendments laid the framework for future legal intervention in the civil rights movement of the twentieth century (Foner, 1988). The intervention of the US Army kept worse human rights violations from happening (Downs, 2015). Even as systems such as convict leasing were created to control the labor of Black southerners and there was no widespread reform of land ownership, some Black people were able to gain property and a measure of economic independence.

However, the failure to secure Black rights had lasting effects that contrasted with African Americans' hope and pride in their economic and social progress (Foner, 1988). The reinvention of justifications for racism in the Jim Crow system and ongoing violence limited Black political participation for decades. The end of slavery did not bring the end of racism or full citizenship and belonging for Black Americans (Manning, 2008). Without military intervention, the support of Northerners, and federal authority, White Southerners were able to develop new systems of racist progress. The failure to reinvent a society based on racial progress meant that racism and White supremacy persisted in the United States.

Inquiry Arc

These primary sources work together to help students grapple with the complexity of racial and racist progress following the Civil War. Students explore change and continuity over time and a range of perspectives as they see African Americans pursuing their hopes for a transformed society in the face of new obstacles placed by White people trying to maintain their power (D2. His.4.9-12). Those circumstances were unique to that time and place but also address the longer context of White supremacy in US history (D2. His.1.9-12). Students can consider the usefulness or limitations of particular sources relating to the intended audience (D2. His.10.9-12 and D2. His.11.9-12). Most of all, students are better able to grasp the complexity of the past as they craft arguments based on evidence that Reconstruction created both gains and losses for Black Southerners (D2. His.16.9-12).

Analyzing these sources will prepare students to move from an academic understanding of sources to consider how they might act upon that knowledge.

Connecting Past and Present

Analyzing emancipation and Reconstruction violence will help students move toward informed action as they consider ongoing effects of racial progress and racist progress. Where do they want to put their energy to create the world they want to live in? Students may consider the reinvention of racist persistence in issues of mass incarceration and prison labor systems, environmental racism, debates over teaching about race in classrooms, and the growth of paramilitary and White supremacist organizations today. (Southern Poverty Law Center) Likewise they may see parallels between past and present forms of racial progress through worldwide racial protests in the summer of 2020, organizations such as Black Lives Matter, battles for economic justice, and ongoing legislation about access to voting rights. Questions that shaped Reconstruction policy continue today in debates over the role of federal, state, and local governments and their interactions, the role of race in shaping public policy, and court cases to determine if policies have either the intention or outcome of racial discrimination. Racism was not just in the past, but students do not have to feel defeated by an inevitable backlash. Instead, they can be prepared to defend against new forms of racist progress today. In teaching this hard history, students will see that democracy and racial progress require constant attention and can consider their own role for activism in shaping their future.

REFERENCES:

Blackmon, D. A. (2008). *Slavery by another name: The re-enslavement of Black Americans from the Civil War to World War II.* Anchor Books.

Downs, G. P. (2015). *After Appomattox: Military occupation and the ends of war.* Harvard University Press.

Foner, E. (1988). *Reconstruction: America's unfinished revolution, 1863–1877.* Harper & Row.

Hahn, S. (2003). *A Nation under our feet: Black political struggles in the rural South from slavery to the Great Migration.* Belknap Press of Harvard University Press.

Kendi, I. X. (2017). *Stamped from the beginning: The definitive history of racist ideas in America.* Hatchette Books.

Manning, C. (2008). *What this cruel war was over: Soldiers, slavery, and the Civil War.* Knopf.

Marshall, A. E. (2010). *Creating a Confederate Kentucky: The lost cause and Civil War memory in a border state.* University of North Carolina Press.

National Council for the Social Studies (NCSS). (2013). *The college, career, and civic life (C3) framework for social studies state standards: Guidance for enhancing the rigor of K–12 civics, economics, geography, and history.* Silver Spring, MD: Author.

Pew Research Center. (2021, August 12). "Deep divisions in Americans' views of nation's racial history—And how to address it." Accessed Aug. 20, 2021 https://www.pewresearch.org/politics/2021/08/12/deep-divisions-in-americans-views-of-nations-racial-history--and-how-to-address-it/

Smith, S. M. (2021). "'They mustered a whole company of Kuklux as militia': State violence and Black freedoms in Kentucky's Readjustment." In A. Domby & S. Lewis (Eds.), *Freedoms gained and lost: Reconstruction and its meanings 150 years later.* Fordham University Press.

Southern Poverty Law Center. "Hate and extremism." Retrieved Aug. 25, 2021, from https://www.splcenter.org/issues/hate-and-extremism.

Anderson, J. to P. H. Anderson (1865, August 7). *Cincinnati Commercial,* reprinted in *New York Tribune,* August 22, 1865.

Bellew, F. (1872, February 24). "Visit of the Ku Klux Klan." *Harper's Weekly.*

"Colloquy with colored ministers" (1865, January 12) in Savannah, Georgia.

Colored Conventions Project, Center for Black Digital Research, Penn State University. https://coloredconventions.org/

Douglass, F. (1865 April). Address to the Massachusetts Antislavery Society.

"Memorial of a committee appointed at a meeting of colored citizens of Frankfort, Ky. and vicinity, praying the enactment of laws for the better protection of life." (1871, April 11) *Index to the miscellaneous documents of the Senate of the United States for the first session of the forty-second Congress and the special session of the Senate, 1871.* pp. 53–56

Mississippi black codes (1865).

Nast, T. (1865). "Emancipation," lithograph. First published in *Harper's weekly* on January 24, 1863.

Nast, T. (1874, October 24). "Worse than slavery." *Harper's Weekly.*

Inquiry Design Model (IDM) Blueprint™			
Compelling Question	How and why in this moment of emancipation do we see both racial progress and racist reinvention?		
Standards and Practices	This project will address the following standards in the NCSS C3 framework: D2.His.1.9-12. Evaluate how historical events and developments were shaped by unique circumstances of time and place as well as broader historical contexts. D2.His.4.9-12. Analyze complex and interacting factors that influenced the perspectives of people during different historical eras. D2.His.10.9-12. Detect possible limitations in various kinds of historical evidence and differing secondary interpretations. D2.His.11.9-12. Critique the usefulness of historical sources for a specific historical inquiry based on their maker, date, place of origin, intended audience, and purpose. D2.His.14.9-12. Analyze multiple and complex causes and effects of events in the past. D2.His.16.9-12. Integrate evidence from multiple relevant historical sources and interpretations into a reasoned argument about the past.		
Staging the Question	Consider times when social "progress" for some groups encountered backlash from other groups. Do expanding human rights always last or can they be overturned?		
Supporting Question 1	Supporting Question 2	Supporting Question 3	
How did formerly enslaved people envision society and practice their freedom after emancipation?	In what ways did racist ideas from slavery persist after emancipation and to what extent were the forms of racism reinvented for that new context?	What was the role of violence in disrupting or establishing the postwar racial and social order?	
Formative Performance Task	Formative Performance Task	Formative Performance Task	
List four hopes and dreams that formerly enslaved people explained for their future lives.	Make a t-chart comparing and contrasting how racist ideas from slavery remained in racist ideas following emancipation.	List four ways that violence impacted the ability of freedpeople to act with "practical freedom."	

Featured Sources	Featured Sources	Featured Sources
• "Colloquy with Colored Ministers," January 12, 1865 in Savannah, Georgia • Letter, Jourdan Anderson to P.H. Anderson, August 7, 1865 • Thomas Nast, "Emancipation," lithograph, 1865 (Library of Congress) • Colored Conventions Project, Center for Black Digital Research, Penn State University. https://coloredconventions.org/	• Mississippi Black Codes 1865 • Frederick Douglass, Address to the Massachusetts Antislavery Society, April 1865 • M.C. Fulton to Freedmen's Bureau Official, April 17, 1866 • Charles Raushenberg to Lieut. O.H. Howard, Nov. 14, 1867, Freedmen's Bureau letters • Thomas Nast, "Worse Than Slavery," *Harper's Weekly*, Oct. 24, 1874	• "Memorial of a Committee Appointed at a Meeting of Colored Citizens of Frankfort, Ky. and Vicinity, Praying the Enactment of Laws for the Better Protection of Life," *Index to the Miscellaneous Documents of the Senate of the United States for the First Session of the Forty-Second Congress and the Special Session of the Senate, 1871* (April 11, 1871): 53–56 • Frank Bellew, "Visit of the Ku Klux Klan," *Harper's Weekly*, Feb. 24, 1872 • Lt. Col. C. S. Brown to Brvt. Brig. Genl. C. H. Howards, "Outrage Reports," Records of the Assistant Commissioner for South Carolina, RG 105: Bureau of Refugees, Freedmen and Abandoned Lands, Oct. 23, 1865 https://ldhi.library.cofc.edu/exhibits/show/after_slavery_educator/unit_nine_documents/document_3 • President Grant's Letter in 1876 to Gov. Chamberlain of South Carolina on the Hamburg Massacre, July 26, 1876 https://www.loc.gov/resource/rbpe.2070020a/?sp=2&st=text

Summative Performance Task	Argument	Construct a written argument (or detailed outline or poster) that addresses why there was both racial progress and racist reinvention during Reconstruction using specific claims and relevant evidence from historical sources while acknowledging competing views. Who was harmed or benefitted from those actions? What were the results for freedpeople's choices and government policies?
	Extension	Imagine how one family of formerly enslaved people might have navigated the choices available to them to celebrate their freedom and how they might have fought back against racial violence or racist policies.
Taking Informed Action		**Understand:** Research an issue that exhibits elements of racial progress and racist progress (e.g., voting rights, the right to protest, mass incarceration or prison labor, racial disparities in housing access or homeownership, environmental racism, learning about race in schools, etc.) **Assess:** Take a position on the issue and analyze who benefits from the power imbalance of racial progress or racist progress. Propose an alternative course of action. **Act:** Draft a letter to your state or federal representative stating your position on the selected issue, including claims and evidence to support your position.

CHAPTER TWO

Dismantling Scarlett O'Hara: How Slaveholding White Women Supported Slavery and Resisted Emancipation

KRISTEN BRILL
Keele University

OVERVIEW

This chapter will combine historical and pedagogical analysis to examine the roles of elite white women in the slaveholding South. Recent historical scholarship has shown many of these women were far from the Scarlett O'Hara archetype of "the southern lady," and instead gained social and economic power from their roles as slaveholders regularly wielding violence against their enslaved persons. This chapter will also offer an interdisciplinary framework, speaking not only to History, but Gender Studies as well. Offering a diverse collection of first-person primary source materials to introduce students to a range of historical methods wedding social, political and intellectual history, this chapter will challenge students to reconsider archetypes and mythologies and to confront some elite white women's roles in resisting emancipation in the slaveholding South.

HISTORICAL CONTEXT AND HISTORIOGRAPHY

In the antebellum and Confederate South, there was a disconnect between the ideal of the powerless yet civilized and refined southern "lady" (i.e., women like Scarlett O'Hara) and the lived experiences of elite white women (i.e., women like Julia Gardiner Tyler) (Scott, 1970, pp. 6–7 and 16–17). Some elite white women were instrumental in the management of plantations, including the supervision and discipline of enslaved persons (Glymph, 2008, p. 31; Glymph, 2019). They also engaged in the broader economic landscape of the plantation; they routinely bought and sold enslaved persons and were influential financial agents in the domestic slave market (Jones-Rogers, 2019, p. 151). As these women were foundational to the managerial and economic operation of the plantation, they wielded power. This notion of power was dependent upon the use of violence against enslaved persons; in turn, elite white women's exercise of violence was essential to the functioning of the slave regime (Glymph, 2008, pp. 26–29; Jones-Rogers, 2019, p. 10). Such sustained and systemic engagement with violence stood in stark contrast to perceptions of women's weakness and gentility. These women were economically and socially invested in sustaining slavery, and stood in opposition to emancipation.

Recent historiography reexamines the mythology of the southern lady to analyze the active, and often eager, roles some elite white women played in sustaining slavery in the nineteenth-century South. Two historians in particular have played crucial roles in reconfiguring ideas surrounding the southern lady and slavery. First, Thavolia Glymph (2008) shows that white women were intrinsic to the management of plantation slavery and were actively engaged in the required systemic violence of the institution. Second, Stephanie E. Jones-Rogers expands on Glymph's work to show how white women gained economic power from slavery: white women bought, sold and perpetuated violence against enslaved persons, and in doing so, worked to shape the domestic slave market economy (Jones-Rogers, 2019, pp. xii–xvi, 151, 156–157, and 180). Both Glymph and Jones-Rogers reveal that southern white women might not have had access to the electoral political sphere, but they did have social and economic power in civic society through slaveholding. The daily lives of these white slaveholding women were far from the idea of the southern lady; these women were central to the operation of southern slave plantations. This is a critical issue in teaching the history of emancipation as it shatters the widespread mythology surrounding the plantation South and women like Scarlett O'Hara; some elite white women were actively engaged with sustaining slavery and resisting emancipation in the slaveholding South.

LESSON PLAN

1. Introduction
   Discussion questions: What do you know about slavery in the antebellum and Civil War South? What do you know about elite white women in the antebellum and Civil War South?

2. Show brief opening clip from *Gone with the Wind* (1939)
   6:27-8:55: Open on Scarlett O'Hara discussing "war, war, war" and close on enslaved field labor on the plantation
   Discussion questions: How do these scenes represent elite white women in the Old South? How do they represent the relationship between slavery and elite white women in the Old South?
3. Brief lecture here on the updated historical scholarship outlining elite white women as violent slaveowners; a direct contestation to the ideal of Scarlett O'Hara
   (use historiography and historical context section above)
4. Group Work Activity: Primary Source Analysis

Primary Source Analysis 1

Julia Gardiner Tyler, *The Women of England Versus the Women of America. Mrs. Ex-President Tyler's Letter to the Duchess of Sutherland on American Slavery* (London, 1853)

After a secret engagement following the death of his first wife, Julia Gardiner married President John Tyler (1841–45) in 1844 and served as First Lady for the remainder of his presidency. The Tylers supported slavery and states' rights; John Tyler was a lifelong slaveowner and his northern-born second wife eagerly adopted the role of the plantation mistress. John Tyler died in 1862, and Julia undertook volunteer work for the Confederacy in the American Civil War. Eight years after she left the White House, she published this letter to the Duchess of Sunderland in response to her work on the Stafford House Address antislavery petition.

> [...]
> It is the province of the women in the Southern States to preside over the domestic economy of estate and plantations of their husbands; it is emphatically their province to visit the sick, and attend to the comfort of all the labourers upon such estates; and it is felt to be but a poor compliment to the women of the South to suppose it necessary to introduce other superintendence than their own over the condition of their dependents and servants.
> [...]
> In morals we believe ourselves quite your equals, and therefore it sounds harshly in our ears to be admonished by you for our sins, real or imaginary. There is a proud heart in the American breast, which rebels against all assumption on the part of others, although they may wear ducal coronets or be considered the stars of fashion in foreign courts. Manage your own affairs as best you may, and leave us to manage ours as we may think proper. Each of us such find abundant employment in the performance of our respective duties. If you wish a suggestion as to the suitable occupation of your idle hours, I will point you to the true field of your philanthropy—the unsupplied wants of your own

people in England. In view of your palaces there is misery and suffering enough to excite your most active sympathies. I remember to have seen lately, that there were in the city of London alone 100,000 people who rose in the morning without knowing where or how they were to obtain their "daily bread"
[...]
Leave it to the women of the South to alleviate the suffering of their dependents while you take care of your own. The Negro of the South lives sumptuously with comparison of the 100,000 white population of London. He is clothed warmly in winter, and has his meat twice daily without stint of bread. Have your working men, women and children as well clothed and as well fed, and then go to the serfs of Russia and the Negros of America.
[...]
The African, and her policy and by her laws, became property. That property has descended from father to son, and constitutes a large part of Southern wealth. We desire no intrusion of advice as to our individual property rights, at home or abroad.
[...]

Key Discussion Questions:

How does Tyler defend slavery and resist calls for emancipation?

How does Tyler admonish England?

For Tyler, what are the roles of southern women in issues surrounding slavery? Do you think all southern women would agree?

Is it important that this letter was published before the Civil War in terms of audience and impact? What kinds of issues should historians be mindful of when examining letters (published and unpublished)?

Tyler was a former First Lady. How significant is this?

Primary Source Analysis 2: Susan Cornwall unpublished diary, Georgia, 1861

Susan Cornwall Diary, 1855–1866. Call Number 01601-z. Southern Historical Collection of the Louis Round Special Collections Library, University of North Carolina at Chapel Hill, Chapel Hill, North Carolina and *Elite Confederate Women in the American Civil War: Lived Experiences in the Nineteenth Century*, ed. Kristen Brill (New York: Routledge, 2021), 23–33.

Writing from Alexander in Burke County, Georgia, Susan Cornwall's unpublished diary provides an intimate study of a rural community 160 miles west of Atlanta on the eve of the American Civil War. While elite white southern women wartime diarists often touched on the issue of slavery, they tended to discuss slavery in terms of their everyday interactions with enslaved persons. Focusing on the perceived lack of intellect and culture in the enslaved, Cornwall commented on slavery beyond her own lived experience. She offered slavery as an institution of benevolent paternalism and mutual betterment, and focused on slavery's effect on southern society as a collective. According to Cornwall, slavery and the Confederacy as a republic founded on the right to own slaves, improved humankind and society as a whole. The below is an excerpt from her unpublished diary, written less than three months before the Battle of Fort Sumter and the start of the American Civil War.

January 31, 1861

[…]

We of the South see nothing now in Union but danger or our sacred rights. The government which has been our pride and our hope is soon to be in the hands of a sectional majority; flushed with a recent triumph so inglorious to them as fatal to our national prosperity. The Black Republicans rejoice that they are to be the instruments of final emancipation for that is undoubtedly their aim in spite of their declaration that they will not interfere with slavery in the states where it exists. But what does a thinking mind see in freedom for the black race?

[…]

At the North where freedom is the deity of the white race and Liberty the watchword which everyone has at his tongue and, how much better is the condition of the negro? Who of all their enfranchised hordes is imbued with a true spirit of independence? Who is qualified to lend his brethren to a higher state of improvement? Who is regarded as a man of wisdom or an oracle of truth? Who has discovered a hidden source from whence to imbibe draughts of knowledge, scientific or literary? Who has invented a machine for lightening the Labors of his oppressed brethren? Who has even contributed his mite to the ardent appeals of would-be philanthropists in behalf of the slave? There is no record of any who have done these things, so common among white men as scarcely to excite a tribute of admiration. There was, it is true, some time back a notorious Fred Douglass, who was taken into the abolition council and instructed to play his part in their infernal designs, but having served them he has gone I suppose into obscurity. We hear of women who have forgotten their sex and in their immodest love of publicity, have mounted the rostrum and poured forth incendiary harangues teeming with falsehood and disgusting revelations of their own depravity; but no black woman has so far belied her sex or forgotten her proper share. In this we discover one cause of hopeful gratulation for the race; tho we blush to remember the shaming contrast to those white speech makers.

While the Northerners profess to see nothing in a state of slavery but degradation for the slave and in the slaveholder we consider it a condition highly honorable to both parties, when viewed in a proper light. This subject has been discussed by able minds, and were I writing for the public eye I would not presume to touch upon it, but I am only penning these sentiments as they occur to my mind without regard to a correct arrangement or a concise style. It is highly probable that another in looking over them would smile at their puerility or sneer at their defects, but I am only writing because <u>I feel like it!</u> So a truce to a criticism.

[…]

Key Discussion Questions

How does Cornwall describe "Black Republicans" and abolitionists? According to Cornwall, does abolition and emancipation benefit society?

How does Cornwall describe slavery? According to Cornwall, does it benefit society? Do you think all southern women would agree?

How do Cornwall's beliefs support the core aims of the Confederacy in the American Civil War?

Is it significant that this is written in an unpublished diary? What kinds of issues should historians be mindful of when examining diaries?

Examining Tyler's letter and Cornwall's diary together, in what ways do these women adhere to the mythology of the southern lady? In what ways do they undermine the mythology of the southern lady?

5. Conclusion

Discussion questions:

Why is the mythology of Scarlett O'Hara and the romanticization of the Old South so enduring? How is historical memory constructed and to what ends?

Can you think of other examples in which the historical narrative has been romanticized in processes of memory?

ASSESSMENT

Traditional Approaches to Assessment

1. Possible Essay Questions
Analyze the relationship between plantation mistresses and enslaved persons in the plantation household.
How important is gender in understandings of slavery and the Old South?
Is the Scarlett O'Hara archetype an accurate description of elite white women in the slaveholding South? Justify your answer.
2. Possible Group Presentation Topics
Roles of women in the Civil War
Slavery in the antebellum South
Abolition movement in the antebellum North

Innovative Approaches to Assessment (these can also be repurposed as group activities in the seminar)

1. Podcast
   Prepare and deliver a 5-minute elevator pitch to National Public Radio (NPR) for a podcast on women and slavery. Consider the following:
   What's the topic of your podcast? A person? An event? A place?
   What's the story arc? How many episodes will your podcast be? What will you discuss in each episode?
   How would you make this material resonate with a contemporary audience? Why should they care about this? Get creative and be bold!
2. Design a Museum Exhibit
   You are a curator for the Smithsonian American Women's History Initiative. You have been asked to design an exhibit on the antebellum plantation household. You have a limitless budget and you are able to procure any historical object or document you desire.
   What documents or objects would you include and why?
   Which individuals would you include and why?
   What will be the overall aims and objectives of the exhibit?
   Would you connect this exhibit to issues in contemporary society? If so, how?
3. Design a Lesson Plan
   You will design a lesson plan to teach a 45-minute outreach session to a class of 6th grade students on the roles of elite white women in supporting slavery and resisting emancipation in the slaveholding South.
   What are your three to five key learning objectives?
   Much of this is quite sensitive material, how would you prepare your students for learning about this violent episode in history?
   What are your three to five key discussion questions?
   Can you think of an interactive way to teach this material?
   How will you evaluate if the students have learned this material?
   Note: It would be ideal if students could actually teach their lesson plans to other students. Peer teaching can foster not only a greater knowledge of the subject material, but a greater independent learning initiative for the peer teacher.

PRIMARY SOURCES READING LIST

Avary, M. L. (1903). *A Virginia girl in the Civil War, 1861–1865*. D. Appleton and Company.*
Bacot, A. (1994). *A Confederate nurse: The diary of Ada W. Bacot, 1860–1863* (J. V. Berlin, Ed.). University of South Carolina Press.

Branch, M. P. (1912). *Memoirs of a southern woman "Within the Lines" and a geographical record*. Joseph G. Branch.*

Butler, L. W. (2107). *The diary of a Civil War bride: Lucy Wood Butler of Virginia* (K. Brill, Ed.). Louisiana State University Press.

Buck, L. (1997). *Shadows on my heart: The Civil War diary of Lucy Rebecca* (E. R. Baer, Ed.). University of Georgia Press.

Chesnut, M. (1905). *A diary from Dixie* (I. D. Martin & M. L. Avary, Eds.). D. Appleton and Company.*

Clay-Clopton, V. (1999). *A belle of the fifties: Memoirs of Mrs. Clay of Alabama covering social and political life in Washington and the south, 1853–66* (3rd ed.). University of Alabama Press.*

Pember, P. Y. (1974). *A southern woman's story: Life in Confederate Richmond* (2nd ed.) (B. I. Wiley, Ed.). Mockingbird Books.

Morgan, S. (1991). *The Civil War diary of Sarah Morgan* (C. East, Ed.). University of Georgia Press.*

*Available on Documenting the American South website, see below.

SECONDARY SOURCES READING LIST

Blight, D. (2005). *Race and reunion: The Civil War in American memory*. Harvard University Press.

Brill, K. (2022). *The weaker sex in war: Gender and nationalism on the Confederate home front*. University of Virginia Press.

Campbell, J. G. (2005). *When Sherman Marched North from the Sea: Resistance on the Confederate Home Front*. University of North Carolina Press.

Cashin, J. E. (2008). *First lady of the Confederacy: Varina Howell Davis's Civil War*. Harvard University Press.

Censer, J. T. (2003). *The reconstruction of white southern womanhood, 1865–1895*. Louisiana State University Press.

Churchwell, S. (2022). *The wrath to come: Gone with the Wind and the lies America tells*. Head of Zeus, 2022.

Clinton, C. (1982). *The plantation mistress: Woman's world in the Old South*. Pantheon Books.

Clinton, C. (1995). *Tara revisited: Women, war and the plantation legend*. Abbeville Press.

Cox, K. (2003). *Dixie's daughters: The United Daughters of the Confederacy and the preservation of Confederate culture*. University of Florida Press.

Edwards, L. (2000). *Scarlett doesn't live here anymore: Southern women in the Civil War era*. University of Illinois Press.

Elder, A. E. (2022). *Confederate widows and the emotional politics of loss*. University of North Carolina Press.

Fox-Genovese, E. (1988). *Within the plantation household: Black and white women of the Old South*. University of North Carolina Press.

Gardner, S. (2004). *Blood and irony: Southern white women's narratives of the Civil War, 1861–1937*. University of North Carolina Press.

Glymph, T. (2008). *Out of the house of bondage: The transformation of the plantation household*. Cambridge University Press.

Glymph, T. (2019). *The women's fight: The Civil War's battles for home, freedom and nation*. University of North Carolina Press.

Jabour, A. (2007). *Scarlett's sisters: Young women in the Old South*. University of North Carolina Press.

Janney, C. E. (2008). *Burying the dead but not the past: Ladies' Memorial Association and the Lost Cause*. University of North Carolina Press.

Jones-Rogers, S. E. (2019). *They were her property: White women as slave owners in the American South*. Yale University Press.

McCurry, S. (2010). *Confederate reckoning: Power and politics in the Civil War South*. Harvard University Press.

McCurry, S. (2019). *Women's war: Fighting and surviving the American Civil War*. Harvard University Press.

Scott, A. F. (1970). *The southern lady: From pedestal to politics, 1830–1930*. University of Chicago Press.

Whites, L. & Long, A. P. (Eds.). (2009). *Occupied women: Gender, military occupation and the American Civil War*. Louisiana State University Press.

Relevant Digital Humanities and Public History Websites

White House Historical Association: First Ladies and Slavery https://www.whitehousehistory.org/the-first-ladies-and-slavery

The White House Historical Association offers information on the role of slavery in the construction of the White House as well as the roles of some Presidents and First Ladies as slaveowners. This might be a good opportunity to consider the significance of slavery to specific Presidents and plantation homes, such as George Washington's Mount Vernon (https://www.mountvernon.org/george-washington/slavery/), Thomas Jefferson's Monticello (https://www.monticello.org/slavery/#:~:text=Slavery%20at%20Monticello,lived%20in%20bondage%20at%20Monticello) and James Madison's Montpellier.

Documenting the American South
https://docsouth.unc.edu/

This digital humanities collection sponsored by the University of North Carolina at Chapel Hill offers first-person accounts of the South, including elite white southerners' diaries (such as Mary Chestnut) and fugitive slave narratives (such as Harriet Jacobs). It also provides full-text versions of pro and anti-slavery nineteenth-century literature (such as *Uncle Tom's Cabin*).

Federal Writers' Project
https://www.loc.gov/collections/slave-narratives-from-the-federal-writers-project-1936-to-1938/about-this-collection/

The Library of Congress digitized first-person narratives of slavery collected through transcribed interviews of the Federal Writers' Project of the Works Progress Administration later renamed the Work Projects Administration (WPA). These sources raise important issues related to memory, mediation and silences in the archive.

REFERENCES:

Glymph, T. (2008). *Out of the house of bondage: The transformation of the plantation household*. Cambridge University Press.

Glymph, T. (2019). *The women's fight: The Civil War's battle for home, freedom and nation*. University of North Carolina Press.

Jones-Rogers, S. E. (2019). *They were her property: White women as slave owners in the American South*. Yale University Press.

Scott, A. F. (1970). *The southern lady: From pedestal to politics, 1830–1930*. University of Chicago Press.

CHAPTER THREE

Jus Post Bellum and the Moral Imperatives of Reconstruction

KENT A. MCCONNELL

THE CHALLENGES OF HISTORICAL INTERPRETATION IN AN "AGE OF FRACTURE"

In the summer of 1989, historian Maris A. Vinovskis published a seminal article entitled "Have Social Historians Lost the Civil War?" The author's findings offered a resounding "yes" to the question (Vinovskis, 1989). Since its publication historians have made significant advances in studying the impact of the war on local communities and individuals, yet considerable work remains. In light of widespread demonstrations in the public square concerning the removal of Confederate monuments it is perhaps time to reconstitute Vinovski's question to ask, "Have classroom instructors "lost" not just the Civil War but also Reconstruction in their curriculum?" To be sure, public rancor over monuments involves much more than a retelling of the past, but it is a topic that might guide educators where to place their priorities in the classroom.

Debate over the removal of Confederate monuments or other symbols of the Old South from public spaces is symptomatic of America's cultural divide and suggests an appreciable shift in understanding of the Civil War's legacy and meaning. In our "age of fracture," as historian Daniel T. Rodgers characterizes it, "nostalgia [exists] on both sides of the 'culture wars.'" Rodgers further suggests the desire for nostalgia has important national implications concerning public memory and politics. "Here history did not unfold step by step, organizing the chaotic patterns of causation and change," the scholar notes, but rather an "alternative vein" of historical interpretation developed where "the boundary between past and present virtually dissolved" (Rodgers, 2011, pp. 221–223). The resulting affect has been the loss of a strange and complicated past. Public discourse around the war's meaning oftentimes reflects the symbolic terrain of present where the deep cultural fault lines of the present are magnified and even fought over. At the 150th anniversary of the start of the Civil War, a Pew Research Center survey found that 56% of Americans understood the war as relevant to today's politics (Drake, 2013). In light of the white nationalists' march in Charlottesville, Virginia and the lamentable responses by some of our democratically elected leadership at the time, perhaps the moment ripe for educators to revisit the lessons of the era that is anything but bygone.

The public vitriol that emerged from these violent clashes necessitated justification and is an indication, even by those whose motives were without ethical sanction, that physical violence needs justification. It is no coincidence in these dialogues of "real world ethics," as ethicist Peter Singer characterizes them, this historical era has become the battleground of contemporary politics (Singer, 2016, "Introduction"). For at the heart of this era's historical lesson rest questions about the nature of justice and what that means for an interracial democracy. Central to this on-going dialogue is the relationship between history, social memory, democratic citizenship, and notions of justice that underpin participation in the liberal state. Thomas Jefferson keenly understood something those protesting around his statue on the campus of the University of Virginia did not; namely, what distinguishes democracy from demagoguery is an informed citizenship. Surely some of this public dialogue has repeated historical "facts" and rehashed moral tropes of the past for the sake of rendering judgments in the present. But the practitioners of this discourse seek an uncomplicated past, one of convenience that relegates ethical questions for the sake of mythology, ideology, or politics, rather than a historical narrative that lays bare moral dilemmas and seeks the humanizing effects of historical understanding, empathy, and mature historical and ethical thinking. Now more than ever it is imperative to complicate our classrooms and a retelling of the nation's past.

A century after Lincoln's election, historian William B. Hesseltine offered an intriguing analysis of Lincoln's plans for Reconstruction. "Reconstruction was, in fact, the basic issue of the Civil War," Hesseltine wrote, arguing the "desire to re-make the South" economically, governmentally, and constitutionally "…had been the reason for beginning the war and for prosecuting it with vigor…" (Hesseltine, 190, p. 12) *Lincoln's Plan for Reconstruction* earned praise among historians for the questions it raised and its insightful analysis, but few scholars agreed with Hesseltine's assertion about the *jus ad bellum*. The war did not start to "remake" nearly any aspect of the South, but it undeniably became such a war and, as Hesseltine insightfully commented, in the course of its prosecution, *jus in bello*, the war became intimately related to the new ends, *jus post bellum*, of ending slavery and citizenship. Failing to secure the full protections of citizenship for Black Americans, one might logically ask, "What happened?".

Herein raises another interpretive issue, what Rodgers' might deem an "alternative vein" of history perspective. Given the perennial themes of American history found in Reconstruction, contemporary students with their acute awareness of racial injustices may be prone to adopt singular explanatory methods when it comes to this era. Students commonly explain the failures of Reconstruction as the problem of race. But what does this mean? While not wrong in identifying "racism" as the major phenomenon in shaping the era, such explanatory models become monolithic because of a failure to appreciate distinctions between the past and present. This interpretation is akin to adage, not analysis. While it is true students' charges of racism may correctly identify the personal dispositions that reflect behaviors and attitudes of many or most of the historical actors, at the same time these models may fail to address the mechanisms of racism through institutional life, economic systems, or partisan politics.

Additionally, racism as a causative force has been adaptive to various social and cultural contexts where it may gain or lose currency alongside other competing claims. The multivalent character of these "isms" is intimately related to issues of causation and contingency which are fundamental elements of retelling a dynamic past. Pure circumstance, an unsettling thought for some, may also be a determinative factor of varying degrees which challenges cultural norms, psychological predispositions, or ideological convictions. As historians and instructors, however, it is our task to provide students the opportunity to develop analytical skills that see the interrelatedness of subjects—even disciplinary fields—while fostering habits of mind that enable them to see topics as interrelated yet analytically distinct and choices as being shaped by multiple factors.

Equipping students with minds that move beyond convenient generalities will not only make them better students of the discipline, but more importantly foster the habits of mind to participate as educated citizens in a democratic project. If as theorist Michael Walzer maintains "…just war theory is a necessary guide to democratic decision-making," then students examining the Civil War Era will benefit greatly from discussing the tensions that existed over the rights of citizenship, the right of self-determination, the equal application of justice, the limits of constitutionalism, and the perpetuation of the Union Walzer, Michael. (2000, p. xvi.). In doing so, they will be better equipped to understand the trajectory of the "moral arc of history," how far the nation has come, and that which remains undone.

JUST WAR THEORY: A GUIDE FOR EXPLORING THE MORAL DILEMMAS OF RECONSTRUCTION

With the growing recognition among educators for the need to diversify voices from the past in recounting America's past, questions remain on how to achieve this objective and to what ends does this plurality serve? In a 2012 article in *The Atlantic*, scholar Ta-Nehisi Coates asked the question "Why do so few blacks study the Civil War?" In his writing Coates recounts that in his youth the Civil War "was always something of a sideshow" to African American history. This understanding was given, not constructed by Coates. "…For my community, the message has long been clear: the Civil War is a story of white people—acted out by white people, on white people's terms—in which blacks feature strictly as stock characters and props" (Coates, 2012). Coates criticism of Civil War historiography is not misplaced, but hopefully is not the final word either.

Periodization, an essential tool of the historian's trade, when skillfully applied can illuminate features of the past in important ways. Like any contouring tool, however, its misapplication can potentially distort or even substantially alter the final form. An argument can be made that a scholarly focus on the American Civil War has distorted its relationship to Reconstruction. With few exceptions, most twentieth-century treatments of the Civil War focused on the war years or in recounting the war developed a narrative thread that considered the causative forces of the pre-war decades. Many of these monographs centered their attention on military campaigns or politics to the exclusion of the experiences of citizens living through the war (Paludan, 1996). Published primary sources have also conditioned our thinking about the interrelatedness of the past. An abundance of Civil War diaries detail events of the war years, but few of these published sources address the aftermath of the conflict. Textbooks, also mirror this pattern of periodization, highlighting the successes of Union victory and its high-minded ideals which stand in stark contrast to the less-than-noble political maneuvers and partisanship that quickly undermined by Reconstruction. Those monographs that have raised issues of just war theory have separated the Civil War from Reconstruction by focusing on issues of causation rather than effects (Lockwood & Harris, 1985). No doubt conceptualizing the relationship of conflict to a postwar society, a dilemma that Albert Schweitzer termed "the problem of peace," is quite challenging; however, in focusing our studies in this way, the issue of race and the meaning of citizenship and civil liberties comes to the fore.

Perhaps another reason Reconstruction has often been overlooked in school curriculums is due to the inconveniences of a singular narrative thread and one of truths this era reveals, namely that the Republic has been profoundly affected by violence. What one historian termed the "many-sided problem of Reconstruction," today proves to be pedagogically challenging given the historical issues and political cross-currents at play (Randall & Current, 1983, p. 359). Tomes like W.E.B. DuBois's (1998) 700-page *Black Reconstruction in America: 1860–1880* or more recently Eric Foner's (1988) 600-page definitive study, *Reconstruction: America's Unfinished Revolution 1863–1877* are both visual and scholarly reminders of the complexity and seemingly limitlessness number of subjects available for discussion. Chief among these topics, however, is the legacy of violence, democracy, race, and justice that emerged from this period.

Just war theory provides an opportunity for educators to weave together several important subjects of this period while attempting to recalibrate contemporary perceptions of the past, particularly as it relates to moral reasoning during the initial formation of America's interracial democratic project. For one, those who engage in historical inquiry care about human activity and its meaning. Peter Verbeek reminds us in his study on war and peace that such inquiries are "crucial for human well-being and survival" (Verbeek in Fry, Douglas P. ed., 2013, p. 64). With this orientation in mind, it is difficult to image how history instructors can avoid questions of ethics and the state while discussing Reconstruction. In his *Liberalism and the Limits of Justice*, author Michael J. Sandel maintains the essential nature of justice to contractarian states. Sandel argues justice "…is not merely one important value among others, to be weighed and considered as the occasion requires, but rather the means by which values are weighed and assessed" (Sandel, 1998, pp. 15–16). This conception of justice as a means to assess the democratic state shortcomings in realizing its professed ideals holds great potential in learning about Reconstruction as it moves us beyond the conveniences of dichotomous thinking. If as Sandel suggests, "Justice is the standard by which conflicting values are reconciled and competing conceptions of the good accommodated if not always resolved," then just war theory provides a revealing pedagogical framework to study this particular era (Sandel, 1998, pp. 15–16).

Additionally, this line of inquiry makes it clear the range of available choices to historic actors faced within a particular historic context. For the Civil War generation opportunities and choices were not measured by two distinctive or unrelated periods, but rather by the continuum of their lives. Once the war had been settled on the battlefield, the question that emerged was, "What did all the killing to achieve?" Here students may explore a range of beliefs Americans held in common and quickly discover it is not only difficult to detach issues of justice and rights from conversations about the common good, but also that given the nature of these issues such detachment is undesirable (Sandel, 2009, p. 251).

Exploration of this question is also an important component of the just war tradition, specifically the notion of *jus post bellum*, a principle first expounded upon by Hugo de Groot, or Grotius, an eminent seventeenth century Dutch-born legal theorist and philosopher. In his work *After War Ends*, philosopher Larry

May seeks to develop a greater appreciation of Grotius's ideas on this relatively neglected aspect of the just war tradition. "The proper moral answer to the question 'why do we fight,'" May writes, "must be 'to achieve a just peace' and in this sense the questions of *jus ad bellum*, which concern the moral basis for initiating war, must be intimately linked to questions of *jus post bellum*, which concern the moral basis for the end of war" (May, 2012, p. 12).

Even with focusing the analytical lens of Reconstruction on issues surrounding *jus post bellum*, the student of history still confronts a wide-open historical terrain where pedagogical goals may get lost. One topic of Reconstruction that lends itself to an exploration of the swirling debates around justice and the political and social cross-currents that informed them are issues pertaining to official government responses, or non-responses, around the treatment of soldiers at the close of the war. Embedded in this debate is the uneven prosecution of justice in American life. The year 1866 is particularly illustrative of systematic racism and its manifestation within dialogues of reconciliation, social stability, or the effort to restore federal power in the South through appeasements to white power and fulfilling the demands of *jus post bellum*. Two focal points of analysis bring these contrasting forms of adjudicating justice into sharp relief; namely, questions around the charge of treason for former Confederate General Robert E. Lee versus the basic protections of citizenship provided for African Americans and black Federal soldiers in Memphis and New Orleans. These critical months foreshadowed the realism that was to come as human agents made concessions and compromises as newly constituted and constitutional state sought "a new birth of freedom" while plotting its way towards the creation of an interracial democracy. For the student of history, no catharsis is to be found in this story, but its exploration will help them to understand the complicated nature of social formation and the dualities that constitute moments of our nation's history (Kennedy, 1998).

LINCOLN'S PRAGMATISM, LEGAL FORMALISM, AND TENSIONS WITH "CHARITY FOR ALL"

At the close of the fighting season in 1861, the *Harrisburg Patriot and Union* expressed the doubts of Northerners about the prospects of restoring an authentic peace. Speaking of the South's disposition towards Northerners, the newspaper suggested "We cannot force them to regard us with affection" (Harrisburg *Patriot and Union*, January 7, 1861; Shankman, 1980, p. 54). The newspaper spoke a simple truth. While the war for the Union was predicated on reunification, it alluded to commonly held doubts about a lasting peace. The reconfiguration wartime objectives involving emancipation, however, linked the challenge of reestablishing "bonds of affection" to issues of human rights and democratic justice for a people once thought of as personal property.

Simply stated wartime objectives not only took on a moral dimension but so did the aims of peace. The dilemma that was recognized in 1861, namely the use of violent force to achieve cultural transformation, did not abate by 1865.

Lincoln reasoned that the moral faculties of white Southerners—or Northerners for that matter—who doubted the original premise equality among the races could in time have their consciousness persuaded based on the lawful implementation of justice and democratic power. What Lincoln plainly saw in 1862/63, somehow was not seen by his fellow countrymen and for Lincoln, the remedy was to reestablish the routines of domestic order and working life among Southerners for them to see the reasonable nature of emancipation. In March, 1865, meeting aboard the *River Queen* with Generals Grant and Sherman, along with Admiral Porter, Lincoln stated he to offer generous terms to the South in order to "get the deluded men of the rebel armies disarmed and back to their homes…" where, Lincoln thought, "…they won't take up arms again. Let them all go, officers and all, I want submission and no more bloodshed.…I want no one punished; treat them liberally all around. We want those people to return to their allegiance to the Union and submit to the laws" (Donald, 1995, p. 574). Herein lies the "tragedy" of the moment or perhaps sheds light on what some have termed Lincoln's Achilles heel, that is his "tragic pragmatism." Lincoln held an abiding faith in the power of rationalism to move people to do what is right with little recognition of the structural impediments and deep roots upon which racism thrived. Moving away from the greater movements of time during Reconstruction enables students to wrestle with these values and judgments, both sharpening their critical thinking skills and appreciating the ethical complexity of the moment.

As a young congressman, Lincoln spoke of the "strict observance of all the laws" suggesting a great reverence for the law which he, influenced by his reading of Cicero, saw as fundamental to the success of any Republic. Delivering an address before the Young Men's Lyceum of Springfield, Illinois, in 1838, Lincoln claimed the law was, "the political religion of the nation" where citizens of the nation should "sacrifice unceasingly upon its altars" (Basler, ed. 1953, Vol. I, pp. 108–115). Despite any possible shortcomings or imperfections, the law buttressed the democratic project and, in Lincoln's mind, enabled the democratic experiment to maintain the bulwark of its egalitarian principles against any of its enemies. This conviction is exemplified in an 1855 letter to his confidant Joshua F. Speed about the existential threats posed to democracy by the anti-immigration party known as the "Know Nothing Party." Cautioning against the "degeneracy" of democratic spirit in the moment, Lincoln decried, "As a nation, we begin by declaring that 'all men are created.' We now practically read it 'all men are created equal, except negroes.' When the Know-Nothings get control, it will read 'all men are created equal except negroes, and foreigners, and catholics.' When it comes to this," Lincoln quipped, "I should prefer emigrating to some country where they make no pretense of loving liberty—to Russia, for instance, where the despotism can be taken pure, and without the base alloy of hypocrisy" (Basler, 1953, Vol. 2, pp. 320–324). Throughout much of Lincoln's life, the moral good of Republics was secured through the application of adjudicated laws. Moral sentiments or intentions, as principled and well-grounded as they might be, could not overturn legal means without due process. Students may object to this reasoned use of the law in penultimate issues of human rights and equality, but as historian Allen C. Guelzo eloquently reminds us, "For the president of the United States to fling legal prudence to the wind on the grounds that he considered something 'morally right' would not give the nation morality, but despotism" (Guelzo, 2004, p. 224).

But as scholar Larry May suggests *jus post bellum* and entailing efforts of reconciliation are "…such an amorphous normative principle that it is unlikely to be instantiated in a system of rules" (May, 2012, p. 101). Any discussions of race, equality, and justice that naturally rise with Reconstruction should also emphasize the confluence of historical forces in the moment that brought about unprecedented social change creating a chasm for civil law to fill. The moral decree of the Emancipation Proclamation culminating in the Thirteenth Amendment, which according to David E. Kyvig was "a dramatic statement of social policy placing the federal government on the side of human rights at the expense of private property rights as they were understood" took two years to be codified into law (Kyvig, 1996, p. 155). The assassin's bullet had long removed Lincoln from earth to witness the culmination of these changes. To borrow a phrase from Lincoln biographer John Burt, there was a "tragic pragmatism" guiding Lincoln's approach to recognizing human rights and establishing an interracial democracy that accentuated problems of black citizenship for those caught in the moment. A kind of legal formalism which guided Lincoln's thinking, a perspective shared by many of Lincoln's time and ours, limited the range of options in dealing with the difficult demands of transitional peace and subsequently dampened enthusiasm among whites to support combating systemic racial inequality.

Herein lies the tensions with Lincoln's Reconstruction program, from its origins it was a radical vision of the liberal state at the time. No doubt it was restrained by a legal formalism which was less than nimble in the moment and conceptions of a moral universe that failed to expediently address civil rights fully. It should be remembered, however, the Emancipation Proclamation which set the course for subsequent Reconstruction amendments were, as historian Eric Foner deems them, "sleeping giants." The amendments revealed the socially restrictive definitions of freedom and equality that had developed as working principles in America up until the mid-nineteenth century. Speaking of Reconstruction's expansive view of citizen's rights as the logical fulfillment of the Revolutionary Period, Foner remarks, "The underlying principles…were striking departures in American law" from earlier generations (Foner, 1998, p. 107). Caught in the midst of these contradictory values were African Americans who initially did not benefit from the legal protections of citizenship in the year following the war. Since notions of citizenship have been historically linked to soldiering since the Revolution, it is no coincidence that Black Union soldiers became the initial symbolic target of white Southerners to disrupt Reconstruction efforts and sought to maintain the status quo of racial division and hierarchy in the South following the war (Resch, 1999, pp.177–201).

Given the appreciable adjustments in Lincoln's thinking about these issues as war necessitated changes, perhaps the president's actions would have met these challenges and his thinking might have continued to evolve, but the answers to these issues we cannot fully know. To be sure, Lincoln was a president not an autocrat. He worked within the limits of the law, with members of Congress who were greatly divided over prosecution of the war and its aims, and had to respond to the Joint Select Committee on the Conduct of the War whose investigative efforts did both "marked harm" and "contributed positively to the war effort" and the Lincoln Administration's efforts (Tap, 1998, pp. 8–9). Still, his conception of the relationship between the law and society restrained him (Donald, 1995, p. 588).

The so-called tragedy of the era was not of Lincoln's making alone, but one of a process that did not adjust to the unprecedented nature of a more egalitarian state and the demands transitional justice would have in order to secure such a state (Fry, 2013). Modern liberal states face similar paradoxes today. As philosopher Larry May writes, "In violent use of force, the chief human rights abridgement risked is the right to life. In nonviolent use of force," May continues, "the chief human rights infringement risked is the right to liberty" (May, 2012, p. 131).

It is revealing of Lincoln's mind and values, however, that the narrative thread of the just war tradition was stitched through this era and additionally was one that was relatively absent in American history prior to the Civil War. Teasing out this subject complicates our understanding of Reconstruction as careful attention needs to be paid to the historical contexts in which its stated objectives were implemented against the range of possible alternative approaches (Starr, 2007, pp. 17–18). A study of external forces that imposed constraints on presidential power encourages students to resist singular explanatory theories about Lincoln's intractable bigotry or his magnanimous character as an emancipator and homespun philosopher (Oates, 1979, p. 61). Through this exploration students may discover the limits of Lincoln's antislavery efforts as they pressed against constitutional constraints of presidential powers, but perhaps more importantly they may see how the collective conditions to ensure "peace" were fraught with contradictions and compromises when it came to issues of justice long after Lincoln was killed.

Further complicating this story is that prior to the Lincoln administration, dialogue about the morality of war was generally divorced postwar realities. In some respects, this statement holds true today. Yet a close examination of Lincoln's thinking about wartime measures reveals a consistent awareness of the correlation between the war and construct a lasting peace. "Lincoln began considering the issues of Reconstruction almost as soon as the war broke out" writes historian Vernon Burton in *The Age of Lincoln*. The author continues by remarking, "Just like war, war's aftermath involved matters of moral integrity and sheer power" and therefore throughout Lincoln's presidency there was an ongoing deliberation about the terms of peace (Burton, 2007, p. 238). Upon hearing of the Lincoln administration's efforts, David Lowry Swain, the one-time governor of North Carolina, simply remarked, "With reference to emancipation, we are at the beginning of war" (Foner, 1988, p. 123). Now, the moral objectives of an existing war had changed, creating a fundamental tension between human rights, civil justice, and the current construction of rights within the liberal state.

Although seventeenth-century Holland may seem historically unrelatable to the lives of Civil War Americans, in terms of ethical thinking about the nature warfare these worlds were, in some sense, not far apart. Some of President Lincoln's "team of rivals" were intimately familiar these intellectual developments in Europe (Witt, 2012, pp.170–219). Henry Halleck, who served as Lincoln's General-in-Chief of all Union armies during the war, published his influential work, *International Law; or Rules Regulating the Intercourse of States in Peace and War* in 1861 recognizing Grotius's contribution to the just war tradition (Halleck, 1861). Francis Leiber, who Halleck and Secretary of War Edwin Stanton solicited in 1862 to give clarity to Enlightenment thinking about the rules of warfare, particularly as related to codes of conduct towards those without national citizenship, ex-slave turned soldier, might find protection under humanitarian restraints of the law, developed his 157 codes concerning the conduct of war with Grotius not far from his mind (Smith, 1956). Popularly known as General Order 100 or Lieber's Code, *Instructions for the Government of Armies of the United States in the Field* outlined the rules of warfare building upon the just war tradition and central to this code was questions of morality. Code 15, for example, states in part, "Men who take up arms against one another in public war do not cease on this account to be moral beings, responsible to one another, and to God." (Lieber, 1898). Lieber's conceptualization of rights and obligations according to author James Childress were "inter-completing." This perspective was not Lieber's alone, but held by many leaders of the Union and Confederate war effort schooled in Enlightenment philosophy. To sever these two notions from one another was to undermine the ethical ground upon which nineteenth-century American based their actions. Obligation, Childress further explains, is the corollary of right and therefore to uphold one's right entails a person's duty (Childress, 1982, p. 128). This corollary was fundamental in the treatment that was to come for former Confederate soldiers, particularly with men like General Lee.

The dilemmas of establishing *jus post bellum* were formalized by Hugo Grotius, the architect of an international legal system who first published *De Jure Bellli ac Pacis* in 1625, in which issues of postbellum morality were central. While recently theorists have drawn distinctions between "intermediate states" and "postbellum states," the problems manifest in creating peaceful states out of warring ones were no less apparent to those fighting the American Civil War. The signing of the Treaty of Westphalia, observes Geoffrey Robertson, was a "'Grotian moment' that produced a new world order" for the West which included the legitimization of war as a means to settle disputes and seek peace (Robertson, 2006, p. 4). This redistribution of political and civic powers spawned intellectual debates, most notably Emer de Vattel's, *The Law of Nations* first published in 1758, that resulted in several important publications concerning individual rights, the obligations of nation states, and the justifications for waging war. Still by the close of the nineteenth century, the problem of transitional justice and a recognition of human rights posed serious problems to liberal state and the just war tradition in the West. As one prominent British barrister wrote at the opening of the twentieth century, "the law recognizes a state of peace and a state of war but that it knows nothing of an intermediate state which is neither one thing nor the other" (Stahn, 2006, pp.158–160).

In many respects it can be said that Lincoln's thinking about war was fundamentally ground in principles that underlie the act of moral judgment, which involves both a "truthful pronouncement on what has been done" and "an effective foundation for what is to be done" (O'Donovan, 2003, p. 15). Nowhere is this ethical formula more evidenced than in the Emancipation Proclamation. "With the Union's triumph," writes Eric Foner, "freedom truly defined the nation's existence." The eminent historian on Reconstruction further adds, "The concrete reality of emancipation posed freedom as a historical and substantive issue, rather than a philosophical or metaphorical one" (Foner, 1998, p. 100). The logical conclusions introduced by the Emancipation Proclamation fundamentally altered notions about *jus post bellum* and by logical extension the prosecution of *jus in bello*. Historian John Fabian Witt maintains that two interrelated but analytically distinct ideals, humanitarianism and justice, has "animated American behavior" around warfare. "In 1862," the author claims, "it was the crisis of slavery and emancipation that called forth the Union's law of war instructions and helped produce the modern laws of war" (Witt, 2012, pp. 7–9). Albeit in its infancy, modern-day just war theory (i.e., *jus ad bellum*; *jus in bello*; *jus post bellum*) was being formulated in the midst of the Civil War and subsequently implemented during Reconstruction.

Transition to the post-war years, as Lincoln defined them, had two primary political and potentially conflicting goals. The first was consolidating Federal power in the South and restoring functioning political institutions within the state. Historians such as William Hesseltine have rightly criticized Lincoln's plan as it relates to white Southerners. He notes, "Lincoln had rested his program on a hope that mystic chords of affection would draw loyal people back into proper political relations to the government," a proposition that was naïve, at best, about the realities of war and the relationship between *jus in bello* and *jus post bellum* (Hesseltine, 1960, p. 30). A second was the recognition of the legal and civil rights, still ill-defined by the administration, of African Americans among white Southerners. While the institution of slavery had been outlawed by Lincoln's administration in the seceding states, the question of legal protections of citizenship for Blacks remained unsettled on paper until the Civil Rights Act of 1866. For more than a year, the peace that followed and rights of American citizenship was disproportionally applied, reflecting the tensions between individual rights and communal justice.

These long months without legal recognition were fraught with peril. Scholar Ruti Teitel highlights one of the fundamental dilemmas surrounding transitional justice is, "the struggle is over the extent to which pre-existing procedures are adhered to or new regime values are advanced." The author continues, "The conception of justice that emerges is contextualized and partial: What is deemed just is contingent and informed by prior justice" (Teitel, 2000, p. 6; p. 215). Lincoln's tendency toward legal formalism coupled with a pragmatism was an outlook shared by many leading Republicans of his time. Theirs was a faith in democratic project writ large, that would ultimately propel white Southerners allegiances and restore the Union on Northern emancipatory terms.

In his planning for Reconstruction, Lincoln firmly believed that the white South would ultimately honor their national commitments. This roadmap for Reconstruction, which was followed to varying degrees by Lincoln's predecessors, was predicated on the belief that the rule of law ground the legal order even in extraordinary times. Great caution, some would say a timidity, was to be taken when applying the law to any historical contingencies (Teitel, 2000). Had Lincoln lived would his presupposition about the law been radically altered given the unprecedented nature of Reconstruction and the accompanying demands of an interracial democracy? It is hard to say, even of this extraordinary man. For as historian Paul Escott reminds us when thinking the so-called revolutionary nature of the war, students of the history should be aware that "for an intelligent understanding of race in U.S. history the proof lies in the policies, not in the supposed but secret noble intentions" (Escott, 2009, pp. 240–241).

History unfolded to bring about both a legal and practical conundrum concerning the enforcement and protection of civil rights for blacks, many of the nation's leaders failed to enact obligations of transitional justice assuring a "new birth of freedom" for African Americans. The year 1866 reveals the deep connection that emerged in America between soldiering and the ability to enjoy the rights of citizenship. In looking at the realities facing Black Union veterans and former Confederate leaders like Robert E. Lee, a sharp contrast can be drawn where issues of jus post bellum came to the fore and justice was denied in both accounts, but in deeply contrasting ways.

LESSONS OF CONTINGENCY: ROBERT E. LEE, SYMBOLISM, AND WHITE SOUTH

On the Sunday following Lincoln's assassination, Northerners gathered to mourn the loss of their fallen leader. At the South Presbyterian Church in Brooklyn, New York, Reverend Samuel T. Spear ascended into his pulpit asking his congregants, "What shall we do with the rebels?" While scholars have for some time recounted these sermons as important mechanisms for transforming the wartime president into a national martyr, a considerable number of these sermons thunderously proclaimed that the path of reunion was one predicated upon a justice that demanded punishment for Confederates like Jefferson Davis, Alexander H. Stephens, and Robert E. Lee (Chesebrough, 1993, 1994; Schwartz, 1991). Like many public leaders in the North, Spear blamed white Southern aristocrats for a war based on the sin of slavery, all the while overlooking the benefits whites enjoyed from the system throughout the nation.

Calls for retributive justice against leading Confederates were common and full of vitriol. Spears's sermon entitled "The Punishment of Treason" captured the sensibilities of many who saw the North as righteous victors who God had ordained to implement justice. The biblical text of Spear's sermon was Psalm 89 verse 14 which reads, "Justice and judgment are the habitation of thy throne: mercy and truth shall go before thy face" (King James Bible, 1769). Given such catastrophic losses on the battlefield throughout four years of fighting, there was little room for mercy among divines like Spear as calls for retributive justice echoed throughout the North. The minister's words mirrored those of some Radical Republicans suggesting the properties of leaders be confiscated, trials for treason should be held, and Confederate leaders be hanged. "Simultaneously with this work," Spear thundered from the pulpit, "I would turn to another class less conspicuous and in some respects less criminal, yet deeply guilty and very dangerous to the public peace; and these men I would *expel* from the country, and confiscate their property for the benefit of the State." Spear continued to share his ideas with the congregation spelling out the multilayered problem of peace. "A third class I would *disfranchise,* making them incapable of wielding any political power or discharging any official duty under the Government of these United States. By these several methods I would *punish* treason according to the gradation of its guilt: and by combining them I would make an utter end of the leading rebel-traitors." He concluded his thoughts with this summary: "In this way I would vindicate the majesty of the law, and protect the masses of the common people, alike Northern and Southern" (Spear, 1865, p. 20).

Concerns about violent social unrest following the war had long been on the minds of Northerners as they fought to negotiate peace. General Ulysses S. Grant wrote to Commodore Daniel Ammen, a childhood friend from Georgetown, Ohio, criticizing fellow Northerners who sought compromising peace terms in a hard-fought war. "It would be but the beginning of the war," Grant speculated in August, 1864. "The demands of the South would know no limits…and they would keep on demanding until it would be better dead than submit longer" (Smith, 2001, p. 382). Months of hard fighting lay ahead, but Grant was in no mode for anything but "unconditional surrender" in 1864.

During the latter-half of his sermon, Spear explained his reasoning around peace terms. An underlying current of this discourse was the necessary measures to take for peaceful reunification, justice, and stemming any potential of continued civil unrest. "Treason is a crime, the highest crime known to man…," the cleric reasoned, "…[it] is the spirit of disorder and hell. It is hence justly regarded as the highest offence which a man can commit against the majesty of law." He concluded, "…if you will not punish traitors, tell me, if you please, what class of criminals you will punish." Drawing an analogy between treason and murder, the minister asked, "Will you hang a plain common man who in a fit of passion kills his neighbor, and leave such a gentleman as Jefferson Davis or General Lee, whose offense consists in trying to kill the State, unscathed by the righteous penalty of law?" (Spear, 1865, p. 21). By war's end, many Northerners were primed for justice. The forethought by Confederate leaders, long-term planning, no just provocation, coupled with armed resistance against popular government for the "despotic and cruel system of slavery," and the mistreatment of Union prisoners, specifically Union soldiers at Andersonville, were all elements that called for justice and "the most condign punishment." In both thought and deed, according to Spear, Lee and others leading southern men were no more than "chivalrous barbarians" (Spear, 1865, pp. 21–26).

Such analogies held symbolic power at the time and for the North, Confederate leaders represented the worst of anti-democratic values. Paul Roscoe's essay on social signaling, conflict management, and the difficulties in structuring peace offers some helpful insights when looking back at Reconstruction. Once emancipation was proclaimed as policy, Lincoln's plan of Reconstruction centralized the issue of human rights. This direction of governance was unprecedented and exposed the inadequacies of the liberal state so deeply divided along racial and economic lines. Roscoe remarks, "Conflicts of interest are managed through elaborate and supposedly 'objective' systems of governmental control: legislative bodies that define legitimate interests and prescribe sanctions for infringing upon them." Yet the realities of life in the South was a small-scale, politically decentralized communities where the mechanisms for maintaining peace were quite different and involved what Roscoe terms, "passionate ethics." Central to this type of intragroup system is the maintenance of peace, which relies heavily on symbolic headmen, who both dispense justice while simultaneously embody its mediation in society. Such systems operate along many socio-economic lines, including race. The author continues, "Passionate ethics esteem the internal harmony of the political community, abjure intragroup violence, and exalt the use of peaceful rather than violent means of advancing the former over the latter. They also have rudimentary judicial systems: headmen, priests, or gathering of peers, before whom complaints can be brought for mediation, arbitration, or adjudication" (Fry, 2013, pp. 476–477).

Given the social realities involving sectional systems of justice, it is no surprise that some of the most virulent post-war debates in 1865 and 1866 surrounded former Confederate soldiers and the swearing of allegiance to the United States in order to regain citizenship. Nor did the problems end once former Confederates pledged to "swallowed the dog." Racial hatred continued to grip both north and south and social stability in the defeated section also was under tremendous pressure from a crippling economic condition, continued animosity towards federal authority, monetary issues, and the legal status and rights of blacks in the region. Service in the war ultimately raised considerable questions for both state and national governments concerning veterans and their families. Power and violence, a point of discussion to follow, were central to this ongoing dialogue.

It is worth noting that Spear's reasoning, although not appropriating the language of the just war tradition, certainly appropriated its concepts. With justice as a central theme, the sermon writer drew a correlation between *jus ad bellum* and *jus in bello*. Developing a course of action for *jus post bellum* in April 1865 was a penultimate problem as Robert E. Lee, like most of his fellow Southerners, remained, in the words of the minister, "conquered, but not converted" to the terms of northern victory (Spear, 1865, p. 32). With Lincoln's skillful political leadership now gone, federal leaders faced two potentially countervailing goals for Reconstruction. The first was the extent to which emancipation and Reconstruction policies could guarantee the rights of citizenship to over four million former slaves. The 13th Amendment, the only constitutional amendment signed by a president, ended the practice of slavery but stopped short of full citizenship leaving black Americans in legal peril as their status remained ill-defined. The second was the restoration of white Southerners to full citizenship. Historian William C. Harris remarks that, "Lincoln's peace terms, except for the addition of the emancipation requirement, had not fundamentally changed since 1861 when, in his July 4 message to Congress, he promised that the government would restore the constitutional rights of Southerners once they had ceased their rebellion" (Harris, 2009, p. 95).

These objectives left many like Spear to ask, "What shall we do with the rebels?" Scholar Colleen Murphy examines the processes of reconciliation emphasizing the development of political principles and the rule of law as they relate to questions of cultural norms. "Of the attitudinal changes that are most important in attaining reconciliation," Murphy writes, "is the attitude toward returning soldiers. And the hardest issue to deal with is that of having positive attitudes towards those soldiers who participated in an unjust war of aggression...against one's own nation or ethnic group" (May, 2012, p. 89). Scholars have long debated both the methods and possible ramifications of what Spear and other northern leaders were suggesting at the time to secure justice. Lee was certainly a symbolic figure, so his treatment in the courts would have social implications. One Confederate soldier near the end of the war recounted in his diary of seeing the "Godlike Lee" near Farmville, Virginia (Levy, 1865, diary entry April 7th). Given such sentiment, the question facing nineteenth-century Americans was "What path does justice follow to secure northern war aims and a lasting peace?"

In thinking about a "morality of peace," Larry May offers six normative principles that must frame the *jus post bellum* discourse. They are: rebuilding of vanquished states and collective responsibility; the law and balancing retributive justice; restitution; reparations; the proportionality principle; and reconciliation. Long before America's civil conflict, Hugo Grotius warned about conflating wartime motives with those of reasoned justice. "For in some cases," Grotius writes, "motives of interest operate distinctly from motives of justice." Drawing the distinction between social justice and motives, Grotius suggests, is fundamental to just war reasoning (Grotius, 1646, p. 170). Extending this premise into peacetime realities, the contemporary ethicist Larry May suggests that in the case of *jus post bellum*, "...not all strategies that promote peace are worth pursuing, especially when pursuit of peace means that justice will not be had" (May, 2012, p. 44). He additionally notes, "...attitudes toward soldiers on both sides during war or armed conflict will affect the ability to achieve reconciliation after war ends" (May, 2012, p. 85).

While contemporary scholarship on the just war tradition provides students of history ample opportunity to explore issues related to justice across many subjects, given the limitations of space it is perhaps helpful to examine the extreme responses to this question. This approach seems most relevant, when it comes to understanding Spear's position and advocacy for Lee's execution for treason, as the power over a citizen's life held by liberal states is the greatest power and should be carefully considered. Highlighting elements of Robert E. Lee's life in the immediate year after the war provides such an opportunity because in a sense, Lee would come to epitomize for many Southerners "their" cause. Lee's case provides one opportunity to explore ethical issues and obstacles, both our own and those of historical actors, to ethical reasoning because as humans, "we have a propensity to respond to the plight of a single identifiable individual rather than a large number of people about whom we have only statistical information" (Singer, 2016, p. 212). It is worth remembering too, that many who advanced theories of execution did not single out Lee alone.

The other extreme response is to simply avoid prosecution altogether. In the case of Robert E. Lee this is what took place, but the key measure here is the idea of premediated and were the actions that lead to this circumstance consciously taken with this objective in mind. In either of these extremes there are consequences to weigh. With his seminal treatment *Practical Ethics*, Peter Singer forwards the concept of justification as an important tool to distinguish broadly based ethical reasoning from those acts an individual alone claim to be moral. Singer writes, "Self-interested acts must be shown to be compatible with more broadly-based ethical principles if they are to be ethically defensible, for the notion of ethics carries with it the idea of something bigger than the individual" (Singer, 1993, p. 10). The conclusion that Lee was symbolic of the Confederate cause and any form punishment would inevitably garner a large and violent response from Southerners is speculative and singularly focused at best. Put bluntly, the foremost concern articulated at the time was a social stability enjoyed by middle- and upper-class whites.

Issues around historical contingency are also an important factor when weighing ethical options and possible outcomes. It is important to remember that Lee wasn't always the "Marble Man" of the southern cause and therefore some form of legal finding might not have resulted in violent social unrest. "From the evidence of Civil War writings prior to the 1870s, Lee did not possess the aura of the invincible military chieftain. Early biographers and historians, North and South, criticized him for major blunders…," writes biographer Thomas Lawrence Connelly. He continues, "But between 1870 and 1885 Lee emerged as the pre-eminent military idol of the South, a man described as invincible on the battlefield. He gained such a grip upon the Southern mind that by 1900 he was the great regional hero, surpassing even George Washington" (Connelly, 1977, p. 4). While not prosecuting Lee and other leaders is judicially difficult to reason, the question of how to handle Lee's case in the immediate aftermath of the war is one involving both judicial and political questions. It is also one that involves *jus post bellum* and proportionality, another concept of just war reasoning.

Justice is not theory but practice and so there are good reasons to focus on larger cultural frameworks when it comes to issues of justice. Ethical reasoning is not based on the principle that one can justify an ethical system, but rather what are the systematic implications of an ethical position. Moreover, feminist scholars have skillfully shown systematic structures that lead to inequality and oppression often maintain the rights of individuals while at the same time denying the possibility of systematic moral infringement upon a community. Writing on issues of individual freedom, scholar Linda Bell reminds us that acts of intimidation or oppression within systems of violence do not have to be overt actions to be measured as harmful or immoral. "First, a focus only on self and individual relationships leaves the larger system of oppression intact and leaves at their mercy all who do not have the wherewithal to protect themselves effectively." Later Bell suggests, "Second, individual solutions may, in fact, ultimately undermine themselves by strengthening the status quo to such an extent that solutions, even of this sort, become more problematic and difficult" (Bell, 1993, p. 27).

Perhaps it is no surprise that at the end of the war, Congressman Thaddeus Stevens, the skillful Pennsylvanian lawyer would insightfully understand the social and legal implications of the moment. For Stevens, given the issue of jus ante bellum, prosecution was not a choice but necessity for justice. In a speech on Reconstruction delivered in Lancaster Pennsylvania in September, 1865, the radical Republican took up the question of the status of former rebels. Stevens told those gathered, "Upon the character of the belligerent, and the justice of the war, and the manner of conducting it, depends our right to take the lives, liberty and property of the belligerent. This war had its origin in treason without one spark of justice." While the congressional leader has been remembered as a bloodthirsty extremist seeking Confederate blood, a portraiture developed in the late-nineteenth century by Southerners and Democrats, in reality Stevens recognized the tenuous nature of the time suggesting moderating forms of justice that might mollify extremes. "Surely, these things are sufficient to justify the exercise of the extreme rights of war—'to execute, to imprison, to confiscate.'" Stevens told the crowd. "How many captive enemies it would be proper to execute, as an example to nations, I leave others to judge." He then offered the audience his opinion on the matter, saying "I am not fond of sanguinary punishments, but surely some victims must propitiate the manes of our starved, murdered, slaughtered martyrs. A court-martial could do justice according to law" (Stevens, 1865). But moderation did not win the day. Why?

Human choice is the story of history, but not everyone shares the same range of options at any given moment, may share the same abilities in response, nor anticipate the potential consequences of their choices and actions. Furthermore, the consequences of some actions are simply unforeseen. Commanding General of the United States Army, Ulysses S. Grant, was undoubtedly a devoted to the Union cause and a faithful companion of President Lincoln. Award-winning biographer David Herbert Donald claims that on several conversations with Grant and others, "Lincoln was not just ordering the generals to follow protocol: he wanted to make sure that any negotiations led not merely to a suspension of fighting but to a peace that would ensure his war aims of Union, Emancipation, and at least limited Equality" (Donald, 1995, pp. 573–574). Evidence shows that despite being called a "butcher" in the press and subsequent histories of the war, the Commanding General measured the cost of human life in the cause. For example on April 7th, 1865, Grant asked Lee to surrender the Army of Northern Virginia writing in part, "I feel it so [Lee's need to surrender after a weeklong series of losses], and regard it as my duty to shift from myself the responsibility of any further effusion of blood by asking of you the surrender of that portion of the Confederate States army known as the Army of Northern Virginia" (Smith, 2001, p. 399). Lee declined the offer.

Two days later, however, Lee accepted the terms offered by Grant and in these conversations, according to historian Jean Edward Smith, Grant "went out of his way to spare Lee embarrassment..." (Smith, 2001, p. 400). On Palm Sunday, April 9, 1865 Lee surrendered to Grant at Appomattox. One Grant biographer writes, "Writing rapidly, he brought the war in Virginia to a close with less than 200 well-chosen words, reflecting the charity that Lincoln desired and his own innate generosity." The last two sentences of Grant's peace terms, Confederate officers could keep side arms and soldiers could keep horses and private baggage, were significantly consequential for the terror campaigns that ensued. Officers and men could return home and "not to be disturbed by United States authority" so long as they observed the terms of their parole and the laws in force where they resided (Smith, 2001, p. 405). Recounting Lincoln's pragmatic approach to political questions coupled with ethicist Peter Singer's idea that "we have a propensity to respond to the plight of a single identifiable individual" it may be that Grant, in the moment, could not have envisioned the implications of these hastily penned words, but his choice was deadly consequential, and in all probability predicated on codes of honor that, at best, focused on the disciplined qualities of soldiering while naively measuring the potential long-term ramifications of allowing a defeated enemy to return home with firearms.

The weight of the white terrorist history that followed in the South does not singularly rest with Grant's actions at Appomattox Court House; however, it was the one step in a process of decisions and actions that seriously jeopardized legal prosecutions of former Confederate insurgents. Mirroring a type of "passionate ethics" which placed soldiering, sacrifice, and honor as qualities of receiving a pardon, Grant's act severely limited the options for working out principles of *jus post bellum* in the courts or on the ground. Power, which might have been redistributed differently throughout the South had Grant followed Lincoln's advice for soldiers to return without arms, would soon come to rest in the armed minority. His involvement with now citizen Lee did not end at Appomattox.

Weeks after the assassination of Lincoln, a Grand Jury in the District Court of Columbia handed down separate indictments against Jefferson Davis and John C. Breckinridge for high treason. According to a report of the *New York Observer and Chronicle*, the court based its charges on the Confederate raid of the city in July 1864, known as the Battle of Fort Stevens. The charge of this "overt act" included the "killing of citizens and destroying property" with Breckinridge being "present in person" and Jefferson Davis being associated with the crime "constructively" (*New York Observer and Chronicle*, 1865; *The Independent*, 1865).

The following month Judge John C. Underwood, a Virginian who remained loyal to the Union during the war, issued an indictment from the bench of the U.S. District Court of Virginia against thirty-seven indictments of treason against former leaders including Robert E. Lee, James Longstreet, and Jubal Early. Also charged were two of Lee's sons, a nephew of the former commander, and several former Confederate governors and other political figures. Underwood issued a two-fold argument against former Confederate leaders who had perpetrated "the most gigantic, bloody and unprovoked crimes that ever cursed the world" (Blair, 2014, p. 239). Although thousands of Confederate soldiers had participated in treasonous activity taking up arms against their country, Underwood absolved them of any crimes based on pragmatic considerations suggesting prosecution of all soldiers was unreasonable and an impractical plan. Contracting case law, which did not grant the notion of accessories when it came to treason, Underwood followed the logic of many Union men at the time suggesting the common soldier was "not morally responsible for the Rebellion" (May, 2012, p. 90). Seeking prosecution of leaders for the immorality of Confederate justifications for war, the judge overturned the earlier paroles granted to Confederate soldiers claiming such protection was a "military arrangement" that did not apply to the civil rights enjoyed by the nation's citizenry (*Philadelphia Inquirer*, 1865; Blair, 2014, p. 239).

Such legal positioning was unsettling to Lee. Writing Grant on June 13, 1865, Lee sought to get clarification on recent indictment for treason issued by Underwood. Lee's letter typified elements of male southern honor that stood in contrast with a kind of obsequiousness that characterized some of his remarks. "I am ready to meet any charges that may be preferred against me, & do not wish to avoid trial," Lee declared, "but if I can correct as to the protection granted by my parole, & am not to be prosecuted." In order to demonstrate his new-found loyalty to the Union and give some assurances to his former battlefield protagonist, Lee wrote, "I desire to Comply with the provisions of the President's proclamation & therefore enclose the required application" (Simon, 1988, p. 150).

Grant wrote assuring Lee of the legal standing of his parole and then campaigned to Federal officials. Writing Secretary of War Edwin M. Stanton, Grant stated, "In my opinion the officers and men paroled at Appomattox C. H. and since upon the same terms given to Lee, cannot be tried for treason so long as they observe the terms of their parole." Grant's plea was not rooted in civil legal arguments, but rather codes of military honor and his individual moral commitments. "Good faith as well as true policy dictates that we should observe the conditions of that convention," Grant suggested. "Bad faith on the part of the Governm't or a construction of that convention subjecting officers to trial for treason, would produce a feeling of insecurity in the minds of all paroled officers and men. If so disposed they might even regard such an infraction of terms, by the Government as an entire release from all obligation on their part" (Simon, 1988, p. 149). Fully aware of Lincoln's admonition of military leaders steer clear of political planning or policies, Grant sought to assure Stanton his recommendation was consistent with the policies of the recently assassinated President. "I will state further that the terms granted by me met with the hearty approval of the President at the time, and of the country generally. The action of Judge Underwood in Norfolk has already had an injurious effect, and I would ask that he be ordered to quash all indictments found against paroled prisoners of war, and to desist from further prosecution of them" (Simon, 1988, p. 149). Grant was not alone in his reasoning about Lee. Henry Halleck, Lincoln's appointed General-in-Chief and solicitor of just war theorist Francis Leiber, agreed with Grant that southern submission to Union peace terms would be expedited by showing leniency to Robert E. Lee (Simpson, 1991, p. 105).

President Andrew Johnson was not persuaded by Grant's views. Although a native of Tennessee, Johnson was from humble origins and prior to politics, he was a tailor by trade. Schooled in the politics of Jacksonian America, Johnson shared few affinities with the slaveholding class and as a Democrat saw himself as representing the country's working class whose lives were made difficult by aristocrats and speculators of industrialism. As an early congressional advocate of the homestead legislation in Tennessee, Johnson was not fond of the planter class and his hatred towards these aristocrats only grew upon Secession. As wartime governor of the state, Johnson made his feelings known claiming to "extend no terms of compromise" to "leading traitors." These sentiments had not changed when Johnson took the oath of office. News of his presidency, Jefferson Davis claimed, would be "disastrous for our people" (Hahn, 2016, p. 299).

News of Grant's position reached Johnson, who refused to entertain the general's views. For four days, between June 16–20, Grant privately campaigned that his general pardon be upheld and that Lee's status as a parole not be overturned unless the former Confederate violate the terms. Finally, in a last-ditch effort to persuade Johnson, Grant threated to resign if Johnson persisted in prosecuting Lee (Simon, 1988, p. 150). In this moment, politics, not justice reigned. Grant biographer Brooks Simpson writes, "Realizing that without Grant's support his administration would be in serious trouble, Johnson backed down. On June 20 Attorney General Speed directed that the proceedings against Lee be dropped" (Simpson, 2000, p. 453). Grant immediately informed his former adversary that all legal proceedings against the former Confederate commander by the federal government would cease. Commenting on the significance of Grant's actions historian William A. Blair writes, "Lee owed Grant a very large debt, which rarely has been acknowledged then or now" (Blair, 2014, p. 240).

Although it would take a while for what Grant measured as an honorable personal gesture to have a larger historical significance, in the end such back-room dealings would prove to be socially transformative, perhaps even revolutionary. "In the entire Confederacy 656 prominent leaders survived the conflict long enough to make post-war readjustments," historian William Hesseltine calculated, "and only 71 of this company failed to regain a substantial portion of the position and prestige they had enjoyed at the Confederacy's peak" (Hesseltine, 1960, p. 16). The symbolism around Confederate leadership mattered significantly. John J. McDermott writes that, "The failure of the United States to implement post-conflict amnesty in a non-partisan manner during the Reconstruction Era exacerbated sectional and political tensions and economic recovery problems" (McDermott, 2009). With Lee out of the picture of possible judicial prosecution of any form, Johnson turned his attention to other members of Confederate leadership, some of whom, like Jefferson Davis, languished in prison for some time. Yet there was growing turmoil among former Unionists.

By mid-1867, Radical Republicans were calling for Johnson's impeachment after he fired Lincoln appointee and Radical Republican, Edwin M. Stanton, the Secretary of War. In the end, the internal partisan politics of the North made it nearly impossible to pursue judiciary measures of justice against the former insurgents (Blair, 2014, p. 247). For his part, Johnson had no temperament to navigate these politics. *A Resolution of Impeachment* against Johnson was passed by the House on February 24, 1868 and that spring a trial ensued in the Senate. In May, thirty-five senators voted to convict the president of "high crimes and misdemeanors," but the vote fell one short of the necessary two-thirds majority to convict. Notably, nineteen "Recusant Republican" senators voted for acquittal. With little more than two months before leaving office, President Johnson offered a Christmas gift to his fellow Southerners, bequeathing a general pardon to all former Confederates on December 25, 1868 which flew in the face of his Radical opponents (Bergeron, 2011, pp. 186–216). The symbolism could not have been clearer. With this stroke of the pen, John Brown remained the only person in United States history to be executed for treason since the adoption of the Constitution (Blair, 2014, p. 234).

ASYMMETRICAL JUSTICE: BLACK SOLDIERS, SYMBOLIC REVENGE, AND THE COMPROMISES OF UNION

Long-time coeditor of the *North American Review* and founder of new *The Nation*, Charles Eliot Norton, expressed his concerns about the status of the nation in his new publication in the fall of 1865. Raising questions about the disposition of southern people and ultimately the realized gains of a Union victory, Norton wrote, "Though the South has sullenly laid down its arms, it has not laid down its hate." The writer warned, "…we have not yet secured a moral Union, a civil unity; we have the harder part of our task before us" (Cimbala and Miller, 2010, p. 173). In the coming year Norton's concerns about securing a "moral Union" proved to be prophetic as southern hatred over the war festered. At the time, many Northerners were responding to Norton's call to ensure the promise of justice and social change. Contrary to the assumptions among some contemporary students, many whites were not indifferent to the plight of the newly freed slaves. Their work for reform, however, became increasingly ineffectual as southern states returned local white legislatures and random violence expanded across the region dampening northern zeal for reform.

1866 proved to be a watershed year. The murderous campaigns on black communities that were so highly prevalent throughout the South in the 1870s, were first tested in places like Tennessee against the greatest symbolic threat for the South, the black Union soldier. Judicial delays or non-responses to former secessionists empowered whites who targeted black communities ultimately leading to what one historian characterized as "…terrorism in service of a coherent cause, the overthrow of Reconstruction, which was beginning [by the early 1870s] to seem plausible" (Lemann, 2006, p. 81). These violent campaigns clearly demonstrated to recalcitrant white Southerners that justice was not equal when it came to race in America and their actions would have little consequence. But how did the nation reach this point? Briefly highlighting two cases in western Tennessee, known as the Fort Pillow Massacre and the Memphis Riots of 1866, are illustrative of the way bureaucratic systems of governance at the federal level could not combat the "passionate ethics" of the South. All the while, the law was largely remained mute in these matters as a fear of another Civil War swirled in the public mind.

At the turn of the twentieth century the British Parliamentarian, Edward Macnaghten recognized the inadequacy of dichotomous thinking about war and peace, particularly as it relates to systems of legal protection. Macnaghten suggested that "the law recognizes a state of peace and a state of war, but that it knows nothing of an intermediate state which is neither one thing or the other" (Stahn, 2006, pp. 158–160). More recently, legal scholar Ruti G. Teitel has acknowledged the inadequacy of the law in transitional states, those moving from war to the routines of a peaceful state, and the need to buttress the law with constituencies to bolster power. "Justice seeking in these periods is fully epiphenomenal and best explained in terms of the balance of power. Law is a mere product of political change" (Teitel, 2000, p. 3). But in nineteenth-century America, the law was perceived not only as foundational, but also having an almost omniscient quality to it that could enable Americans to adjudicate their way out of any problem.

Certainly, the law had power, but so did the people. As Hannah Arendt suggested long ago, power, in essence, is the instrument of rule and it can be done by the many or the few (Arendt, 1970, pp. 35–42; Starr, 2007, pp. 17–18). In the postwar South, who or what would rule was up for debate in 1866, but soon a minority of violent white men would appropriate power in a measure of non-democratic rule. It was the recent past that provided this roadmap.

THE MASSACRE AT FORT PILLOW: BUREAUCRACY, POLITICIZATION, AND OBFUSCATION

"The Battle of Fort Pillow" as it was once known, took place just over a year before Lincoln's assassination. The encounter was prompted by an expedition launched by Confederate General Nathan Bedford Forrest, who would serve as the first grand wizard of the Ku Klux Klan, and his cavalry were foraging for manpower and supplies on behalf of the Confederate cause. As Union General William Tecumseh Sherman gathered forces and supplies in Chattanooga for his upcoming Atlanta Campaign, Forrest decided to carry out a series of raids to disrupt Sherman's preparations. Fort Pillow, which stood on a bend in the Mississippi River a day's ride north of Memphis, contained a garrison of more than five hundred troops who primarily consisted of southern Unionists, deserters from the Confederate Army, and African Americans.

With estimates of 1,500 to 2,500 cavalrymen, the Confederates surrounded the fort and commenced firing. At mid-afternoon, Union Major William Bradford who was now in command of the fort after its commander was killed by a sniper's bullet, called for a one-hour cease fire after Forrest demanded the fort's surrender. Fearing the probability of Union reinforcements, Forrest told Bradford fighting was to resume in twenty minutes ignoring the initial request. In their final assault, Forrest's men dismounted from their horses charging Union forces on the ground. The Union men were caught off guard and proved to be no match to the assailants. When Forrest's men breached the fort's defenses, the fighting degenerated into chaos and murder as no quarter was given to black Union troops. Between 277 and 295 Union troops were killed, most of whom were African American, verses only fourteen Confederates. Recounting the events out west, the *Franklin Repository* published a story entitled "Rebel Atrocities" (1864, p. 8). The article detailed the "butcheries at Fort Pillow" and characterized them as "fiendish atrocities" and a "shameless violation" of the rules of warfare. Writing to Secretary of War William Stanton shortly after the Fort Pillow Massacre General Sherman stated the unvarnished truth, "I know well the animus of the Southern soldiery [towards blacks] and the truth is they cannot be restrained" (Tap, 1998, p. 195).

Within days news of the Fort Pillow Massacre reached the east coast. Attending the Sanitary Fair of Baltimore on April 18, 1864, Lincoln was compelled to address news of the massacre to the assembled crowd, attempting to assure the public justice would be carried out. "There seems to be some anxiety in the public mind whether the Government is doing its duty to the colored solider," Lincoln acknowledged suggesting that African American soldiers now fighting in the Union effort, should be afforded "all the protection given to any other soldier." "The difficulty," Lincoln continued, "is not stating the principle, but in practically applying it. It is a mistake to suppose the Government is indifferent to this mater, or is not doing the best it can in regard to it." The president went on to distinguish between fearing the worst and knowing factually what is true. Lincoln assured the crowd, "If there has been a massacre of three hundred there, or even the tenth part of three hundred, it will be conclusively proved; and being so proved, the retribution shall as surely come. It will be matter of grave consideration in what exact course to apply the retribution; but in the supposed case, it must come" (Holzer, 2011, pp. 240–242).

As Lincoln promised, a Congressional investigation did ensue; however, in the animus of sectional division and war, the results were quickly discredited as being politicized and, in this atmosphere, policies were easier to draft than execute. Led by two Republicans, Senator Benjamin F. Wade and Representative Daniel W. Gooch, the committee heard startling details about what transpired that day. Although the sworn testimony of nearly ninety white and black Federal soldiers and a few civilians overwhelmingly demonstrated war crimes had been committed, the committee's findings and recommendations for stronger punishment against such crimes were quickly deemed "partisan" by Southerners and Democrats in the North who sought to use the report as an example of Radical Republican extremism.

The hearings generated much public interest and on May 3, Lincoln gathered his Cabinet asking each member for their response on how to handle the situation. On May 5, 1864, the Senate ordered that over 20,000 additional copies of Report No. 65 of the Congressional Committee on the Conduct of the War be printed for free distribution to the general public. The following day, the Cabinet gathered again to discuss their ideas. The range of response to the massacre by the members mirrored that of the general public. "Every cabinet official agreed that the Richmond government should first be given the chance to disavow the massacre and to acknowledge the legitimacy of black soldiers," writes historian Bruce Tap. "Although a variety of opinions was expressed, two general viewpoints emerged. Seward, Stanton, Chase and Secretary of the Interior John P. Usher favored man-for-man retaliation" (Tap, 1998, p. 200).

Upon the completion of the meeting, Lincoln sat down and drafted instructions for Secretary of War Edwin M. Stanton. The memo forestalled any response by the United States government until July 1st or hearing from the Confederacy. Should no response be given before or by July 1, Lincoln declared, "such action as may then appear expedient and just [be taken]" (Basler, Volume VII, 1953, pp. 345–346). The next day, July 7, Lincoln received a first-hand report on the Battle of the Wilderness. Although two days later he transmitted to the Senate through the Attorney General his ideas on "rights of colored persons in the army or volunteer service," and followed up this measure on May 17 instructing Secretary Stanton to "notify the insurgents" of the position of the government of the United States in these matters, the orders were never signed and therefore never sent (Baringer, 1991, pp. 256–258).

THE MEMPHIS "RIOT": 1866 AND THE LESSONS OF A RECENT PAST

According to philosopher Larry May, "Political conciliation involves bring parties to the point where they have respect for each other's rights and can live peaceably together." Fundamental to May's conception of reconciliation is the recognition of equal status before the law and that human rights are protected. Equally important, the philosopher remarks, is an understanding of "what could and should have been done to prevent the violence" (May, 2012, pp. 85–86). That black soldiers would be the target of southern reprisals after the war was obvious before peace terms at Appomattox and Fort Pillow was one massacre where the government had first-hand accounts of such violent reprisals based solely on race (Dobak, 2011, p. 469). Fort Pillow, however, was not the only sign at the time.

Despite the public outcry around events in Tennessee, Confederate leadership would not give assurances to Union leaders that blacks in the ranks would be treated justly. During the Siege of Petersburg (June 9, 1864–March 25, 1865) Confederate forces slowly winnowed to the point where Lee, facing a severe manpower shortage, approached Grant about an informal "man for man exchange" of prisoners on the Petersburg front in the fall of 1864. Seizing the opportunity, Grant agreed with the stipulation that African American soldiers be exchanged on the same basis as their white counterparts. Lee declined the offer writing, "Negroes belonging to our Citizens are not Considered Subjects of exchange and were not included in my proposition." The transmissions ended with Grant insisting that "all soldiers be treated equally" (Smith, 2001, p. 387; Simon, 1988, pp. 258–263). While Grant and others demonstrated on paper their concerns for black soldiers, their deeds to assure such treatment fell short.

As summer turned to fall and with bureaucratic delays mounting the initial response to the question, "What shall we do with the rebels?", was becoming increasingly clear: the Confederacy's top government officials, not the soldiers, were the target of the Federal efforts to prosecution for treason. Still, considerable legal debate accompanied these maneuverings. With President Johnson's May 29th *Proclamation Pardoning Persons Who Participated in the Rebellion* coupled with Grant's steady assurances and efforts, Lee moved west in the summer of 1865 to take up residence in Lexington, Virginia to head the economically strapped, Washington College. On October 2, 1865, the same day he was inaugurated as president of Washington College, Lee signed his Amnesty Oath and thereby coming into full compliance with the provision of Johnson's proclamation.

Late in the fall, Lee was asked to be interviewed before the Joint Committee on Reconstruction. That winter, Lee headed North to appear before the Joint Committee on February 17, 1866. Understanding the theatrics involved, Lee's responses were measured. Much of the questioning centered upon the "affections" of the southern people, the prospect of continued violent civil unrest towards Federal authority, and the status of local courts to prosecute for treason. With this questioning, Lee let it be known that state representatives were to blame for secession, not soldiers, but also that prosecution at the local level for any such charges would be challenging (*Report*, 1866, part II, pp. 129–136). Questions were also raised about Lee's responsibility in the conduct of the war and in particular, the degree of Lee's knowledge concerning conditions at Confederate prison camps such as Andersonville, Belle Isle, Libby Prison and Salisbury.

As the hearing came to an end, Michigan representative Jacob Merritt Howard turned his line of questioning to the status of African Americans in the South. Lee's responses were telling. When Howard asked, "Suppose an amendment should, nevertheless, be adopted, conferring on the blacks the right of suffrage, would that, in your opinion, lead to scenes of violence and breaches of the peace between the two races in Virginia?" Lee responded, "I think it would excite unfriendly feelings between the two races. I cannot pretend to say to what extent it would go, but that would be the result" (*Report*, 1866, p. 134). Moments later, Missouri representative Henry Blow asked Lee about his feelings to the presumed dwindling number of African Americans in the state. "Do you not think that Virginia would be better off if the colored population were to go to Alabama, Louisiana, and the other southern States?" asked Blow. "I think it would be better for Virginia if she could rid of them," responded Lee. In revealing language that indicated not only his attitudes towards racial equality and the humanity of blacks, but also the times in which he was living Lee continued, "That is no new opinion with me. I have always thought so, and have always been in favor of emancipation—gradual emancipation" (*Report*, 1866, p. 136). Through violent force and now what would shortly become law, the war had simply replaced these notions of "emancipation." But southerners like Lee were still not "converted."

Lee's response was but one expression on the national stage that could be found throughout the South. Months earlier in Tennessee, a state Supreme Court justice wrote Major General George H. Thomas complaining about affects members of the 101st United States Colored Infantry were having on local blacks. Receiving particular consternation from the judge was the commanding officer who, "regards himself as the guardian of the negroes and this necessarily makes them insolent." He continued, "If the colored soldiers were removed, the negro population would be more obedient to the laws" (Dobak, 2011, p. 469).

A few short weeks after Lee's testimony, the 39th United States Congress overturned President Andrew Johnson's veto passing the *Civil Rights Act of 1866* that declared all persons born in the United States as citizens of the nation. The New England Methodist newspaper, *Zion's Herald and Wesleyan Journal*, gleefully reported "The passage of the Civil Rights Bill by both Houses of Congress…is an event in the legislation of this country which causes great joy to all who place justice and right above a temporizing policy." (*Zion's Herald*, April 18, 1866). The article continued, "To the freedmen it is only a simple act of justice, and the nation owes it, in consistency with itself and in the solemn duty to God, to see that all which that bill proposes is sacredly carried out." The article closed by recalling, "It is a happy coincidence that it passed the House of Representatives on the first anniversary of Lee's surrender of the rebel army to the *inevitable Grant*" (*Zion's Herald*, April 18, 1866). These rapid advances in legislation for citizenship of African Americans were now more threatening than ever to the chances of restoring the old social order in the South. To stem the tide of legislative advances, white Southerners resorted to vigilantism to reestablish the old social order.

In the immediate aftermath of the war, Union soldiers and officers occupied the South and had to effectively create and administer policies and orders on the ground to preserve order and peace until civil governments were effectively reestablished. Because of the breadth of these demands in the field, historian Michael Lind asserts that "Radical Reconstruction, for any purpose, was doomed to fail because of the lack of adequate force" (Lind, 2004, p. 221). The author points out that a rapid postwar demobilization effort on the part of Federal Government shrank the number of Union soldiers in the South from over one million troops in May, 1865 to fewer than 200,000 by that November.

As the number of Union forces were in decline, the timing and attack on black Federal soldiers in Memphis were no coincidence. The opportunity for such backlash was bolstered as demographic changes resulting from the war exacerbated racial tensions. War refugees and now freepersons of color were flooding into urban centers like Nashville and Memphis to find land and employment in 1866. Before the war, Memphis had fewer than 4000 blacks subserviently living among the white population. This figure increased fourfold by the summer of 1865 and represented more than half of the city's overall population of 27,703 citizens

(Lovett, 1979, pp. 9–33; Zuczek, 2006, pp. 400–401). Contraband camps such as Camp Dixie, Camp Shiloh, and Camp Fiske transformed Memphis's landscape during the war and by 1865 the lands in these camps were being leased or sold to newly freed blacks by former owners or the Treasury Department in lieu of federal taxes. This new demographic structure served to heighten tensions in the region (Lovett, 1979, p. 9).

In this intermediate state of postbellum politics, Johnson appointed provisional governors and explicitly ordered military commanders in the region to assist them. Martial law for the South remained in place as economic opportunities remained scarce and threatened social stability. During the fall harvesting season of 1865, a Freedman's Bureau official wrote of these growing pressures commenting that "quite a large number of vagrants were arrested by the colored troops, & by force of arms, were sent to the country to work on the plantations" (Dobak, 2011, p. 462). Such scenes presumably made it clear among locals, that African Americans, if given the opportunity, would use the imprimatur of Federal authority to overturn lines of authority that had stood for generations. Many thought so-called "Negro rule" must be stopped.

Given interactions like these, it is no surprise reports from white southerners reached Johnson's desk alleging the Freedmen's Bureau being mismanaged and that black troops in the South were disturbing the peace. In response, Secretary of War William Stanton dispatched George Gordon Meade, hero of Gettysburg and now the commander of the Military Division of the Atlantic from Virginia to the South Carolina, to resolve any disputes. Meade traveled to the South Carolina, where he found that black troops poorly officered and in ill-health. Meade denied the claim that black soldiers were encouraging idleness among laborers or fomenting hostility among the freedmen towards the planter class. In a conciliatory move toward local whites, however, Meade restored civil rule, not military jurisprudence, to all cases not involving blacks and left freedmen under the protection of the army's system of provost courts. Perhaps even more importantly, Meade conceded that black troops in the state were better stationed along the coast, "where they will be measurably removed from contact with the whites" (Graf, 1987, p. 199).

Benjamin F. Perry, acting Provisional Governor, responded to the proposal expressing the "earnest desire to get rid of all negro troops entirely" but suggested such a process would need to take place gradually as to not "offend public sentiment at the North." The proposed changes did not stop there. Meade halted the confiscation and redistribution of abandoned lands to former slaves in the region. Moreover, he recommended that the Bureau come under direct military control and that these measures would assure the avoidance of "any conflict of authority, arising from the construction of laws and orders" (Graf, 1987, p. 199). As the authority of black Union soldiers were curbed and their interaction among whites restricted, they became an easy target for white Southerners.

Major General George Stoneman, Jr., commanding the Department of Tennessee headquartered in Memphis was stationed at Fort Pickering. On his watch, Memphis contained a large black veteran population, hundreds of them stationed at the fort. This included men of the 3rd U.S. Colored Heavily Artillery who had never seen combat. Given the expressed concerns circulating in official orders, Stoneman decided to turn over control of law enforcement in Memphis to the civil authority in May. Ironically, when the riot broke out, the city asked for help from Stoneman who suppressed the white rioters using Federal troops.

According to a New York publication, the events of May 1, 1866 started as a street brawl between Irish police and reportedly small group of reportedly drunk African Americans "such as might occur any day in Philadelphia or New York and create in itself no disturbance." In reality these men were not intoxicated African Americans roaming the streets, but rather recently discharged soldiers of the Third United States Colored Heavy Artillery regiment, who were being harassed for wearing Union blue in a downtown area. Fighting for the lives the newly mustered Union veterans sought refuge in nearby Fort Pickering where, upon arrival, they were disarmed by Captain Allyn's garrison. In turn, Allyn dispatched two squads of Regulars to disperse the crowd and patrol the streets of Memphis (Hardwick, 1993, p. 120). As darkness fell, a white mob descended upon the local black community terrorizing and murdering residents.

During the roughly forty-eight hours of social anarchy, forty-six blacks and two whites lay dead. The violence did not stop there. In the mayhem seventy-five other persons received bullet wounds while roving gangs raped at least five black women, robbed over one hundred individuals of cash, and left ten others severely beaten. *The Independent* graphically detailed the pretext of police actions and the resulting African American carnage. As police "entered the houses, pretending to search for rioters" from the previous evening, the slaying of innocence began. With the pretext of an "investigation," the newspaper reported, "They shot men and women in bed. They dragged little children from under the bed, and clubbed their brains out on the spot," the report claimed. "The police, in well-authenticated instances, stood by, and in others assisted in this robbery and murder." The events closed with "scarcely an arrest" being made "except of 'rioting nagers'" (*The Independent*, 1866). Additionally, 91 houses, 4 churches, and 12 schools were destroyed (Ryan, 1977). Martial law was declared and order reestablished on the third day, but the impact of random and lawless violence had changed future prospects of what was possible in the South using violent acts to redistribute the power away from the law (Ryan, 1977).

Writers agree the origins of the violence was multi-causal; however, the timing was not purely coincidental. The previous day the last of the black troops in the city serving the Federal forces had been mustered out of service and became civilians of the United States. As Kevin R. Hardwick's skilled treatment of the riots notes, "As soon as these men lost the protection, and the ability to protect others, that their status as Union soldiers afforded them, they became vulnerable to white repression" (Hardwick, 1993, p. 120). Systems for ensuring the application of the law were absent in the moment. Still, a bigger problem faced those seeking transitional justice and that was the corruption of systems already in place. The issue was not lost on a New York publication which sharply contrasted the civil rights enjoyed by whites in the South versus blacks. Memphis was where "…Irish police have been in the habit of making frivolous arrests among the negroes," the story noted, "and handling them roughly, and taking personal property from them, on the pretense of recovering stolen goods" (*The Independent*, 1866). Now "suspicion" of riotous activity by blacks provided white police officers to "recover stolen goods" for their own benefit. Even the *Daily Argus*, a decidedly conservative and anti-black newspaper, admitted the riots had created a "standing animosity" between the police and the local African American population (Ryan, 1977, p. 244).

Stories in newspapers of varying political persuasions made it challenging for citizens across the country to understand the reasons for the violence. Expressions of racism were clearly apparent in a number of these accounts, but newspapers also preyed upon anti-immigration sentiment, classism, governmental ineptitude, temperance, and kind of "natural" lawlessness among the landless. That summer newspaper audiences in Montana were met with the headlines "Terrible Riot in Memphis—Unprovoked Slaughter of Blacks." The *Montana Post* went on to report, "There has been a terrible riot of the low whites of Memphis directed against the negroes: on Tuesday, they murdered fifteen of them; on Wednesday the blacks sought for arms to defend themselves at Fort Pickering, but were warned off…" (*Montana Post*, May 19, 1866). The *Chicago Tribune* (1866) claimed that only, "vagabond whites participated in the riot, and all the best citizens depreciate it, but were powerless to repress it." The *Montana Post* closed its coverage suggesting a South in dire straits, "the dead bodies of negroes lay along South Street as they fell; the negroes went beyond the city limits, homeless and defenseless; the riot was unprovoked and carried on by the lowest whites, while the drunken Mayor babbled of insurrection and armed a posse of degraded followers" (*Montana Post*, May 19, 1866).

While civil rights abuses had been happening throughout the nation in the postbellum, the events that transpired on the first three days of May begged questions concerning the moral architecture of not only of the "new birth of freedom," but also *jus post bellum*. Historian Stephen Ash maintains, "The riot can be seen both as a continuation of older forms of racial brutality and as a harbinger of a new kind of violence: the organized terror Southern whites would carry out against blacks well into the twentieth century" (Ash, 2013, p. xiv). The "natural fruits" of a "new 'policy'" had been "lately reaped" in the South, New York's *The*

Independent sardonically noted in the late spring of 1866. "The popular name for it is a 'negro riot,'" here the article continued, "—the true name is *negro massacre*." With the surrender of Lee's Army at Appomattox still fresh in the memories of Northerners, the newspaper reported two days of "pillaging, burning, and slaying" had engulfed the black community in Memphis, while "nothing...bore even the semblance of a riot" on part of local blacks.

Yet again lawless violence ushered in a public debate about the Federal government's ability to secure civil liberties in the face of terrorism. Like Fort Pillow, investigative committees were formed but their reports became mired in bureaucratic channels producing few results. Members of the Special Committee of the House reached Memphis on May 22, 1866 to investigate. Upon arrival they found a second commission had also been set up by General Stoneman. Serving on this second commission was the superintendent of the Freedmen's Bureau for the District of Memphis, officials from the army, as well as, Marcus Joseph Wright, a lawyer and citizen of Memphis who formerly served as Brigadier General in the Rebel army, and was asked by Stoneman to serve "in order to insure a fair hearing on the part of the citizens of Memphis."

Ultimately the reports generated served as nothing more than paper walls against the violence on the ground. It is revealing that although Stoneman was no friend of the South, his appointment of Wright bespeaks of the increasingly irreconcilable tensions of the day and are suggestive that the war for *jus post bellum* was far from realized. The pressing question of the day for those in power remained the same at the end of 1866 as it did in April, 1865, "What shall we do with the rebels?" To the surprise of many white Americans at the time, and perhaps today, the tensile strength of the nation's "bonds of affection," were deceptively weak when it came to issues of human equality or the realization of an interracial democracy. Too often as this history demonstrates, individual appeasement lead to unintended consequences or clear-eyed efforts of systematic change which empowered those who threatened violence and moved the ability to rule away from the law.

CONCLUSION

These forms of lawless violence perpetrated against blacks and a select number of whites in the South, only grew throughout the period of Reconstruction. Within a month of the Civil Rights Bill passing through Congress, the Memphis Riots broke out. Later violence in New Orleans flared which was particularly poignant given this city was the site of Lincoln's ten-percent plan and first efforts to reconstruct the Union during the war (Weigley, 2004, p. 351). After the symbolic pillars of Union victory fell, the violence against blacks increased for years along racial lines creating its own set of symbolic mean. Had the nation's "moral war" secured a just peace? Louis Hartz's writings provides a partial answer to the question in noting that, "...the way in which a culture distributes the legitimate use of force is a clue to its ethical life" (Hartz, 1969, pp. 123–124).

If political and social order (i.e., peace) is the aim of war, then Reconstruction should be weighed in any calculation about the Civil War and its aims. While Lincoln's assassination at the end of war certainly complicates judgments about the proposed course of Reconstruction, on a theoretical level the moral ends a war produces are so intimately bound to questions concerning its stated purposes that, "the principles of governing a just peace seem relevant to whether a war should be initiated at all" (May, 2012, p. 2). This question of *jus ad bellum* may provide for a fruitful discussion in some classrooms about the nature of warfare and democracy, but ultimately historical studies must grapple with the realities of what transpired, not what might or should have happened.

Should the Civil War be characterized as a "moral war"? The simple answer is "yes" but an important element of this characterization is to tease out the implications of the question for whom and at what cost? If we take the calculation of *jus post bellum* seriously, it is important to discuss the fact that unchecked white southern vigilantism fundamentally impacted and restricted the civil liberties of countless black Americans for decades to come as local, state, and Federal judiciary systems failed to adapt to the moment at hand. The war irrevocably changed black lives for the better, but is was no revolution for the North measured by *jus post bellum* criteria. In the end, the use of violence to reconstitute the legislative system among states in the South won the day. For many contemporary students of all races, this story is nothing new, but history is not fiction and cathartic uplifting narratives do not usually win the day. Herein lies ultimate power in the study of history I believe.

Beyond the humanitarian concerns and principles of equality this history raises, perhaps the important lesson to be gleaned from this epoch is about the limited nature of the law to respond to unprecedented circumstances and human folly. According to Carsten Stahn, an associate legal officer for the International Criminal Court, dualist conceptions that fail to recognize the interrelationship between armed violence and the restoration of peace are "increasingly anachronistic" today. Looking at the past enables our students see the perils that come with intermediate post-war states and the adaptive measures, based on principle and law, that it takes to sustain peace (Stahn, 2006, pp. 158–160). As students of history, it is also important to recognize that what we see so clearly today, was an anathema to many Americans in the past. A lesson to be learned from this historical tale is not only a reflection of the moral universe inherited by the nineteenth century, but it is also one of our own preconceptions. One of many "tragedies" of the Civil War and Reconstruction is that upstanding citizens did not act on the social imperatives of the day, leaving behind or reconfiguring their sense of "rights" and "obligations." But how could they given our limited horizons of cause and affect? Of this dilemma, John Burt writes "...conflicts over moral issues are so entangled with the weaknesses of human nature that all outcomes are tragic and no agents are pure...and a shared legacy of unending inner conflict over the issues that divided the outward belligerents ultimately demands an un-self-righteous rapprochement with the former enemy" (Burt, 2013, p. 649).

Instead of encouraging our students to chastise those in the past and perhaps lose the lessons of history, it is worth reminding them of their own historical journey in the larger trajectory of human history with all its limitations. In his 1950s essay, *The Rebel: An Essay on Man in Revolt*, the French philosopher Albert Camus claimed his contemporaries were not entirely to blame for history because they did not start history. At the same time, Camus emphasized no innocence was to be found because humans continue history. Recognizing our collective reality, Camus recognized the reality of our lived history. "'We are' in terms of history, and history must reckon with this. 'We are,' which must in its turn keep its place in history. I have need of others who have need of me and of each other. Every collective action, every form of society, supposes a discipline, and the individual, without the discipline, is only a stranger, bowed down under the weight of an inimical collectivity" (Camus, 1991, p. 297). At its best an intimate study of the past may provide one avenue for realizing our shared humanity in the face of our inimical collectivity. Considering *jus post bellum* in light of the Civil War and Reconstruction is one of these moments.

REFERENCES:

Primary Sources

Basler, Roy P. (1953). *The Collected works of Abraham Lincoln*. Volumes I–VIII. New Brunswick, NJ: Rutgers University Press.
Chicago Tribune, (May 18, 1866).
Franklin Repository, (May 11, 1864).
Grotius, Hugo (1646). *The law of war and peace*. Three Books. Amsterdam: The House of Johan Blaeu.
Halleck, Henry (1861). *International law; or Rules regulating the intercourse of states in peace and war.* New York: D. Van Nostrand.
Harrisburg *Patriot and Union* (January 7, 1861).
The Independent ...Devoted to the Consideration of Politics, Social and Economic Tendencies, History, Literature, and the Arts (June 1, 1865).
The Independent ...Devoted to the Consideration of Politics, Social and Economic Tendencies, History, Literature, and the Arts (May 31, 1866).
Leiber, Francis (1898). *General orders 100: Instructions for the Government of Armies of the United States in the Field*. Washington, DC: Government Printing Office.

Levy, Eugene H. (1865). Diary. Small Collections, SC-7005, American Jewish Archives, Hebrew Union College, Cincinnati, OH.
The Montana Post, (May 19, 1866).
New York Observer and Chronicle, (June 1, 1865).
Philadelphia Inquirer, (June 8, 1865)
Report of the Joint Committee on Reconstruction at the First Session Thirty-ninth Congress (1866). Washington, DC: Government Printing Office.
Simon, John Y. (Ed.). (1988). *The papers of Ulysses S. Grant, Volume 15: May 1 – December 31, 1865*. Carbondale and Edwardsville: Southern Illinois University Press.
Spear, Rev. Samuel T. (1865). *The Punishment of Treason: A Discourse Preached April 23d, 1865, in the South Presbyterian Church of Brooklyn*. Brooklyn, NY: "The Union" Steam Presses.
Stevens, Thaddeus (1865). "Reconstruction, Speech of the Hon. Thaddeus Stevens, delivered to the City of Lancaster, September 7, 1865." Lancaster, PA: Examiner and Herald Print.
Zion's Herald and Wesleyan Journal. (April 18, 1866).

Secondary Sources

Arendt, H. (1970). *On violence*. Houghton Mifflin Harcourt Publishing.
Ash, S. V. (2013). *A massacre in Memphis: The race riot that shook the nation one year after the Civil War*. Hill and Wang.
Barginer, W. E. (1991). *Lincoln day by day: A chronology 1809–1865*. Morningside Press.
Bell, L. (1993). *Rethinking ethics in the midst of violence: A feminist approach to freedom*. Rowman & Littlefield Publishers, Inc.
Bergeron, P. H. (2011). *Andrew Johnson's Civil War and reconstruction*. University of Tennessee Press.
Blair, W. A. (2014). *With malice toward some: Treason and loyalty in the Civil War Era*. University of North Carolina Press.
Burt, J. (2013). *Lincoln's tragic pragmatism: Lincoln, Douglas, and moral conflict*. The Belknap Press of Harvard University Press.
Burton, O. V. (2007). *The age of Lincoln*. Hill and Wang.
Camus, A. (1991). *The rebel: An essay on man in revolt*. Vintage Books.
Cimbala, P., & Miller, R. M. (Eds.). (2010). *Reconstructing America: The great task remaining before us: Reconstruction as America's continuing civil war*. Fordham University Press.
Coates, T. (2012). "Why do so few blacks study the Civil War?" *The Atlantic*. http://www.theatlantic.com/magazine/archive/2012/02/why-do-so-few-blacks-study-the-civil-war/8831/
Chesebrough, David B. (1993). "'His own fault': Rev. Charles H. Ellis of Bloomington sermonizes on the assassination of Abraham Lincoln." *Illinois Historical Journal*, 86(3), 146–158.
Chesebrough, D. B. (1994). *"No sorrow like our sorrow": Northern Protestant ministers and the assassination of Abraham Lincoln*. The Kent State University Press.
Childress, J. (1982). *Moral responsibility in conflicts: Essays on nonviolence, war, and conscience*. Louisiana State University Press.
Connelly, T. L. (1977). *The marble man: Robert E. Lee and his image in American society*. Louisiana State University Press.
Dobak, W. A. (2011). *Freedom by the sword: The U.S. colored troops, 1862–1867*. Center of Military History.
Donald, D. H. (1995). *Lincoln*. Simon & Schuster.
DuBois, W. E. B. (1998). *Black Reconstruction in America: 1860–1880*. The Free Press.

Drake, B. (2013). Gettysburg Address: Americans still find the Civil War relevant to today's politics. *Pew Research Center*, November 19, 2013. http://pewrsr.ch/I0vyRE

Escott, P. D. (2009). *"What shall we do with the Negro?": Lincoln, white racism, and Civil War America*. University of Virginia Press.

Foner, E. (1998). *The story of American freedom*. W.W. Norton & Company.

Foner, E. (1988). *Reconstruction: America's unfinished revolution 1863–1877*. Harper & Row Publishers.

Fry, D. P. (Ed.). (2013). *War, peace, and human nature: The convergence of evolutionary and cultural views*. Oxford University Press.

Guelzo, Allen C. (2004). *Lincoln's Emancipation Proclamation: The end of slavery in America*. Simon & Schuster.

Graf, L. P. (Ed.). (1987). *Advice after Appomattox: Letters to Andrew Johnson, 1865–1866*. University of Tennessee.

Hahn, S. (2016). *A nation without borders: The United States and its world in the age of civil wars, 1830–1910*. Viking Press.

Hardwick, K. R. (1993). 'Your old father Abe Lincoln is dead and damned': Black soldiers and the Memphis Race Riot of 1866. *Journal of Social History 27*(1), 109–128.

Harris, W. C. (2009). *Lincoln's last months*. Harvard University Press.

Hartz, L. (1969). A comparative study of fragment cultures. In H. D. Graham & T. R. Gurr (Eds.), *The history of violence in America: Historical and comparative perspectives*. Frederick A Praeger.

Hesseltine, W. B. (1960). *Lincoln's plan of Reconstruction*. Quadrangle Books.

Holzer, H. (Ed.). (2011). *Lincoln on war: Our greatest Commander-in-Chief speaks to America*. Algonquin Books.

Kennedy, D. M. (1998). The art of the tale: Story-telling and history teaching. *Reviews in American History, 26*(2).

Kyvig, D. E. (1996). *Explicit and authentic acts: Amending the U.S. Constitution, 1776–1995*. University Press of Kansas.

Lemann, N. (2006). *Redemption: The last battle of the Civil War*. Farrar, Straus, and Giroux.

Lind, M. (2004). *What Lincoln believed: The values and convictions of America's greatest president*. Doubleday.

Lockwood, A. L., & Harris, D. E. (1985). *Reasoning with democratic values, Volume 1: 1607 – 1876*. Teachers College Press Columbia University.

Lovett, B. L. (1979). Memphis riots: White reaction to blacks in Memphis, May 1865 – July 1866. *Tennessee Historical Quarterly, 38*(1), 9–33.

May, L. (2012). *After war ends: A philosophical perspective*. Cambridge University Press.

McDermott, J. J. (2009). Reconstruction and post-Civil War reconciliation. *Military Review, 89*(1).

Oates, S. B. (1979). *Our fiery trial: Abraham Lincoln, John Brown, and the Civil War Era*. University of Massachusetts Press.

O'Donovan, O. (2003). *The just war revisited*. Cambridge University Press.

Paludan, P. S. (1996). *A people's contest: The Union and Civil War, 1861–1865* (2nd ed.). University of Kansas Press.

Randall, J. G., & Current, R. N. (1983). *Lincoln the President: Last full measure*. University of Illinois Press.

Resch, J. (1999). *Suffering soldiers: Revolutionary War veterans, moral sentiment, and political culture in the early republic*. University of Massachusetts.

Robertson, G. (2006). *Crimes against humanity: The struggle for global justice* (3rd ed.). The New Press.

Rodgers, D. T. (2011). *Age of fracture*. The Belknap Press of Harvard University Press.

Ryan, J. G. (1977). The Memphis Riot of 1866: Terror in a black community during Reconstruction. *The Journal of Negro History, 62*(3), 243–257.

Sandel, M. J. (1998). *Liberalism and the limits of justice* (2nd ed.). Cambridge University Press.

Sandel, M. J. (2009). *Justice: What's the right thing to do?* Farrar, Straus, and Giroux.

Schwartz, B. (1991). Mourning and the making of a sacred symbol: Durkheim and the Lincoln assassination. *Social Forces, 70*(2), 343–364.

Shankman, A. M. (1980). *The Pennsylvania antiwar movement, 1861–1865*. Fairleigh Dickinson University Press.

Simpson, B. D. (1991). *Let us have peace: Ulysses S. Grant and the politics of war and reconstruction, 1861–1868*. University of North Carolina Press.

Simpson, B. D. (2000). *Ulysses S. Grant: Triumph over adversity, 1822–1865*. Houghton Mifflin Company.

Singer, P. (2016). *Ethics in the real world: 82 brief essays on things that matter*. Princeton University Press.

Singer, P. (1993). *Practical ethics* (2nd ed.). Cambridge University Press.

Smith, J. E. (2001). *Grant*. Simon & Schuster.

Smith, W. (1956). *Professors & public ethics: Studies of northern moral philosophers before the Civil War*. Cornell University Press.

Stahn, C. (2006). "'Jus Ad Bellum,' 'Jus In Bello,' 'Jus Post Bellum?' Rethinking the concept of the law and armed force," *Proceedings of the Annual Meeting (American Society of International Law), 100*.

Starr, P. (2007). *Freedom's power: The true force of liberalism*. Basic Books.

Tap, B. (1998). *Over Lincoln's shoulder: The Committee on the conduct of the war*. University of Kansas Press.

Teitel, R. G. (2000). *Transitional justice*. Oxford University Press.

Vinovskis, M. A. (1989). Have social historians lost the Civil War? Some preliminary demographic speculations. *The Journal of American History, 76*(1), 34–58.

Walzer, M. (2000). *Just and unjust wars: A Moral argument with historical illustrations* (3rd ed.). Basic Books.

Weigley, R. F. (2004). *A great Civil War: A military and political history, 1861–1865*. Indiana University Press.

Witt, J. F. (2012). *Lincoln's code: The laws of war in American history*. Free Press.

Zuczek, R. (Ed.). (2006). *Encyclopedia of the reconstruction era, Volume 2: M-Z and primary documents*. Greenwood Press.

CHAPTER FOUR

A Reconstruction Timeline

JENICE L. VIEW

It is false to discuss the politics and economics of the Reconstruction Era and its aftermath in terms of a binary. Legal and political decision making rarely address anything other than the ethics and morality of property, bodily autonomy, labor, capital, and land. In effect, slavery was both a business at the microeconomic (plantation) level, and a global political-economic system (Halpern & Del Lago, 2002, p. 138), so its dismantling required attention to both.

The economics of the system of slavery impacted the North and South. One southerner calculated that 7 million northern, British, and French people depended on their existence by keeping 3 million Blacks enslaved (Baptist, 2014, p. 350). Prior to the start of the Civil War, northern U.S. and British textile mills relied on the more than 100,000 days of enslaved labor annually to produce 15 million pounds of cotton, amounting to 5% of the nation's entire gross domestic product and enabling New England's textile owners to become the wealthiest people in the free states (Baptist, 2014, pp. 317, 321, 325). As the federal government enabled the westward theft of Indian lands, southern production of cotton grew to 1.65 billion pounds, or two-thirds of the global demand for cotton. By 1860, Connecticut joined seven southern states as one of the eight wealthiest, and was the most industrialized. The 3.2 million enslaved people had a "market value" of $1.3 billion in 1850, one-fifth of the nation's wealth and nearly the entire gross national product (Baptist, 2014, p. 352). As literal battlegrounds for the expansion of slave economies, the western territories were the centerpiece of the so-called Sectional Debate. By the end of the Civil War, the North, the South, the Midwest, and the West sought a hasty restoration of cotton production, preferably by Black labor (Foner, 1988, p. 479).

It is also ahistorical to suggest that the assigned period of the Reconstruction Era is self-contained (e.g., Downs & Masur, 2017). Attempts to dismantle the socio-economic system of slavery began with the first enslaved person fleeing enslavement and the first effort to assist the fugitive to safety, sometime between 1619 and 1865. It was against the law to teach enslaved people to read in every southern state, typically to keep them economically dependent on whites, yet there is ample evidence of organized literacy activities led by both enslaved and free Blacks prior to 1865 (e.g., Williams, 2005, pp. 7–29). Of the over 100 historically Black colleges and universities (HBCUs) formed in the U.S., five were formed before the start of the Civil War. Many free Blacks were skilled, non-agricultural workers prior to the Civil War, and the ranks of Black skilled workers increased with the start of the war. For example, Union officers used the First Confiscation Act of 1861 to put countless Black escapees (perceived as confiscated Confederate "property" or "contraband") to work on the Union side of the battle. As they grew dependent on the labor, even those Northerners hostile to the idea of civil rights for Blacks argued that their labor for the Union merited their freedom (Halpern & Dal Lago, 2002, pp. 387–396). President Lincoln's 1863 Emancipation Proclamation accelerated this push, leading thousands more Black people in Confederate states to seek refuge and join forces with Union soldiers as armed fighters and spies. Nevertheless, white northerners were hostile to the migration (or federal placement) of newly freed Black people into northern states in the early years of the war (Dattel, 2009, p. 211), a sentiment that extended through the formal end of Reconstruction in 1877. Again, the sentiment had as much to do with anti-Black attitudes as with maintaining the cotton economy on which the north depended, this time with free Black labor (Dattel, 2009, p. 213). For simplicity, however, this chapter/lesson contrasts politics and economics in an annual timeline of events and decisions between 1865 and 1877, with hints about the precursor events and the aftermath.

This is not as tidy as implied, since the newly freedpeople of the Reconstruction Era were clear about the intersectional nature of their condition, placing education, land ownership, fair contracts, voting rights, and jury service as equally important aspects of their self-determination (Sterling, 1976, pp. 1–66; Williams, 2005, p. 5). The evolution of attitudes such as the nature and purpose of social hierarchies (e.g., Piketty, 2020, p. 7), the role of government in the economy, immigration policies, the definition of freedom, and U.S. imperialism into Indian lands all played a role in both sides of the pairing. Similarly, the events of the Sectional Debate prior to the Civil War fed Reconstruction policies and events and extended for at least twenty years after the formal 1877 end of the Era, at least until the 1896 *Plessy v. Ferguson* decision.

And, as with all discussions of race in the United States, the Black-white binary is a false construction. The first racialized conflicts began with the 15th century British, French, Spanish, and Portuguese imperial encounters with the Indigenous peoples of what became North, South, and Central America. The conflicts were exacerbated by the introduction in the 17th century of enslaved Africans to the European colonies. The war between the U.S. and Mexico from 1846 to 1848 drastically changed the borders of what had been Mexican land. The importation of Chinese labor to work on southern plantations following emancipation increased the number of Chinese laborers already working in the western mines and on the railroads since the early 19th century. Therefore, the Reconstruction Era was a continuation of multiracial arguments and violence (legal and extralegal) about the social construction of race, whiteness, and supremacy.

Therefore, the timeline tactic intends to draw a visual that explores the possibility of cause and effect. It is, by no means, comprehensive and invites the learner to research the connections and tentacles more deeply. In the same way that southern states determined that literacy would make Black people unfit to be enslaved, and as Frederick Douglass understood the pathway from slavery to freedom was literacy, any events on the timeline related to Black education are considered economic events, particularly the founding of historically Black colleges and universities. Similarly, any event related to labor, land, bodily autonomy, capital, and debt are grouped with economic events.

A teacher may use this timeline at the beginning or the end of a unit on Reconstruction. Using the inquiry design method, the guiding questions for examining this timeline are: 1. To what extent did one part of the pair (political or economic events) influence the other? and 2. What is the legacy, if any, of these political and economic events? Some of the relevant primary sources for exploring these questions can be found in the references cited.

The relevant NCSS Standards include:

> D2.His.1.6-8. Analyze connections among events and developments in broader historical contexts.
>
> D2.His.2.6-8. Classify series of historical events and developments as examples of change and/or continuity.
>
> D2.His.1.9-12. Evaluate how historical events and developments were shaped by unique circumstances of time and place as well as broader historical contexts.
>
> D2.His.2.9-12. Analyze change and continuity in historical eras.
>
> D2.His.3.9-12. Use questions generated about individuals and groups to assess how the significance of their actions changes over time and is shaped by the historical context.

D2.His.4.6-8. Analyze multiple factors that influenced the perspectives of people during different historical eras.

D2.His.4.9-12. Analyze complex and interacting factors that influenced the perspectives of people during different historical eras.

D2.His.14.6-8. Explain multiple causes and effects of events and developments in the past.

D2.His.14.9-12. Analyze multiple and complex causes and effects of events in the past.

D2.Civ.2.6-8. Explain specific roles played by citizens (such as voters, jurors, taxpayers, members of the armed forces, petitioners, protesters, and office-holders).

D2.Civ.2.9-12. Analyze the role of citizens in the U.S. political system, with attention to various theories of democracy, changes in Americans' participation over time, and alternative models from other countries, past and present.

D2.Civ.10.6-8. Explain the relevance of personal interests and perspectives, civic virtues, and democratic principles when people address issues and problems in government and civil society.

D2.Civ.10.9-12. Analyze the impact and the appropriate roles of personal interests and perspectives on the application of civic virtues, democratic principles, constitutional rights, and human rights.

D2.Eco.9.6-8. Describe the roles of institutions such as corporations, non-profits, and labor unions in a market economy.

D2.Eco.9.9-12. Describe the roles of institutions such as clearly defined property rights and the rule of law in a market economy.

D2.Eco.1.6-8. Explain how economic decisions affect the well-being of individuals, businesses, and society.

D2.Eco.1.9-12. Analyze how incentives influence choices that may result in policies with a range of costs and benefits for different groups.

Sample vocabulary for this lesson includes:

Convict leasing: Using prison labor to make profits for private companies. In the 19th and 20th centuries, state government prison systems paid employers a fee to feed and transport imprisoned people to work in coal mines, sawmills, railroad camps, cotton fields, and other industries while the employer reaps all the profits. Typically, the leased convicts were Black and male, convicted of petty crimes for extreme sentences. (e.g., Oshinsky, 1996, pp. 40–53).

Lynching: The public killing of a person who has not been given due process for an accused crime. The victims of lynching in the 19th and 20th centuries were typically Indigenous, Black, Latinx, Asian, and immigrants, with most of the victims being Black. The executions were public spectacles, sometimes including refreshments and postcards of the victims' remains.

Scab labor: Non-union workers who are recruited to break labor union strikes. "Crossing the picket line" and doing the work of striking organized laborers is considered a violation of solidarity among working people against employers.

Scalawag: Southern white members of the Republican party. This derogatory term was leveled at white people who shared the anti-slavery attitudes of freedpeople, and who advocated the civil, political, and economic rights of Blacks.

Table 1: Pre-Reconstruction timeline showing political and economic events of importance.

	Pre-Reconstruction Era	
Year	Political	Economic
1830-1865	• 1830–1893: Colored Conventions began to address freedom from enslavement, constitutional rights, and Black self-help (Bracey, Meier, & Rudwick, 1970, pp. 51–66) • 1862: The Homestead Act gave citizens or future citizens up to 160 acres of "public" land; over 270 million acres of Indian land was distributed in this way • 1863: Emancipation Proclamation was President Lincoln's tactic for freeing only those enslaved in the Confederate states to work and fight for the Union • 1863: Frederick Douglass advocates for the arming of Black troops to fight on the Union side	• 1837: Cheyney University (PA) was founded by Quakers as "The Institute for Colored Youth" 1851: Minor Normal School (Washington, DC; became the University of the District of Columbia) 1854: Lincoln University (PA) the first degree granting HBCU 1856: Wilberforce University and Payne Theological Seminary (Ohio) 1857: Harris-Stowe State (MO) and 1862: LeMoyne-Owen College (TN) were among the first of the historically Black colleges and universities (HBCUs)

(continued)

Table 1: *Continued*

	Pre-Reconstruction Era	
Year	Political	Economic
	• 1863–65: The military experience of Black people strengthened their visions for freedom (e.g., Berlin et al., 1992, pp. 187–233)	• From 1861 to 1890, 11.3 million European immigrants arrived in the U.S. and moved westward (Dattel, 2009, p. 268)
		• 70% of the cotton imported textile mills in Europe came from the U.S. South (Piketty, 2020, p. 232)
		• Black people—enslaved and free—engaged in a range of literacy activities (Williams, 2005, pp. 7–29)
		• Wartime wage labor introduced formerly enslaved people to a degree of autonomy (Berlin et al., 1992, p. 182)
		• American Indians were engaged in the Civil War on both the Union and Confederate sides, hoping to protect their lands, their way of life, and improve the treatment they received from whites (U.S. Department of the Interior, 2013, p. 8)
		• 1861: Virginia lost 1/3 of its land and population when West Virginia split off to create a separate, Union-allied state
		• 1862: The first Black seamen's union is formed in New York
		• 1863: Black refugees began establishing schools at their own expense (Williams, 2005, p. 5)
		• 1864: The federal government destroyed Navajo communities and livelihoods for the Long March of 8,500 people from Arizona to prison camps in New Mexico
		• 1864: The Sand Creek (Colorado) Massacre killed 450 Cheyenne and Arapahoe

Table 2: Reconstruction Era timeline showing political and economic events of importance.

Reconstruction Era 1865–1877		
Year	Political	Economic
1865	• 13th Amendment formally abolished slavery while permitting involuntary servitude as punishment for "duly convicted" criminals • Pres. Johnson pardoned all southern whites except Confederate leaders and wealthy planters, restoring political rights and all property; only Confederate president Jefferson Davis served time in jail for rebelling against the Union • Northern abolitionists posted $100,000 bail for Jefferson Davis's treason trial, seeking a "peaceful reunion" of the nation (Dattel, 2009, p. 228) • Colored (Freedmen's) Conventions in Louisiana, Virginia, Tennessee, Missouri, Arkansas, South Carolina, and North Carolina and in the free state of Kansas called for education, voting rights, education, and jury service (Colored Conventions, n.d.) • Over 2000 Black men held local political offices, 600 state offices, and 17 at the federal level, including two U.S. Senators, through 1900 • All northern states—except Minnesota and Iowa—voted to deny voting rights to Blacks • Two to three Black people per week were lynched in the South (Downs & Masur, 2015, p. 7), every week during the Reconstruction period	• Immediately after emancipation, formerly enslaved people sought land, voting rights, and universal education for themselves and their children to lead self-determined lives • President Johnson denied to former Confederates property rights to "own" formerly enslaved people • Compensating enslavers for the loss in "property value" would have cost the federal government $9.2 billion in 1862 dollars (Piketty, 2020, p. 237) • Southern states sharply increased taxes on land to compensate for lost revenue due to emancipation (Dailey, 2000, p. 29) • General Sherman issued Special Field Order 15 to rid himself of the "nuisance" of 40,000 Black refugees, by authorizing up to 400,000 acres of land in South Carolina and Florida (40 acres per person) belonging to white farmers (Dattel, 2009, p. 243; Berlin et al., 1992, pp. 43, 68, 175–176) • Freedmen's Bureau bill intended to offer a one-year transition the nation from a slave economy to wage economy by administering confiscated land, documenting the violation of Reconstruction laws, and providing resources for freedpeople (Downs & Masur, 2015, p. 13)

(continued)

Table 2: *Continued*

Reconstruction Era 1865–1877		
Year	Political	Economic
		• First set of Black Codes enacted to regulate the behavior and labor of freedpeople including the requirement that a freedman sign an annual labor or apprenticeship contract or face arrest as a vagrant
		• 100,000 of the region's 120,000 skilled workers in the South were Black (Hill, 1977, p. 11)
		• Blacks were pushed out of jobs that they had formerly dominated as enslaved people, such as tobacco, carpentry, and caulking (Hill, 1977, p. 11)
		• Black workers were barred from industrial labor in the south, particularly the textile industry
		• In South Carolina, all freedmen had to pay a fee to do any work other than farming (Dattel, 2009, p. 252)
		• The New York Chamber of Commerce advised that the repayment of federal war debt depended on cotton exports (Dattel, 2009, p. 229)
		• Enticement laws passed by 10 southern states make it a crime to hire away a laborer under contract to another employer
		• Vagrancy laws enacted in every southern state except Texas and Arkansas, causing the arrest of any man without a labor contract and subjecting him to convict leasing
		• Bowie State University (MD) is founded

Table 2: *Continued*

	Reconstruction Era 1865–1877	
Year	Political	Economic
		• Clark-Atlanta University (GA) is founded
		• Shaw University (NC) was founded
		• Virginia Union University is founded
1866	• Massacres of Black people in Memphis (TN) and New Orleans (LA), killing over 100 people, were organized by white elected officials (Sterling, 1976, pp. 91–92)	• Black workers in Louisiana, Mississippi, Georgia, Virginia and Alabama went on strike for better working conditions (Murolo et al., 2001, p. 94)
	• Colored (Freedmen's) Conventions continued to push for civil, political, and economic rights for freedpeople	• Black women with weapons in the South Carolina lowcountry beat back an attempt by a Confederate widow to reclaim her husband's farmland and reinstate slave labor conditions (Arnesen, 2007, pp. 17-19)
	• Frances Ellen Watkins Harper advocated for voting rights for Black men and women (Foner, 1988, p. 448; Kendi, 2016, p. 246)	
		• The National Labor Union is formed in Baltimore. It preached labor solidarity across gender and race lines, and across all types of labor, except for its racism toward Chinese labor (Murolo & Chitty, 2001, pp. 101–102)
		• The extended Freedmen's Bureau bill removed any provision related to land allocation for freedpeople
		• Only 2,000 freedmen families were able to secure permanent ownership once whites reclaimed title to the South Carolina and Florida land Sherman had designated in his "40 acres" authorization (Painter, 1976/1986, p. xi)
		• Educational clauses were built into labor contracts between freedmen and planters

(continued)

Table 2: *Continued*

	Reconstruction Era 1865–1877	
Year	Political	Economic
		• Scalawags attempted to farm the land of former Confederates to maintain the cash crops (Foner, n.d.)
		• Black skilled labor (mechanics, blacksmiths, plasterers, painters, stone masons, etc.) outnumbered white skilled workers in most southern states and were able to negotiate better working conditions than were former agricultural workers (Hill, 1977, pp. 11–12)
		• The Southern Homestead Act set aside 3 million acres of poor quality for which freedmen could pay $5 per acre
		• Black soldiers in Arkansas purchased 30 acres of land to build a school for freedpeople, Southland Institute (Williams, 2005, p. 58)
		• At least 500 "native" (Black-homegrown) schools were documented throughout the South, not including the Sabbath schools (Anderson, 1988, pp. 7–9; Williams, 2005, pp. 7–38)
		• Edward Waters College (FL) was founded
		• Fisk University (TN) was founded
		• Lincoln University of Missouri was founded
		• Rust College (MS) was founded

Table 2: *Continued*

	Reconstruction Era 1865–1877	
Year	Political	Economic
1867	• Reconstruction Acts—Deployed U.S. military rule of 5 southern districts until ratification of 14th amendment and the adoption of new state constitutions • Five states—Mississippi, South Carolina, Louisiana, Alabama, and Florida—had Black electoral majorities, joining the Republican Party • Hundreds of Black men served as elected officials at the local, state, and national levels, many of them formerly enslaved • The Ku Klux Klan formed to "maintain the supremacy of the white race," its membership growing to 500,000 men over the next five years (Sterling, 1976, p. 366) • Widespread violence against and harassment of Black voters and Black office holders existed throughout the South • Black communities armed themselves, formed fraternal organizations, and organized defense committees (or state militia in Republic controlled states) against Klan violence • The Grange is formed to advocate for the concerns of small, white farmers who mistrusted railroad companies and major industrial corporations, and who excluded Blacks	• Educational clauses were built into labor contracts between freedmen and planters (Williams, 2005, p. 71) • A cooperative of freedpeople forms on land formerly owned by Jefferson Davis' family • Federal aid to railroads, including the impressment of Chinese workers that went on strike for higher wages (Murolo & Chitty, 2001, p. 121) • Black labor associations begin to form all over the country; one example was the Colored Caulkers Trade Union Society in Baltimore, a cooperatively owned and operated shipyard (Foner, 1988, p. 480) • All 80,000 acres of land reverted from Black workers to former Confederate owners, except for land held by federal government • Alabama State University was founded • Barber-Scotia College (NC) was founded • Fayetteville State University (NC) was founded

(continued)

Table 2: *Continued*

	Reconstruction Era 1865–1877	
Year	Political	Economic
		• Howard University (Washington, DC) was founded
		• Johnson C. Smith University (NC) was founded
		• Morehouse College (GA) was founded
		• Morgan State University (MD) was founded
		• St. Augustine College (NC) was founded
		• Talladega College (AL) was founded
1868	• 14th Amendment provided U.S. citizenship to all except for Indigenous Peoples, and by asserting equal protection under the laws, revoked the Black Codes • Election of Ulysses Grant as president • Political assassinations against Black office holders, white Republican supporters, and Black voters rose	• Convict leasing began in Mississippi with the state government paying employers a fee to feed and transport imprisoned people to work for free while the employer reaps all the profits • Hampton Normal and Agricultural Institute (now University) was founded in Virginia primarily to train Black teachers for common schools (Anderson, 1988, p. 34)
1869		• Alabama, Louisiana, and Texas enact policies to terminate the employment of freedpeople whose children attend school, partly to use child labor (Anderson, 1988, p. 23) • 4,000 freedmen obtained land through the Southern Homestead Act, barred from obtaining land from the Homestead Act of 1862

Table 2: *Continued*

	Reconstruction Era 1865–1877	
Year	Political	Economic
		• The transcontinental railroad was completed, having displaced American Indians from 150 million acres of their ancestral lands (U.S. Department of the Interior, 2013, p. 182; Murolo & Chitty, 2001, p. 113), and expanding the demand for southern cotton
		• The Knights of Labor is formed for all workers regardless of nationality, race, creed, sex, and skill (Murolo & Chitty, 2001, pp. 122–127; Sinyai, 2006, pp. 21–23)
		• The Colored National Labor Union is formed with delegates from 18 states (Murolo & Chitty, 2001, pp. 102–103) after being rebuffed by white labor unions (Sterling, 1976, pp. 281–283)
		• Claflin University (SC) was founded
		• Dillard University (LA) was founded
		• Simmons College (KY) was founded
		• Tougaloo College (MS) was founded
1870	• 15th Amendment: voting rights to all men, including free Black men in the north (Rosado et al., 2022, p. 22); strongly opposed by white suffragist women (Making good the promises) • Enforcement Acts targeting the violence of the Ku Klux Klan	• Every former Confederate state was re-admitted to the Union, having ratified the 14th and 15th Amendments, rescinded the Black Codes, recognized labor's right to organize, abolished imprisonment for debt, and eliminated property requirements to vote and hold office. • Southern states began building public hospitals, orphanages, asylums, and the first free public schools (Murolo & Chitty, 2001, p. 94)

(continued)

Table 2: *Continued*

Reconstruction Era 1865–1877	
Year Political	Economic
• Rampant corruption in New York, Washington, DC, and throughout the South included land swindles, theft, fraud, and bribery that impacted the Democratic and Republican parties nationwide	• Congress chartered the Freedmen's Savings Bank to encourage freedpeople to purchase land; in its 42 branches, over 44,000 freedpeople deposited over $12.5 million, to purchase land, homes, seed, animals, and equipment (Sterling, 1976, p. 259)
	• Freedman and Army veteran Henry Adams and his committee of 500 began documenting labor abuses and organizing throughout the south (Bracey et al., 1970, pp. 161–166)
	• A report by the National Teachers Association documents that state and local funding for Black schools in the south was inadequate and not equal to funding for white schools; Black congressmen advocated for a national education bill to equalize school funding
	• Industrialization increased with the transcontinental railroad, steel mills, and the expansion of oil drilling
	• From the 1870s to the 1890s, Mexican Americans were lynched in Texas, California, Arizona, and Colorado by white supremacists
	• Allen University (SC) was founded
	• Benedict College (SC) was founded
1871 • Northern whites adopted an attitude of Social Darwinism, or survival of the fittest (Kendi, 2016, pp. 264–267)	• Samuel Gompers, later the president of the American Federation of Labor, began organizing against Asian workers in the West
	• Alcorn State University (MS) was founded

Table 2: *Continued*

	Reconstruction Era 1865–1877	
Year	Political	Economic
	• The Ku Klux Act imposed fines and imprisonment to those who intended to deny equal protection under the law to Blacks and to overthrow the state Reconstruction governments, and gave the President power to send in federal troops to enforce the law	
	• Neither the Freedmen's Bureau nor the U.S. Army could stop the violence of the Ku Klux Klan and other white supremacy organizations as countless acts of arson, rape, murder, and beatings were targeted at Black people	
	• Congress eliminated the treaty system that dealt with each Indian nation as a sovereign nation, to hasten negotiations of land for railroad construction (Foner, 1988, p. 463)	
1872	• Re-election of Ulysses Grant as president	• Black schools in Washington, DC were the best in the nation (Sterling, 1976, p. 295)
		• South Carolina State University was one of only two in the South to be racially integrated
		• Between 1862 and 1872, the federal government awarded over 100 million acres of land and millions of dollars toward railroad construction, but no land to freedpeople (Foner, 1988, p. 467)

(continued)

Table 2: *Continued*

	Reconstruction Era 1865–1877	
Year	Political	Economic
1873	• Colfax (Louisiana) Massacre was "the bloodiest single act of carnage in all of Reconstruction (Foner, 1988, p. 530)." On Easter morning, Democrats shelled the courthouse where 61 armed Black Republicans were protecting reelected officials, and publicly executed the 37 survivors in the town square (Kendi, 2016, p. 252). • The Supreme Court decided in Slaughterhouse Cases that the rights of citizens were under state, not federal, control, and the 14th amendment, protected property rights (Foner, 1988, pp. 529- 531, 533) • Northern states (Pennsylvania, New York, Ohio, etc.) began to prohibit racial discrimination in public places and to provide schools for Black children (Foner, 1988, p. 471)	• Just as the U.S. became second only to Britain in manufacturing production (Foner, 1988, p. 461), the Panic of 1873–79 led to a major economic depression in North America and Europe, closing 5000 U.S. businesses, wiping out local and national unions, and creating countless unemployed industrial workers with no refuge to family-owned farms (Murolo & Chitty, 2001, pp. 103–104; Sinyai, 2006, p. 19) • The Freedmen's Bureau was dismantled • The Cherokee and Choctaw grant land and partial rights to those they formerly enslaved, making them the only freedpeople to receive 40 acres; The Chickasaw resisted because slave-holding whites had not similarly granted land to freedpeople (Sterling, 1976, p. 247) • Bennett College (NC) was founded • University of Arkansas—Pine Bluff was founded • Wiley College (TX) was founded
1874	• By year's end, Alabama, Arkansas, and Texas were in Democratic control, leading to more violence against Blacks and Republicans • Northern states began to criminalize unemployment by passing vagrancy laws, and Indiana adopted a convict leasing system to support the manufacturing of railroad cars (Foner, 1988, p. 519)	• Midwestern states and Kansas competed for the cotton market supported by railroad construction (Dattel, 2009, p. 233) • Louisiana, Arkansas, Florida, and Mississippi state school superintendents were Black men, serving all the state's children (Sterling, 1976, p. 308)

Table 2: *Continued*

	Reconstruction Era 1865–1877	
Year	Political	Economic
	• The northern press began to express the belief that Blacks in the south were incapable of self-determination (Foner, 1988, p. 526)	• The Freedmen's Savings Bank failed, due partly to making large, unsecured loans the railroads (Foner, 1988, pp. 531–532)
		• Florida's Black legislators won laws that supported better working conditions for timber workers and longshoremen
		• The Grange supported setting the wages of Black laborers, and the abolition of schooling for Blacks to have greater control of Black labor (Foner, 1988, p. 549)
1875	• Civil Rights Acts were intended to protect Black access to public accommodations and to provide federal restitution	• Alabama A&M University was founded
		• Huston-Tillotson University (TX) was founded
	• Mississippi adopted the "Shotgun Plan" using thousands of former Confederate military men to "carry the election peaceably if we can, forcibly if we must." President Grant rebuffed Governor Ames' request for federal protection, stating "the whole public are tired out with these annual autumnal outbreaks in the South." (Sterling, 1976, pp. 439–445)	• Knoxville College (TN) was founded
1876	• Cruikshank decision of the U.S. Supreme Court demolished the Enforcement Acts, which required the federal government to enforce the 13th, 14th, and 15th amendments and permitted local enforcement of crimes against Blacks (Foner, 1988, p. 531)	• The Lakota Sioux, Northern Cheyenne, and Arapaho Indians won a victory against the U.S. in the Battle of Little Big Horn
		• The Southern Homestead Act was repealed
	• South Carolina, Arkansas, Mississippi, and Louisiana were the only states still under Republican control (Foner, 1988, p. 539)	• Meharry Medical College (TN) was founded
		• Prairie View A&M (TX) was founded

(continued)

Table 2: *Continued*

	Reconstruction Era 1865–1877	
Year	Political	Economic
	• South Carolina witnessed a massacre in the all-Black town of Hamburg during election season by 3,000 white men	
	• Outnumbering whites in South Carolina's upcountry, armed Black women patrolled the polling places on Election Day (Sterling, 1976, p. 470)	
	• Presidential campaign of Hayes (R) and Tilden (D) ends in a bargain that ends federal military occupation of the south	
1877	• 22 Black men held federal offices	• Henry O. Flipper was the first Black man to graduate from West Point Military Academy
	• Federal troops were being redirected away from the south to fighting American Indians in the west	• In Nicodemus, Kansas, Black homesteaders were assisted by the Osage and Potawatomi Indians in setting up an all-Black community (U.S. Department of the Interior, 2013, p. 192)
		• The price of cotton had fallen 50% from 1872 prices, increasing the number of white tenant farmers and sharecroppers and low wage textile workers
		• The national Republic Party focused attention on protective tariffs, banks, and railroads
		• Black Republicans maintained a focus on land, schools, civil and voting rights
		• Every southern state, except Virginia, adopted the practice of leasing Black prisoners to companies seeking labor

Table 2: *Continued*

	Reconstruction Era 1865–1877	
Year	Political	Economic
		• A national railroad strike included 100,000 Black and white workers (half of the nation's total) from Baltimore, Buffalo, Albany, St. Louis, and Chicago (Murolo & Chitty, 2001, p. 107) • Jackson State University (MS) was founded • Philander Smith University (AR) was founded

Table 3: Post-Reconstruction timeline showing political and economic events of importance.

	Post-Reconstruction	
1878–1896	Political	Economic
	• 1879–1883: The state of Virginia was governed by a coalition of Black and white Republicans and white Democrats called the Readjuster Party that sent 18 Republicans to Congress • 1883: US Supreme Court declared the Civil Rights Act of 1875 unconstitutional • 1887: Mound Bayou, MS was formed as an all-Black town (Bracey et al., 1970, p. 157)	• 1878: the Panic of 1873 hit bottom with the failure of 10,000 businesses • 1879: Large numbers of Blacks—as many as 20,000 known as Exodusters—fled the South for Kansas in pursuit of "their three central preoccupations—earning a living, voting in peace, and seeing their children educated." (Bracey et al., 1970, pp. 167-169; Murolo & Chitty, 2001, p. 97; Painter 1976/1986, p. 43) • 1880: In Alabama, North Carolina, and Florida it was a criminal act for a Black man to change employers without permission (Blackmon, 2008, p. 54)

(continued)

Table 3: *Continued*

Post-Reconstruction	
• 1890: The Force Bill was defeated, ending Republican efforts to enforce the 13th, 14th, and 15th Amendments • 1890: Mississippi, followed by the other southern states, included anti-poor literacy tests and poll taxes in their new state constitutions as barriers to voting • 1890: The National Women's Suffrage Association forms, barring Black women • 1892: The number of documented lynchings peaked at 255 this year, with hundreds documented by Ida B. Wells between 1888 and 1896 (Kendi, 2016, p. 274; Downs & Masur, 2015, p. 7) • 1892: Anna Julia Cooper published *A voice from the South*, advocating Black women's education • 1892–1896: The Populist Party ran candidates for president and secured congressional seats and 8.5% of the popular vote • 1895: Frederick Douglass dies • 1895: Booker T. Washington articulates the Atlanta Compromise, arguing that Black people should not push for equality, if white people would allow Black people to continue their agricultural and manual labors in peace • 1896: U.S. Supreme Court upholds state laws for "separate but equal" public accommodations	• Between 1881 and 1897, workers engaged in over 18,000 labor strikes for higher wages, a shorter workday, and other goals • By the 1880's, tens of thousands of Black workers belonged to all-Black trade unions (Arnesen, 2007, p. 49) • Formerly enslaved Booker T. Washington founded Tuskegee Institute (now University) in Tuskegee, Alabama (Anderson, 1988, pp. 33–78) • 1884: One-third of Exodusters acquired their own land (Murolo & Chitty, 2001, p. 97) • Between 1885 and 1900, more than 2,500 Blacks were lynched (Murolo & Chitty, 2001, p. 119) • 1886: The Knights of Labor lost over 500,000 members in two years, partly due to its insistence on a fully inclusive union (Sinyai, 2006, p. 25) • 1886: The American Federation of Labor forms, barring Black membership • 1889: The People's (Populist) Movement organized to assert power over the monopolists in the railroad, banking, and landholding industries; it excluded sharecroppers and tenant farmers and Blacks • 1890: Over 90% of Blacks lived in the south, 80% of whom lived in rural areas; 82% of Black farmers rented their homes and property, and only 3.7% of them produced any crop other than cotton or corn (Boston, 1997, pp. 158–159; Murolo & Chitty, 2001, p. 118)

Table 3: *Continued*

Post-Reconstruction	
• 1896: The National Association for Colored Women is formed to "defend Black womanhood, challenge discrimination, and lend power to self-help efforts." (Kendi, 2016, p. 275)	• By 1890, 25 all-Black towns were formed in Oklahoma Territory (Bracey et al., 1970, p. 157) • 1890: American industrial production was greater than that of Britain, France, or Germany (Sinyai, 2006, p. 17) • Skilled, unemployed Black men were increasingly used as "scab labor" around the country when white workers went on strike, deepening racial animosities (Arnesen, 2007, p. 42–45) • 1890: The Brotherhood of Locomotive Trainmen in Houston, Texas demanded that all Black workers be replaced with whites (Hill, 1977, p. 15) • 1890: Most labor unions all over the U.S. excluded Blacks • 1890s: A few labor unions organized interracial organizations—Knights of Labor; The Brotherhood of Timber Workers; the Industrial Workers of the World [Wobblies]; and the early United Mine Workers (Hill, 1977, p. 16) • In the early 1890s, declining agricultural prices, high interest on debts, and the high cost of transporting goods caused massive bankruptcy and foreclosures of family farms in the South and Midwest

(continued)

Table 3: *Continued*

Post-Reconstruction
• 1893: The economy crashed, leading to a depression lasting until 1897 that was especially hard on small farmers, small businesses, and wage workers (Murolo & Chitty, 2001, p. 134)
• Membership in the Knights of Labor fell from 750,000 in 1886 to 20,000 by 1896
• Between 1878 and 1896, 30 HBCUs were founded including: Selma (AL), Livingstone (NC), Southern (LA), Morris-Brown (GA), Spelman (GA), Tuskegee (AL), Lane (TN), Paine (GA), Virginia State, Arkansas Baptist, Virginia University of Lynchburg, Shorter College (AR), University of Maryland Eastern Shore, Kentucky State, Florida A&M, Central State (OH), Savannah State (GA), North Carolina A&T, Delaware State, West Virginia State, Elizabeth City State (NJ), Winston-Salem (NC), Clinton College (SC), Texas College, Fort Valley State (GA), Bluefield State (WV), South Carolina State, Oakwood College (AL), and Langston (OK)
• By the end of the 19th century, the rates of Black literacy had grown from 5% literate in 1860, to 30% in 1880, to nearly 70% by 1896 (Anderson, 1988, p. 31)

REFERENCES:

Anderson, J. A. (1988). *The education of Blacks in the South, 1860–1935*. The University of North Carolina Press

Arnesen, E. (Ed.). (2007). *The Black worker: A reader*. The University of Illinois Press.

Baptist, E. E. (2014) *The half has never been told: Slavery and the making of American capitalism*. Basic Books.

Berlin, E., Fields, B. J., Miller, S. F., Reidy, J. P., & Rowland, L. S. (1992). *Slaves no more: Three essays on emancipation and the Civil War*. Cambridge University Press.

Blackmon, D. A. (2008). *Slavery by another name: The re-enslavement of Black Americans from the Civil War to World War II*. Random House.

Boston, T. D. (Ed.). (1997). *A different vision: African American economic thought*. Routledge.

Bracey, J. H., Meier, A., & Rudwick, E. (Eds.). (1970). *Black nationalism in America*. Bobbs-Merrill Co.

Colored Conventions Project. (n.d.). Retrieved from https://coloredconventions.org

Dailey, J. (2000). *Before Jim Crow: The politics of race in post-emancipation Virginia*. The University of North Carolina Press.

Dattel, G. (2009). *Cotton and race in the making of America: The human costs of economic power*. Ivan R. Dee

Downs, R. P., & Masur, K. (2017). *The era of reconstruction*. U.S. Department of the Interior. National Park Service. Retrieved from https://www.nps.gov/subjects/nationalhistoriclandmarks/upload/Reconstruction.pdf

Foner, E. (1988). *Reconstruction: American's unfinished revolution, 1863–1877*. Perennial Classics.

Foner, E. (n.d.). U.S. Department of the Interior. National Park Service. *Reconstruction*. Retrieved from https://www.nps.gov/articles/reconstruction.htm

Halpern, R., & Dal Lago, E. (Eds.). (2002). *Slavery and emancipation*. Blackwell Publishers.

Hill, H. (1977). *Black labor and the American legal system: Race, work, and the law*. The University of Wisconsin Press.

Kendi, I. X. (2016). *Stamped from the beginning: The definitive history of racist ideas in America*. Nation Books.

Murolo, P., & Chitty, A. B. (2001). *From the folks who brought you the weekend: A short, illustrated history of labor in the United States*. W.W. Norton.

Oshinsky, D. M. (1996). *"Worse than slavery:" Parchman farm and the ordeal of Jim Crow justice*. The Free Press.

Painter, N. I. (1976/1986). *Exodusters: Black migration to Kansas after reconstruction; The first major migration to the north of ex-slaves*. W.W. Norton.

Piketty, T. (2020). *Capital and ideology*. Harvard University Press.

Rosado, A., Cohn-Postar, G., & Eisen, M. (2022). *Erasing the Black freedom struggle: How state standards fail to teach the truth about Reconstruction*. Zinn Education Project.

Sinyai, C. (2006). *Schools of democracy: A political history of the American labor movement*. Cornell University Press.

Sterling, D. (Ed.). (1976). *The trouble they seen: The story of Reconstruction in the words of African Americans*. Da Capo Press.

U.S. Department of the Interior. National Park Service. (2013). *American Indians and the Civil War.*
Williams, H. A. (2005). *Self-taught: African American education in slavery and freedom.* The University of North Carolina Press.

CHAPTER FIVE

Drawing Conclusions: Using Political Cartoons in the Classroom to Analyze Reconstruction Era Images of African Americans

TIM DORSCH

Political cartoons often can depict complex viewpoints about historical events and people with a simple illustration and few words. By analyzing these sources, students can improve their understanding of the Reconstruction era by examining the marginalized place of African Americans in the historical narrative. By the end of the nineteenth century, many Americans viewed the Reconstruction era negatively, and criticized the role that African Americans played in it. Although historians today disagree with this old view, students can study political cartoons in order to examine why those viewpoints formed as well as how they changed over time.

Prevalent in a variety of newspapers during the middle to late nineteenth century, political cartoons commented on social and political issues often highlighting partisan perspectives present at the time. Students can use political cartoons as primary sources to analyze the continuities and changes in the image of African Americans during Reconstruction. This can help them to better understand how the optimism about racial equity many shared following the Civil War shifted to the inequality synonymous with the late nineteenth century and early twentieth century.

This chapter first explains how to effectively analyze political cartoons in order to understand their content and context. Second, the chapter provides examples of political cartoons and organizes them in a few groups for analysis. The first group of sources reveal that some cartoonists consistently published unfavorable views of African Americans throughout Reconstruction as a means to undermine calls for their equality. The remaining analytical groups highlight the works of political cartoonist Thomas Nast which changed significantly throughout the Reconstruction era. His early works forward a positive image of African Americans to support their struggle for full citizenship, but over time he used their image more as a tool to back his cartoon's points rather than to improve their status. By the end of Reconstruction, many of Nast's cartoons depicted African Americans with negative stereotypes, a direct contradiction of his earlier work. Analyzing the given sources can lead students to find answers to questions like, what beliefs existed about African Americans during Reconstruction, how did they shift over time, and what caused this change in stance?

USING POLITICAL CARTOONS IN THE CLASSROOM

The educational strategy described in this chapter helps teachers guide students through analysis of political cartoons as primary sources in a way that examines popularly held stances and contextualizes the images within history. Before getting into the specific examples, this section provides an overview of the process students can use to analyze cartoons as well as the strengths, weaknesses, and broader historical perspectives to think about when using the source.

Political cartoons are interesting primary sources to analyze because the illustrators made them with the purpose of either swaying or cementing the viewpoints of the observers. The artist often achieved this by simplifying the subject matter to make his side appear as common sense, while portraying the other side as ridiculous and wrong. Cartoonists used many strategies to connect with their audience and push their agenda, including using popular cultural references, imbuing characters with heroic or villainous traits, as well as generalizing groups of people and their ideas. Identifying these strategies helps to unlock the analytical potential of the source.

How to Analyze a Political Cartoon

In order to glean the most possible information from a political cartoon have students use an analytical process, like the one explained below, for each example. Before studying the content of the source, begin with a pre-analysis of the date, cartoonist, and the newspaper. Whenever possible, include this citation information with the cartoons because it establishes the context as well as the perspective that the student attempts to find (Table 1).

Follow this up with the detailed analysis of the political cartoon and its meaning. An effective way to study the cartoon itself starts with reading all included

Table 1: Pre-analysis

	Importance	Questions to Ask
Date	To situate the political cartoon within the events of that time.	What important events are happening at the time? What events have recently happened? To what is the cartoon responding?
Cartoonist	To understand the perspectives and opinions of the maker of the source.	Who made the cartoon? What stances does the artist usually take?
Newspaper	To know the political leanings of the newspaper and the intended audience.	What agenda does the newspaper have? Who owns and edits the newspaper? Where was it published? Who is the audience? How well does the agenda of the newspaper fit the opinions of the cartoonist?

Table 2: Cartoon Analysis

	Importance	Questions to Ask
Captions/ Labels	To understand how the textual elements support the purpose of the cartoon. To identify subjects within the cartoon.	What text is under or within the cartoon? Who/What is speaking? What people/objects have a label? Is it quoting someone or something of note? Is the use of text genuine or sarcastic?
People and Symbols	To analyze the subjects and topic of the cartoon, as well as determine how the cartoonist meant to use them.	What people or characters are included? What symbols are used, and what do they stand for? Are there any commonly used symbols (like Uncle Sam)? Is each element portrayed in a positive or negative way? Why?
Subject Matter Analysis	To understand the purpose of the cartoon. To create a full picture from the contextual information, text, people, symbols, and purpose of the cartoon.	What argument does the cartoon make? What does it support and/or attack? What perspectives does it show and/or ignore? Is the focus of the cartoon political, social, a combination, or something else? Do any background or secondary details help support the point? Why is this stance important historically?

text and identifying any people or symbols. This assists in building a good overview of the topic and not missing any important elements. From here make an informed analysis of what the cartoonist actually argues about the issue, the purpose of the cartoon, and its historical importance (Table 2).

Some simpler political cartoons may not always require following this full process step by step to understand them, but until students become comfortable with analyzing the source, it helps to start out referring to a guide. The teacher can fill in some details to assist students when using more complex cartoons. Cartoonists often used caricatures of congressmen or newspaper editors but did not label them. Giving the name, position, and political party of subjects, which students may not recognize, helps streamline the analytical process.

Source Usage and Perspectives

Through this analytical strategy, students can learn a lot about the historical era and its issues from these images, however, make sure they recognize the strengths and weaknesses of political cartoons as a source. Keep in mind that these visuals have a bias and push an agenda. They give a small snapshot of the topic from a specific perspective but can oversimplify issues in order to make their point. Cartoons stand as a great window into the partisan opinions held at that time, and by using examples from Republican, Democratic, and independent newspapers, a researcher can learn from comparing and contrasting the varied arguments. These illustrations visually represent groups of people as the cartoonists viewed them or as they wanted the public to view them. Using caricature in this way helps the observer to easily understand the subject and point of the image, but for that same reason cartoons also become an ideal medium for forwarding stereotypes. They show a wide audience a flattened, and often inaccurate, version of the subjects. As historians know, just because a source is biased or inaccurate does not make it unusable. Recognizing the bias and finding out the reasons why a cartoonist may have purposefully pushed a stereotype, or an inaccurate account, can give the researcher insight into the feelings and motivations of the cartoonist and people from that time.

In order to use political cartoons as an examination of popularly held stances of the time, including how they shifted or remained consistent, make sure that students establish a background knowledge of the era. Build their understanding of the era's timeline, important events, legislation, and people if you expect students to fully analyze cartoons on their own. Teachers can also use cartoons to introduce new topics to students if the teacher assists in guiding the analysis.

The instructor should ensure that students think about the different perspectives held by people at the time, keeping in mind that variations in people's viewpoints stem from many reasons, such as political leanings, location, race, gender, and socioeconomic status to name a few. Have them consider the experiences of Northerners or Southerners, residents of urban or rural areas, men and women, people who were white, black, Asian, or Native American, people who were wealthy or poor, and think about how their everyday life shaped their opinions as well as how they would likely view a cartoon.

When examining perspectives the teacher can introduce students to some historiography of the Reconstruction era with regards to African American images. Historiography, or the study of how historical coverage has changed over time, will help them learn about commonly accepted ideas and understandings from different time periods. It also can reiterate that the prevailing viewpoints of today did not always have support, and that the work of historians often reflected the time when they lived.

Modern interpretations of emancipation and Reconstruction highlight the agency exercised by African Americans as well as contextualize their varied experiences. Historians accomplish this through using a variety of sources and methods to cover the subject, including studies of culture, literature, personal writings, discourse, and memory history, which all can help to tell about diverse experiences in a meaningful way. Some, like Baker (2007) and Muhammad (2010), ask questions aiming to explain the creation and proliferation of prevailing African American images during and after Reconstruction, and draw connections between the images and the sentiments of the time.

This broader scope of history did not always exist. In the late nineteenth century United States, the descriptions and arguments used by some historians when describing the image and place of African Americans pushed negative stereotypical portrayals. These images worked to undercut the standing of African Americans and create a narrative of their inability to use the rights which came with citizenship. For instance, the journalist James S. Pike wrote many articles which became the book *The Prostrate State* (1874). This account stressed inferiority of African Americans and the role of corrupt government ruining Southern life. Explanations like this began, in a widespread and public manner, to blame the failures of Reconstruction on a supposed incapacity of African Americans. Later historians like William Dunning (1907) further codified these beliefs and kept them alive well into the middle of the twentieth century. Leftover ideas from theses early interpretations still inform public opinions even if they no longer fit in the historical narrative.

An overview of historiography will help the teacher guide students through conversations about why historical perspectives and methods change over time. A few important works which help create a foundation of today's scholarship include Du Bois (1935), Franklin (1961), Cruden (1969), and Foner (1988).

One of the most useful historical skills for a student to possess is the ability to draw connections between different eras. If they can identify popular beliefs from one time and compare them with those from other eras in United States history, they can really start to understand how the nation changed or stayed the same. Along with other sources, cartoons help show how beliefs, ideas, and stereotypes formed and passed on, as well as if they strengthened or faded over time. For instance, the teacher can return to these Reconstruction era sources in order to make comparisons when covering later units or studying current events. Now having covered an analytical process for political cartoons and some historical strategies and perspectives to keep in mind when teaching with the source, the next section focuses on specific examples and the trends one can identify by studying them.

POLITICAL CARTOON EXAMPLES

Middle to late nineteenth-century newspapers utilized political cartoons to attach powerful visuals to political and social opinions, and this helped inform Americans' stances on issues. For this reason, students can analyze a selection of political cartoons from the mid-1860s through the early 1880s as primary sources to learn about opinions and debates surrounding African American rights, as well as examine the creation, continuity, and change of their public images. Research supports that some cartoonists consistently showed African Americans in a negative light, stereotyping them as simpleminded, lazy, and only able to fill servile jobs. More interestingly, other cartoonists like Thomas Nast came out in favor of emancipation and expanded rights for African Americans during and shortly after the Civil War only to pivot to a less accepting stance in the later years of Reconstruction. Nast's earlier art showed Black Americans as respectable, honest, and a functioning part of the American political system. Later in the 1870s the cartoons of Nast more often showed stereotypical views of African Americans including exaggerated lips, noses, dialects, and portrayals as pawns rather than equal citizens with their own agency.

These sources provide a good starting point for critical conversations about the era, including driving questions such as: Shortly after the Civil War, what did varying cartoonist's works reveal about opinions of African Americans gaining citizenship? How and why did Nast's coverage of African Americans change over time? How did negative images work to differentiate African Americans from other groups? How do the opinions forwarded in political cartoons compare with other types of sources?

Consistently Negative Images

This section will first examine a few examples from cartoonists and newspapers that consistently used negative images of African Americans through the entire emancipation and Reconstruction era. The purpose of these aimed to either oppose the end of slavery and the goals of Reconstruction, or push the idea that African Americans could not participate in American society as equals. To achieve these ends, illustrators used stereotypes based on claims of laziness, inability to learn, cultural incompatibility, and physical differences.

A cartoon titled "Quashee's Dream of Emancipation" (1863) appeared in the popular northern publication, *Frank Leslie's Illustrated Newspaper*, during the Civil War. This six- paneled cartoon showed what a slave, with the derogatory generic name Quashee, believed life after emancipation would include. These dreams contained scenes of making his old master work for him, serving in congress, sitting with his feet up as a white woman waited on him, watching the opera from a stage-box, and working in a ritzy clothing store. The cartoon worked to craft a stereotype of African Americans as trying to get out of hard work, demanding exalted positions, and an inability to fit into existing white society. Cartoonish depictions of cranial proportions and ridiculous clothing choices, such as oversized collars, served to differentiate between the races, and suggested that people should not take these dreams seriously. Elements of the cartoon also worked to stoke anger or fear in the audience. For instance, many white working-class men feared they would lose their jobs and positions in society if slavery ended. The last panel shows the man awakening tied to a whipping post "to find emancipation hasn't much altered his position after all" (Quashee, 1863). This works to reinforce the idea that upward mobility for African Americans would remain a dream.

A later example from *Frank Leslie's Illustrated Newspaper*, showed General Sheridan using federal troops to allow two Black men to attack and rob a white man with impunity. It quoted a "Radical Journal" which stated, "The negro must be protected from all hazards" (Sheridan's Ride, 1875). Although the meaning of the quote dealt with the hazards of hate group violence, the cartoon interpreted it to suggest it meant protecting illegal actions. The purpose of Sheridan bringing troops into Louisiana in January of 1875 stemmed from the state governor William Kellogg asking for federal assistance. He required troops once before in September of 1874 when an armed insurrection of White League members sought to remove Republican lawmakers. When the state legislature reconvened in January of 1875, fears of Democratic attempts to seize disputed seats led to calling up federal troops again. Reflecting the feelings of those people who did not support Reconstruction, this cartoon made the actions out as an overreach of a tyrannical government which aimed to protect criminals at the detriment of good citizens. It cast African Americans as violent criminals, and the government as meddling where it did not belong. The proliferation of ideas like these in Louisiana and around the nation helped to halt federal enforcement efforts, reestablish Democratic control in the south, and undermine equal rights.

Some newspapers printed illustrations of racial stereotype jokes. These often did not include any direct political commentary, but still stigmatized races and ethnicities within a medium that influenced a wide audience. Although present in some newspapers from the Civil War on, the frequency of these depictions increased significantly in the late 1870s through the 1890s. Many cartoons made stereotype jokes about African American culture and work ethic, as well as loving and stealing watermelons and chickens. The physical representations stereotyped exaggerated hair, head shape, mouths, and splayed feet. One example created by E. S. Bisbee (1883) for *Puck* Magazine used many of these stereotypes to craft an extremely flattened and derogatory depiction. The title "A suggestion for a southern scarecrow" is printed above an African American man perched on a pole in a watermelon patch (Bisbee, 1883, p. 39). The artist proposes being a scarecrow as a suitable job for Black people. This illustration works to depict African Americans as massively different from and inferior to white Americans.

Such depictions became a normalized image of African Americans to many Americans, the effects of which last far beyond the end of Reconstruction. If using examples like these in the classroom, it may prove helpful to discuss how stereotypes develop and the influence they have. Also, discussion about how stereotypes from that time influence those still prevalent today can highlight connections over time.

Thomas Nast Cartoons

Analysis of cartoonist's images that always focused on negativity and inequality show some commonly held stances from the time, but more context and understanding of the era comes from cartoonists whose portrayals changed as Reconstruction progressed. A prime example of a shifting image presents itself in the works of Thomas Nast. When studying his works it helps to ask, how did his coverage change, and why did that change occur?

Compared to contemporary cartoonists, Nast usually posited a more positive image of African Americans, but his portrayals did change over time and based on context. Nast gained prominence in the post-Civil War era, during which he strongly supported most Radical Republican stances. He consistently backed legislation granting rights, and decried Southern, Democratic, or hate group attempts to oppose them. As time passed, support of Radical Republican ideas waned in the public as well as in the Republican Party. Nast stuck with his more radical stances longer than most party members, at times causing tension with more liberal Republicans, however by the later 1870s negativity crept into many of his depictions of African Americans.

The following sections detail the rather positive image of African Americans seen in Nast's earlier works, which over time shifted to depictions that used

African Americans to make a larger political or social point, before succumbing to growing negativity and stereotype. Each section contains a few political cartoon examples along with analysis to help explain the purpose and context of the cartoon.

Positive Images:

Shortly after the Civil War, Nast praised the work of the Union Army and painted a positive picture of the constructive changes which could occur in the United States. He supported the Radical Republican ideas about Reconstruction and civil rights legislation, and his cartoons at this time often showed African Americans in a positive way, suggesting the possibility of equality within society.

For instance, on the first page of a two-page cartoon, Nast (1865) depicted an upset Lady Liberty having to accept the pardons of Confederate leaders, captioned "I shall trust these men" (p. 488). The second page, which represented enfranchisement, showed Lady Liberty standing beside a solemn and respectable African American soldier. This veteran, who lost a leg in the war, stood above the caption, "and not this man?" (p. 489). The cartoon admonished trusting ex-Confederates, who often received leniency for their actions during the war, while showing that African Americans who served honorably during the war deserved equal rights. The cartoon, which noted the soldier's active role and sacrifice for the United States during the war, showed him as deserving the right to vote. Nast displayed strong support for African American citizenship and their capability of making informed decisions as involved members of American society.

In 1870, Nast (1870) created a cartoon depicting the first African American Congressman, Hiram Revels, sitting in his Senate seat and talking with other legislators. The importance of this cartoon came from the positive way the drawing portrayed Revels, who had the poise and dignity of an esteemed member of government. Several other congressmen even circled around Revels' desk to speak with him. It showed that Nast wanted the public to see Revels as an equal and capable Senator. The depiction of his race in this cartoon was not a means of diminishing his respectability or his ability to fulfill his job. In the foreground, only Jefferson Davis dressed as Iago, the antagonist from Shakespeare's play Othello, seems bothered by Revels. Davis, who served as the former president of the Confederacy as well as a past senator from Mississippi, comes across as petty and wrong for his anger towards the senator (Image 1).

The teacher can contextualize this cartoon to help students recognize the political influence that many African American men exercised by voting after the passage of the fifteenth amendment. Their voting in the early 1870s helped to shift longtime Democratic strongholds across the south to Republican control, and elected African American representatives to many levels of government. This

Image 1: Thomas Nast. (1870, April 9) Time works wonders. *Harper's Weekly 14*(693), 232. Retrieved from https://www.loc.gov/pictures/item/93508073/

power waned when violence, court rulings, and poor enforcement of laws led to the disenfranchisement of most African Americans by the later 1870s.

The previous cartoons showed images of African Americans as capable and deserving of equal rights, but keep in mind that the cartoonist usually had a purpose for including any subject in an illustration. The favorable portrayal of African Americans often used them as the protagonist compared to the foil of southerners with Confederate sympathies. The two aforementioned examples make genuine arguments that African Americans deserved the right to vote and fit in as active member of society, however some later cartoons used decent portrayals of African Americans more as a tool to accentuate the problems of other groups of people, rather than to focus on improving their status.

Purposeful Positivity:

By the mid-1870s many of Nast's cartoons used a positive or neutral image of African Americans to serve another purpose such as supporting a political or social point. He often did this to highlight the violence of groups such as the White League, the KKK, or southern Democrats. This likely came from his desire to influence the audience to see the threats and killings as unjust attacks on African Americans. Although many of Nast's depictions during this time did not stand out as negative, the images of black people started to become more of a political tool rather than a genuine portrayal of a group of people.

A cartoon from February of 1875 depicted a black man surrounded by a burned schoolhouse and a few corpses while looking down the gun barrels of White League members (Nast, 1875, February 5). The man does not have negative physical attributes, but he existed as a stand in. The illustration attacked the terror tactics used by white groups but used the African American man more as a tool to make the point than as a citizen working to improve his conditions.

In another cartoon the following year Nast drew the smoldering remains of schools, homes, and churches as well as a pile of dead African Americans murdered by the White League. In the center a disheveled but honorable black man mourns on his knees with his eyes turned towards the heavens. Nast (1876) included the questions, "Is this a republican form of government? Is this protecting life, liberty, or property? Is this the equal protection of the law?" (Image 2). The cartoon focused as much on the detrimental effects of hate groups to the nation and government as it did on the rights of African Americans, using their image to further a political point. Nast made the scene as a way to critique the stance and words of L.Q.C. Lamar, a Democratic House of Representatives member from Mississippi, who opposed African American voting rights and did little to curb the violence. The cartoon placed the African American man in a sad situation but showed him as requiring someone else's assistance rather than having the ability to help himself. Images depicting African Americans as active agents grew increasingly rare as Reconstruction wore on, more often placing them in the roles of victims in need of assistance or easily available pawns to be used.

Nast sometimes used respectable images of African Americans as a way of disparaging the South and their restriction of rights. In an 1878 cartoon, he depicted L.Q.C. Lamar, now the Senator from Mississippi, conversing with an upstanding black man. Lamar's statement regarding "the right of the people of

Image 2: Thomas Nast. (1876, September 2) Is this a republican government. *Harper's Weekly* 20(1027), 712. Retrieved from https://www.loc.gov/item/96509623/

the south to self-government" is questioned by an African American man who asks, "Whom do you mean by the people?" Lamar responds, "How dare you wave the bloody shirt again" (Nast, 1878, p. 1016). Waving the bloody shirt refers to people, often politicians, invoking emotional responses from an audience by bringing up those killed during the Civil War. People usually used this phrase to call out one's opponents for continually bringing up old losses as a way of gaining support. In this cartoon however, the man asks a legitimate question concerning rights, only to be met with diversionary tactics. Nast uses this cartoon to refute the idea that enough had been done by the government with regards to Reconstruction. He contended that southerners like Lamar incorrectly believed that beyond emancipation African Americans should not expect better treatment or equal rights. Nast utilized an image of a black man to show another group, in this case Southern politicians, as bad.

Growing Negativity over Time:

Over time, a higher percentage of Nast's cartoons covering African Americans included negative depictions. Even though most of his works still supported equal rights, fewer of them actually showed African Americans as equals. This shift becomes apparent when comparing two cartoons commenting on African Americans in the South from nearly twenty years apart. The first cartoon, which came out in January of 1863, right after the Emancipation Proclamation, showcased "the emancipation of the negroes" with "the past and the future" (Nast, 1863, pp. 56–57). Nast drew the "past" tile with whippings, brandings, slave auctions, and attack dogs, while in the "future" tile he drew scenes of African Americans living peacefully, going to school, and getting paid for their work. Only a very small sketch in the bottom showed field work, in which the workers and the overseer tip their hats at each other. The daily life scenes encircled an image of a family, well dressed, sitting together in a furnished home. The family depiction differed very little from an idealistic image of any American family of the time (Image 3).

Nineteen years later, in January of 1882, Nast again drew a cartoon comparing the 1860s South with a later time and commented on the place of African Americans in that society. In this illustration, he showed a scene from 1861 with a personification of King Cotton sitting upon a throne of cotton bales, pressing down an African American under his foot. The other scene, representing 1882, celebrates how much the Southern economy has grown, but contains only African Americans lifting large loads of cotton in the fields. The main part of the cartoon focuses on a lady, the "Queen of Industry or, the New South" (Nast, 1882, p. 17). She works at a new mechanized spinning machine. Where the 1863 cartoon brought up social and economic growth as goals for the South, the second lauds industrial progress but forgets the social advancement of African Americans, placing them in an agricultural labor scene differing little from one depicting the pre-Civil War era.

A Nast cartoon from March of 1874 depicts African American legislators in a very different light from his 1870 drawing of Hiram Revels. The cartoon "Colored Rule in a Reconstructed(?) State," focuses on Black legislators arguing in an undignified manner. They raise clenched fists, and yell at each other disrupting the session. They wear formal, but exaggerated clothing, and stand out for

Image 3: Thomas Nast. (1863, January 24) Emancipation. *Harper's Weekly* 7(317), 56–57. Retrieved from https://www.loc.gov/item/2002695553/

beady eyes and cartoonish oversized mouths. The caption reads, "The members call each other thieves, liars, rascals, and cowards." Columbia, an embodiment of the United States says, "You are aping the lowest whites. If you disgrace your race in this way you had better take seats" (Nast, 1874, p. 229). Although this cartoon points out the childish actions of the legislators of both races, the focal point rests squarely on the African Americans. Unlike the respectable portrayal of Revels four years earlier, the Black legislators come across as buffoonish and fundamentally different from the white representatives (Image 4).

In 1879, Nast printed a cartoon titled "The color line still exists in this case," showing support for an equal rights cause, but depicted it in a way that painted the characters in a negative light. It commented on the unfairly enforced literacy requirements for voting in the South. Nast drew a white southerner, "Mr. Solid South," who wrote a notice on a wall, stating, "Eddikashun qualifukashun: the blakman orter be eddikated afore he kin vote with us wites." (1879, p. 59). This stressed the way that race rather than education stood as the real obstacle to get to the polls, but unlike earlier examples the African American is not a dignified man but a stereotypical caricature lurking around the corner. Although Nast pointed out and disagreed with unequal treatment, the depiction he used undercut any arguments of equality (Image 5).

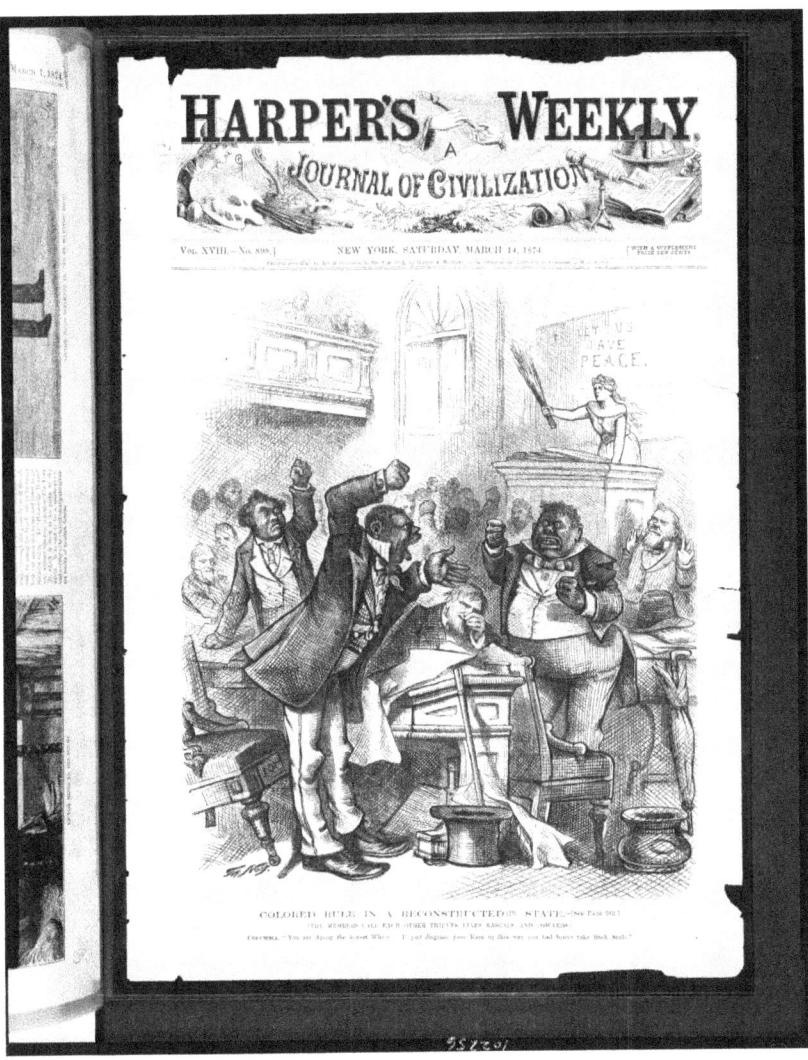

Image 4: Thomas Nast. (1874, March 14) Colored Rule in a reconstructed state. *Harper's Weekly* 28(898), 229. Retrieved from https://www.loc.gov/resource/cph.3c02256/

Nast, an enthusiastic supporter of legislation granting equal treatment of African Americans during the late 1860s and early 1870s, did not sing the praises of the passage of the Civil Rights Act of 1875. The act tackled a large and important issue, aiming to guarantee "the full and equal enjoyment of the accommodations, advantages, facilities, and privileges of inns, public conveyances on land or water, theaters, and other places of public amusement [...] to citizens of every race and color, regardless of any previous condition of servitude" (The Civil Rights

Image 5: Thomas Nast. (1879, January 18) The color line still exists—in this case. *Harper's Weekly*, *23*(1151), 52. Retrieved from https://www.loc.gov/pictures/item/2002710390/

Act of 1875, para. 2). Nast seemed to focus on criticizing negative aspects of the bill rather than supporting it as an attempt to curb segregation and enforce equality. This noticeably broke from his stance in the years directly following the Civil War.

The cartoon titled "Civil Rights (?)" shows an African American man at the registration desk of a hotel. He has a large sly smile and bends over slightly with his back turned to the counter, waiting to get thrown out of the establishment. The white worker, however, graciously opens the registration book and extends a pen to sign in. The bottom quotation reads "Waiting for a Five-Hundred-Dollar Kick," suggesting that he wanted to get kicked out in order to receive money (Nast, 1875, April 17, p. 328). This cartoon commented on the part of the Civil Rights Act of 1875 which stated that if an owner denies service based on race, he "shall, for every such offense, forfeit and pay the sum of five hundred dollars to the person aggrieved thereby" (The Civil Rights Act of 1875, para. 3). The cartoon ignored any civil rights benefits afforded by the act, and instead commented on how greedy people would use this to create problems for monetary gain.

Nast took another jab at the Civil Rights Act of 1875 by drawing an African American man standing before St. Peter at the gates of heaven, with a smile ear to ear, holding the text of the bill. He states, "Hi, Massa Peter, you can't objec' to open de gates fo' me now!" (Nast, 1875, April 3, p. 288). Nast used this religious analogy to make light of segregation and the anti-discrimination law.

After African Americans had the right to vote for several years, Nast made some depictions of them as pawns used for political purposes. More of his cartoons from the later years of Reconstruction disregarded the agency of African Americans in making their own choices, instead showing them voting at the behest of some other group. Nast (1867) did have more positive images early on, such as his illustration from March 16, 1867, showing a black man freely casting his ballot. However, by the early 1880s Nast's published opinion on the African American vote shifted significantly. He drew a cartoon in July of 1881 in which two southerners representing two ideologically different Democrats, one labeled "bourbon" and the other "anti-bourbon," aim pistols at each other, while each pulling on the arm of a limp, broad faced black man with a tag captioned "a vote" stuck in his hat (Nast, 1881, p. 452). This suggested that the voter had no opinion, and only voted for the party that someone forced upon him.

By 1885, long after many people had given up on equal rights and began to accept that expansion and enforcement of African American rights had faded, Nast drew a few cartoons which reflected this mindset. It is hard to prove if this reflected his true feelings, or if like many times before, he negatively portrayed one group to assist in attacking another, but Nast published a cartoon which posited violence against Blacks as an overused trope brought up by newspapers to stir up problems. In an August 1885 illustration, he sketched a desperate *Tribune* writer clinging on the arm of a southern farmer, pleading for him to use violence against African Americans so the writer could have a good story. The caption reads, "South: I should like to oblige you by killing a few negroes, Mr Tribune, but I am too busy" (Nast, 1885, p. 576). This cartoon implied that the South had returned to business as usual, that issues of violence did not exist, and that newspapers wanted to suggest ongoing violence for political reasons. The title, "A dead issue" backs up this assertion that people should shift their attention on to other topics.

Over the duration of Reconstruction, the images of African Americans drawn by Nast slowly trended away from citizens deserving equality towards flattened stereotypes lacking agency. This mirrored the stances of many other cartoonists, writers, and members of the public. For this reason, his political cartoons stand as a useful source when looking into the shift of African American images, and the subsequent widespread acceptance of the more negative ones, from the 1860s through the end of the Reconstruction era and beyond.

CONCLUSION

In the classroom, political cartoons as a source can help students to improve their historical thinking and analytical skills. They serve as a window into partisan opinions of the time, some of which lost popularity while others became mainstream. By studying a selection of political cartoons from the 1860s through the early 1880s, students can learn about crafted images of African Americans during Reconstruction as well as how prevailing views changed over time. This approach leads students to think beyond the legislation and political events often considered central themes of the Reconstruction era, and guides them to examine diverse perspectives as well as the influences of broad social trends.

The references section contains a list of all the cartoons used in this chapter and links to their images online. A lesson plan is included to provide an example of how a teacher may cover Reconstruction era images with political cartoons. Along with using the cited selections, the teacher can include other popular cartoons by searching websites such as hathitrust.org, loc.gov, or harpweek.com.

REFERENCES:

Baker, B. (2007). *What reconstruction meant: Historical memory in the American South.* University of Virginia Press.

Bisbee, E. S. (1883, March 21). A suggestion for a southern scarecrow. [Cartoon] *Puck*, *13*(315), 39. Retrieved from https://babel.hathitrust.org/cgi/pt?id=mdp.39015038641539&view=2up&seq=44

Cruden, R. (1969). *The Negro in reconstruction.* Englewood Cliffs: Prentice-Hall.

Dunning, W. A. (1907). *Reconstruction, political and economic: 1865–1877.* Harper and Brothers.
Du Bois, W. E. B. (1935). *Black reconstruction.* New York: Harcourt Brace and Company.
Foner, E. (1988). *Reconstruction: America's unfinished revolution, 1863–1877.* Harper and Row.
Franklin, J. H. (1961). *Reconstruction: After the civil war.* University of Chicago Press.
Muhammad, K. (2010). *The condemnation of Blackness: Race, crime, and the making of modern urban America.* Harvard University Press.
Nast, T. (1863, January 24). Emancipation. [Cartoon] *Harper's Weekly, 7*(317), 56–57. Retrieved from https://www.loc.gov/item/2002695553/
Nast, T. (1865, August 5). Franchise—And not this man. [Cartoon] *Harper's Weekly, 9*(949), 488–489. Retrieved from https://www.loc.gov/item/2010644408/
Nast, T. (1867, March 16). The Georgetown election—The negro at the ballot-box. [Cartoon] *Harper's Weekly, 11*(533), 172. Retrieved from https://www.loc.gov/pictures/item/2010652200/
Nast, T. (1870, April 9). Time works wonders. [Cartoon] *Harper's Weekly, 14*(693), 232. Retrieved from https://www.loc.gov/pictures/item/93508073/
Nast, T. (1874, March 14), Colored Rule in a reconstructed state. [Cartoon] *Harper's Weekly 28*(898), 229. Retrieved from https://www.loc.gov/resource/cph.3c02256/
Nast, T. (1875, February 6), The target. [Cartoon] *Harper's Weekly, 19*(945), 124. Retrieved from https://babel.hathitrust.org/cgi/pt?id=mdp.39015030616422&view=2up&seq=121
Nast, T. (1875, April 3). The Jubilee, 1875. [Cartoon] *Harper's Weekly, 19*(953), 288. Retrieved from https://babel.hathitrust.org/cgi/pt?id=mdp.39015030616422&view=2up&seq=274
Nast, T. (1875, April 17). Civil Rights. [Cartoon] *Harper's Weekly, 19*(955), 328. Retrieved from https://babel.hathitrust.org/cgi/pt?id=mdp.39015030616422&view=2up&seq=311
Nast, T. (1876, September 2). Is this a republican government. [Cartoon] *Harper's Weekly, 20*(1027), 712. Retrieved from https://www.loc.gov/item/96509623/
Nast, T. (1878, December 21). Poor ignorant black man wants to know. [Cartoon] *Harper's Weekly, 22*(1147), 1016. Retrieved from https://babel.hathitrust.org/cgi/pt?id=mdp.39015034617483&view=2up&seq=904
Nast, T. (1879, January 18). The color line still exists—in this case. [Cartoon] *Harper's Weekly, 23*(1151), 52. Retrieved from https://www.loc.gov/pictures/item/2002710390/
Nast, T. (1881, July 9). The next political condition—south. [Cartoon] *Harper's Weekly, 25*(1280), 452. Retrieved from https://babel.hathitrust.org/cgi/pt?id=pst.000020243258&view=2up&seq=36
Nast, T. (1882, January 14). The queen of industry, or, the new South. [Cartoon] *Harper's Weekly, 26*(1308), 17. Retrieved from https://www.loc.gov/pictures/item/2013648370/
Nast, T. (1885, August 29). A dead issue. [Cartoon] *Harper's Weekly, 29*(1497), 576. Retrieved from https://babel.hathitrust.org/cgi/pt?id=mdp.39015012334440&view=2up&seq=546
Pike, J. S. (1874). *The Prostrate State: South Carolina under Negro Government.* D. Appleton and Company.
Quashee's dream of emancipation. (1863, March). *Frank Leslie's Illustrated Newspaper.* Retrieved from https://www.americanantiquarian.org/Freedmen/Intros/questions.html
Sheridan's Ride (1875, January 16). *Frank Leslie's Illustrated Newspaper, 39*(1007), 320. Retrieved from https://babel.hathitrust.org/cgi/pt?id=pst.000020241384&view=2up&seq=65
The Civil Rights Act of 1875, 18 Stat. 335. (1875) https://www.senate.gov/artandhistory/history/common/image/Civil_Rights_Act_1875.htm

	Inquiry Design Model (IDM) Blueprint™		
Compelling Question	Throughout the Reconstruction era, to what extent did political cartoons shape the image and treatment of African Americans?		
Standards and Practices	D2.His.2.9-12. Analyze change and continuity in historical eras. D2.His.4.9-12. Analyze complex and interacting factors that influenced the perspectives of people during different historical eras. D2.His.9.9-12. Analyze the relationship between historical sources and the secondary interpretations made from them D2.His.10.9-12. Detect possible limitations in various kinds of historical evidence and differing secondary interpretations. D2.His.12.9-12. Use questions generated about multiple historical sources to pursue further inquiry and investigate additional sources.		
Staging the Question	Analyze and discuss the different images forwarded by the two political cartoons: A. "The Georgetown election—the negro at the ballot box" and B. "The next political condition—South".		
Supporting Question 1	Supporting Question 2	Supporting Question 3
---	---	---
How did political cartoonists show African Americans as capable or incapable of being equal citizens?	How did African American images change over time in Thomas Nast's cartoons?	How did stereotypes diminish positive images of African Americans and cement negative images?
Formative Performance Task	Formative Performance Task	Formative Performance Task
Construct a T-chart to organize the ways that cartoons showed African Americans as capable or incapable of using equal citizenship.	Make a timeline which identifies important events during Reconstruction and situates the images found in Nast's cartoons within the era.	Develop an evidence based claim that explains how stereotypes diminish positive images of African Americans and cement negative images.
Featured Sources	Featured Sources	Featured Sources
Source A: Bisbee, E. S. (1883, March 21) A suggestion for a southern scarecrow. *Puck* *13*(315), 39.	Source A: Nast, T. (1863, January 24) Emancipation. *Harper's Weekly* *7*(317), 56–57.	Source A: "Widespread and Pervasive Stereotypes of African Americans" Article from NMAAHC.

DRAWING CONCLUSIONS | 113

Inquiry Design Model (IDM) Blueprint™		
Source B: Quashee's dream of emancipation. (1863, March). *Frank Leslie's Illustrated Newspaper.* Source C: Sheridan's Ride (1875, January 16). *Frank Leslie's Illustrated Newspaper 39*(1007), 320. Source D: Nast, T. (1863, January 24) Emancipation. *Harper's Weekly 7*(317), 56–57. Source E: Nast, T. (1865, August 5) Franchise—and not this man. *Harper's Weekly 9*(949), 488–489. Source F: Nast, T. (1867, March 16) The Georgetown election—the negro at the ballot-box. *Harper's Weekly 11*(533), 172. Source G: Nast, T. (1870, April 9) Time works wonders. *Harper's Weekly 14*(693), 232.	Source B: Nast, T. (1865, August 5) Franchise—and not this man. *Harper's Weekly 9*(949), 488–489. Source C: Nast, T. (1867, March 16) The Georgetown election—the negro at the ballot-box. *Harper's Weekly 11*(533), 172. Source D: Nast, T. (1870, April 9) Time works wonders. *Harper's Weekly 14*(693), 232. Source E: Nast, T. (1874, March 14) Colored Rule in a reconstructed state. *Harper's Weekly 28*(898), 229. Source F: Nast, T. (1875, February 6) The target. *Harper's Weekly 19*(945), 124. Source G: Nast, T. (1875, April 3) The Jubilee, 1875. *Harper's Weekly, 19*(953), 288. Source H: Nast, T. (1875, April 17) Civil Rights. *Harper's Weekly, 19*(955), 328. Source I: Nast, T. (1876, September 2) Is this a republican government. *Harper's Weekly 20*(1027), 712. Source J: Nast, T. (1878, December 21) Poor ignorant black man wants to know. *Harper's Weekly 22*(1147), 1016.	Source B: Bisbee, E. S. (1883, March 21) A suggestion for a southern scarecrow. *Puck 13*(315), 39. Source C: Quashee's dream of emancipation. (1863, March). *Frank Leslie's Illustrated Newspaper.* Source D: Sheridan's Ride (1875, January 16). *Frank Leslie's Illustrated Newspaper 39*(1007), 320. Source E: Nast, T. (1874, March 14) Colored Rule in a reconstructed state. *Harper's Weekly 28*(898), 229. Source F: Nast, T. (1875, April 17) Civil Rights. *Harper's Weekly, 19*(955), 328. Source G: Nast, T. (1878, December 21) Poor ignorant black man wants to know. *Harper's Weekly 22*(1147), 1016. Source H: Nast, T. (1879, January 18) The color line still exists—in this case. *Harper's Weekly, 23*(1151), 52.

	Inquiry Design Model (IDM) Blueprint™			
		Source K: Nast, T. (1879, January 18) The color line still exists—in this case. *Harper's Weekly*, *23*(1151), 52. Source L: Nast, T. (1881, July 9) The next political condition—south. *Harper's Weekly*, *25*(1280), 452. Source M: Nast, T. (1882, January 14) The queen of industry, or, the new South. *Harper's Weekly*, *26*(1308), 17. Source N: Nast, T. (1885, August 29) A dead issue. *Harper's Weekly*, *29*(1497), 576.	Source I: Nast, T. (1881, July 9) The next political condition—south. *Harper's Weekly*, *25*(1280), 452. Source J: Nast, T. (1885, August 29) A dead issue. *Harper's Weekly*, *29*(1497), 576.	
Summative Performance Task	Argument	Construct an argument (e.g., essay, poster, detailed outline) that uses evidence from historical sources to discuss to what extent Reconstruction era political cartoons shaped the image and treatment of African Americans.		
	Extension	Identify what stereotypes exist in current day political cartoons and the influence those images may have on the way the public views groups of people.		
Taking Informed Action	Understand: Find and analyze an illustrated or crafted image of an African American that people may have seen at some point during the 20th or 21st century. Assess: Using evidence from the inquiry, analyze similarities and differences between the selected image and political cartoon portrayals. Act: Present your analysis of the image to the class.			

CHAPTER SIX

Representations of Reconstruction: Social Transformations and Textbook Portrayals of the Past

ADAM J. SCHMITT[1] AND ASHLEY TOWLE[2]
[1]Department of Teacher Education, University of Southern Maine
[2]Department of History, University of Southern Maine

INTRODUCTION

In many history classrooms, textbooks serve as the primary tool teachers use to build student content knowledge and communicate historical understanding about the past. Textbooks are typically written in ways that position the information they contain as an objective retelling of what happened in the past. As Apple and Christian-Smith (1991) remind us, though, textbooks are "the results of political, economic, and cultural activities, battles, and compromises. They are conceived, designed, and authored by real people with real interests. They are published within the political and economic constraints of markets, resources, and power" (pp. 1–2). Textbooks, in other words, are not the neutral source of information they are often perceived to be.

Textbook representations of the past are not conjured out of thin air. Rather, they are most typically authored, or at least connected to, academic historians whose narrative choices reflect historiographic conceptions of the past and then updated by editorial boards as new editions are published (Loewen, 1995/2007). In this chapter, we position the American history textbook as the primary source of analysis for examining the connection between historiographic shifts in the academic field of history and the representation of the past present in textbooks, using Reconstruction as a case study.

Reconstruction is a fitting time period for this study as perhaps no era in United States history has been revised and reinterpreted so vigorously. At its most basic level, Reconstruction was the process of reintegrating the former Confederate states back into the United States. Yet this was not a simple process. The return of the Southern states to the Union hinged on three interrelated questions: what would be the status of the four million formerly enslaved people that gained their freedom as a result of the Emancipation Proclamation and the Thirteenth Amendment; how would the war-ravaged Southern economy and political landscape be rebuilt; and how would Americans come together to unify the nation after four long years of bloodshed and death. The historiography of Reconstruction, and how historians have interpreted the way in which those questions were addressed, has shifted over time. Drawing from Segall's (2006) conception of critical history, the purpose of this chapter is not to claim that there is one best way for interpreting and understanding Reconstruction. Rather, our focus is on using Reconstruction as a means of understanding history as a constructed reality that reflects larger societal discourse at the time of its creation.

CRITICAL HISTORY AND TEXTBOOKS

At the K-12 level, history is often taught in one of three ways: through a collective memory approach, where a "best version" of history is the focus and overarching narratives, often focused on themes such as progress or expanding rights, are enshrined; through a disciplinary approach where students employ the tools of the historian to analyze sources and make evidence-based claims about the past; and a postmodern approach, focused more on the relationship between power and knowledge, particularly who has the power to make claims about what is worth knowing (Seixas, 2000). Segall (2006) refers to the postmodern approach as "critical history" and argues that such an approach is not "simply interested in studying the past itself and for itself…" but rather is "interested in how and why particular pasts are constructed, legitimated, and disseminated by various discursive communities" (p. 129). A critical history approach focuses on the narratives that are put forward about the past in order to understand "why and how it gains its authority and is believed to be true, by whom, and for what and whose purposes" (p. 138). By delving into the power dynamics that enter into the production and dispersal of a historical narrative, a critical approach to history allows those who use it to better understand how the discipline of history is constructed. Such an approach helps move consumers of history, such as students, away from the concept of an objective, correct, and complete retelling of the past and towards a more nuanced understanding of history's subjectivity and connection to the sociocultural milieu that impacts its construction.

Textbooks are a means through which we can see this construction occurring. As Werner (2000) explains, textbook representations of the past are always partial. The construction of any historical text "involves complex choices about what ideas and perspectives to include and exclude… and how to put them all together to achieve a relatively smooth and believable presentation" (Werner, 2000, p. 196). This process can be observed through comparing different versions of textbooks, as new editions of popular textbooks are frequently published and are often revised to incorporate new perspectives, sources, or historiographic developments. Content analysis of textbooks has been a frequently used method of understanding how particular events, people, individuals, or issues are framed and taken up within history classrooms Despite the proliferation of work on textbooks, there has been little focus on Reconstruction specifically. Schramm-Pate (2006) conducted an analysis of two regional history textbooks and found that their Reconstruction coverage reproduced perceptions of a North/South cultural divide and reinforced geographically biased assumptions about the meaning of the time period.

Although there is not much literature on textbook coverage of Reconstruction, there are other textbook studies that help inform our study. There are several studies that highlight representations of race, racism, and Black historical figures in American history textbooks and the ways in which textbook representations rob those topics and people of nuance. These studies include examinations of how Martin Luther King, Jr. is stripped of his complexity and radicalism, in combination with the Civil Rights Movement being isolated from contemporary issues of racial justice Aldridge (2006) and Schocker and Woyshner's (2013) finding that general American history textbooks lack representation of Black women, in comparison to Black history textbooks.

There are also studies that find that even when racial inclusion increases, it still does so in problematic ways that elevate dominant, progress-oriented narratives at the expense of members of marginalized groups. In a survey of 50 history textbooks from 1860 to 2016, Jimenez (2020) examined the use of passive and active voice when discussing groups/individuals that were experiencing suffering. Jimenez found that suffering rhetoric and the use of active voice was most commonly used when discussing the experiences of whites, especially elite whites, while passive voice, which obscured perpetrators, was more commonly used for members of marginalized groups. Somewhat similarly, in their analysis of textbook representations of racial violence, Brown and Brown (2010) found that while there has been increasing coverage of racial violence in textbooks, that violence is often portrayed as the result of individual choices and actions as opposed to a result of larger, institutional structures that sanction and reward racial violence.

We see this chapter as a means to fill a gap in the existing scholarship by examining the nature of how Reconstruction is represented in textbooks and connecting that representation to the historiography of Reconstruction and the social milieu that plays a role in how that era is perceived.

THE HISTORIOGRAPHY OF RECONSTRUCTION

Historians have identified three primary camps of historical interpretation of the Reconstruction era. The first, known as the Dunning School, looms large in American popular memory and has proven difficult to dispel. The Dunning School was named after Columbia University historian William A. Dunning. Writing from 1897 to 1920, Dunning and his followers argued that Reconstruction had been a tragedy for the United States. Their interpretation was rooted in white supremacy and contended that African Americans were unfit for freedom, let alone citizenship and voting rights. Indeed, they argued, the only reason Black people secured these rights was a result of vindictive and power-hungry Northerners who hoped to make Black voters do their bidding in subjugating the South. As Dunning (1907) noted, "few episodes of recorded history more urgently invite thorough analysis and extended reflection than the struggle through which the southern whites, subjugated by adversaries of their own race, thwarted the scheme which threatened permanent subjection to another race" (p. xv). The scholarship that Dunning School historians churned out gained a popular audience with the 1929 publication of journalist Claude G. Bowers' *The Tragic Era*. Bowers used dramatic and vivid prose to depict the apparent horrors of Reconstruction. He noted that unscrupulous "emissaries of hate and sedition" from the north aroused the "passions, cupidity" and "hate of the negroes" in their attempts to gain their votes and wield power over white southerners (pp. 199–200). These sentiments gained traction in the American public with the release of blockbuster films such as *The Birth of a Nation* (1915) and *Gone with the Wind* (1939).

Not all historians, however, agreed with the Dunning School. In particular, W. E. B. DuBois pushed back against this tendentious interpretation and argued that Reconstruction was not the tragedy that Dunning et al. described. In *Black Reconstruction in America*, DuBois (1935) centered the experiences and contributions of African Americans to the rebuilding of the Union. He argued that "white historians have ascribed the faults and failures of Reconstruction to Negro ignorance and corruption. But the Negro insists that it was Negro loyalty and the Negro vote alone that restored the South to the Union; established the new democracy, both for white and black, and instituted the public schools" (p. 637). According to DuBois (1935/2017), the Dunning School had been blinded by racism. The intent of his work was to "tell this story as though Negroes were ordinary human beings, realizing that this attitude will from the first seriously curtail my audience" (p. xxv).

In the 1960s, with the Civil Rights Movement in full swing and African Americans demanding that the federal government enforce the promises of the Fourteenth and Fifteenth Amendments, historians looked at Reconstruction with fresh eyes. Following DuBois' lead, these historians, known as revisionists, countered the argument that Reconstruction was a tragic era. They argued that Reconstruction had seen remarkable advances in interracial democracy and social and economic progress for black people. As the Jim Crow regime in the South crumbled, so too did the historical arguments used to support white supremacy. No longer did historians depict African Americans as inept and incapable of wielding the vote and the rights of citizenship. Under the revisionists' pen, Radical Republicans, Freedmen's Bureau agents, and African Americans became the heroes of Reconstruction and the protectors of American democracy.

On the heels of this flurry of celebratory scholarship of Reconstruction came the postrevisionists. Postrevisionist historians contended that Reconstruction was actually far too conservative and did not address the most pressing issues facing the United States. These historians argued that Republican policy makers failed to pass land reform measures that would give teeth to freedpeople's new civil and political rights. Countering Dunning and revisionist historians' characterization of the era as transformative and radical, postrevisionists maintained that not much had actually changed as a result of Reconstruction. African Americans were still denied political rights and the planter class remained in power; the New South looked much like the Old.

In an attempt to synthesize this varied scholarship, Eric Foner published *Reconstruction: America's Unfinished Revolution, 1863–1877*. Foner's (1988) work took a broad view of Reconstruction. Like the revisionists, he treated African Americans as autonomous political actors and argued that the Reconstruction era was a tremendous period of progress that advanced interracial democracy. Yet, he also employed arguments by the postrevisionists that the era did not go far enough in securing and protecting the rights of African Americans. For Foner, Reconstruction was an "unfinished revolution" in which the promises of the Fourteenth and Fifteenth Amendments would not be realized for over 100 years. Since its publication in 1988, *Reconstruction* has been the foundational text for interpreting this pivotal era.

METHODOLOGY

The goal of our study is to examine the connection between the political and social transformations that impact how historians interpret the past, in this case Reconstruction, and the extent to which those interpretive shifts are taken up in textbook portrayals of the past. The questions that guided our study were

1. What is the connection between historiographical shifts in understanding Reconstruction and textbook portrayals of that time period?
2. What is the potential impact textbooks portrayals of Reconstruction may have on student understanding of the issues related to that event?

Our study focuses on high school American history textbooks taken from three time periods that roughly correspond with the shifts in historical thinking about Reconstruction noted above: The Progressive Era (1920s), The Civil Rights Era (1960s/70s) and the Multicultural Turn Era (1990s-present). Due to library access restrictions stemming from the COVID-19 pandemic, our analysis focused on textbooks that were accessible via our institutional library system, U.S. history teachers we have worked with, and through digitized full-text copies available via Google Books and the Hathi Trust. These access restrictions were especially restrictive for accessing books from the Civil Rights Era. Therefore, that section focuses specifically on changes between editions of Thomas Bailey's *American Pageant*. Please see the Appendix A for more information about the textbooks we analyzed.

We utilized literary analysis for our analysis of the textbook samples. The first phase of analysis focused on the historiography of Reconstruction and the identification of salient themes we observed as interpretations of Reconstruction shifted. We then took those themes, which included the aims of Reconstruction, the portrayal of African Americans, the portrayal of Radical Republicans, the nature/role of white supremacy during Reconstruction, and the nature of Reconstruction's failure, and placed them at the center of our textbook analysis. We also took other text features, such as titles, visuals, and sidebars, into account to understand how Reconstruction was being framed more holistically and to account for how various text features worked together to shape understanding.

FINDINGS

Overall, our findings indicate that textbook representations of Reconstruction reflect dominant contemporaneous academic thinking during the Progressive Era and Multicultural Turn Era, with less of a connection being seen during the Civil Rights Era. In this section we provide an overview of how Reconstruction is presented within each of our chosen timeframes and how they reflect dominant social discourse of the time.

The Progressive Era

Progressive Era textbooks present a consensus about the objectives of Reconstruction. In general, they note that the major issues facing Americans at the beginning of the era concerned how to bring the former Confederate states back into the Union and whether former Confederates should be punished or not. They also contend that determining the political and economic position of formerly enslaved people was of the utmost importance. The means by which the federal government addressed these issues also follows a similar interpretation in each of the textbooks reviewed. The texts highlight the leniency of President Andrew Johnson's reconstruction plan to bring the Confederate states back into the Union and offer a sympathetic portrayal of Johnson, noting that he was in a "peculiarly hard and trying" position to "undertake the delicate and difficult work of reconstruction" (Montgomery, 1920, p. 328).

Progressive Era textbooks place the blame for Reconstruction going awry on the vindictiveness of Radical Republicans. As one textbook noted, "Some of the northern leaders, especially Thaddeus Stevens of Pennsylvania, wanted to punish the people of the southern states…" (Hart, 1920, p. 371). The ratification of the Fourteenth and Fifteenth Amendments affixed the status of African Americans as citizens and granted them political rights, but the intentions behind the passage of these amendments are characterized as malicious and nefarious. According to Beard and Bagley (1925), with the Fourteenth Amendment, the "federal government sought to force manhood suffrage, white and black, on the South." (p. 437). Beard and Bagley (1920) noted that Republicans favored expanding the suffrage to black men because "it meant a huge increase in the vote cast for their party" (p. 432).

Granting African Americans voting rights, these textbooks argue, was particularly egregious because of the ineptitude of African Americans and their lack of experience with freedom and democracy. *History of the United States* characterized Black people as "poverty-stricken ignoramuses" (Fite, 1923, p. 417). Another noted that "men who could not read or write and who had never had a dollar before were elected to state legislatures to aid in restoring order to the stricken land" (Beard & Bagley, 1920, p. 435). In this narrative, African Americans became the political pawns of unscrupulous "carpetbaggers" and "scalawags" whose only agenda was to acquire power and wealth at the expense of subjugated white southerners. For these reasons, Beard and Bagley (1925) observed, "the southern cup of bitterness was full indeed" (p. 439).

It was because of these heavy-handed actions that southerners were impelled to take action. Hart's (1920) explanation of the rise of the Ku Klux Klan is representative. "To break the hold of the negro Republican vote, several secret societies were formed by the southern whites, of which the most famous was the Ku-Klux Klan" (p. 396). Textbooks characterize the Klan as a jocular organization that used trickery to intimidate African Americans from the polls. Hart explained the Klan's methods as such, "at first it consisted of young men who thought it a kind of joke to ride about the country rigged out as headless ghosts and thus to frighten the negroes. This practice quickly grew into a system by which many negroes and some whites were whipped, driven out of the country, or shot" (p. 396). In these narratives of the rise of the Klan, there is limited emphasis on the deadly violence the organization employed or the effect of that violence on African American families and communities. Instead, the Klan is depicted as the savior of the South and the restorer of white rule.

Progressive Era textbooks reflect dominant social understandings of Reconstruction during the 1920s and 30s. Written during a time period of extensive legalized segregation in the form of Jim Crow and during a resurgence of Ku Klux Klan activity, these texts simultaneously serve as a reflection of dominant, white conceptions of Reconstruction, as well as a means to construct/reproduce those conceptions. The message these chapters communicate to all readers, regardless of race, is that African Americans are unfit for the responsibilities of citizenship, which is the exclusive domain of whites. In addition, whites who support African Americans' civil rights are doing so only out of self-interest.

The Civil Rights Era

The Civil Rights Era editions of *American Pageant* we analyzed share some similarities with Progressive Era textbooks in that both agree that the major issues facing the United States at the end of the Civil War were how to bring the South back into the Union, how to restore the war-ravaged Southern economy, and how to ensure the freedom of newly freed people. In *The American Pageant's* third and fourth editions, there is a clear nostalgia and sympathy for the Old South, as Bailey (1966, 1971) notes, "not only had an age perished but a civilization had collapsed, in both its economic and its social structure. The moonlight-and-magnolia Old South of ante-bellum days had gone with the wind" (1966, p. 461; 1971, p. 489). By 1979, this phrase had the caveat that the moonlight-and-magnolias South was "largely imaginary" (Bailey & Kennedy, 1979, p. 430). The task of restoring this "prostrate" region to the Union fell to Andrew Johnson, whom Bailey depicts as a hard-nosed, uncompromising champion of states' rights and the Constitution. According to Bailey (1966), Reconstruction was doomed to fail under Johnson, as "a reconstruction policy devised by the angels might well have failed in his tactless hands" (p. 466). Johnson's blunders, however, were not the ultimate cause of the demise of Reconstruction.

Just as with Progressive Era textbooks, the cause of the failure of Reconstruction, according to the Civil Rights Era textbooks we analyzed, often falls at the feet of spiteful and power-hungry Republicans. Republicans had grown accustomed to the power they held in Congress and were reluctant to relinquish it with the return of the Southern states to the Union. The black vote became their "ace in the hole" to maintain their authority (Bailey, 1971, p. 496). There is some acknowledgment that Republicans were motivated by idealistic intentions to expand democracy, but largely *American Pageant* emphasizes the self-interest of Republicans.

As with Progressive Era textbooks, *American Pageant* depicts African Americans as unprepared for freedom, citizenship, and suffrage. "The sudden thrusting of the ballot into the hands of the ex-slaves... set the stage for stark tragedy. As might have been foreseen, it was a blunder hardly less serious than thrusting overnight freedom upon them" (Bailey, 1966, p. 475). Both the 1966 and 1971 editions of *American Pageant* likened freed African Americans to orphaned children turned loose to do as they pleased. By 1979, this comparison of Black people to children was removed from the chapter, but Bailey and Kennedy still maintained that "blacks had suffered many cruelties during slavery, but one of the cruelest strokes of all was to jerk them overnight from chains to freedom without any preparation or safeguards" (p. 430). The result of these measures was the same as Progressive Era textbooks reported: corrupt governments in the South led by "much-maligned 'scalawags' and 'carpetbaggers,' who in turn used the Negroes as political henchmen" (Bailey, 1971, p. 500). While Bailey (1971) depicts the Reconstruction governments as being crooked, there are some caveats to the contributions African Americans made when granted the right to vote, including the election of more than a dozen black Congressmen, "who as a group did creditable work" (p. 499). The textbooks also note that the state constitutions these bi-racial governments passed had some "desirable legislation and introduced many overdue reforms" (Bailey, 1966, p. 476).

The outcome of these overwhelmingly corrupt governments, however, was the same as Progressive Era historians had argued; white Southern men were compelled to resort to violence to oust African Americans and their cronies from power. "Deeply embittered, otherwise decent Southern whites resorted to savage measures against Negro-carpetbag control" (Bailey, 1971, p. 504). Similarly, these textbooks first emphasize the trickery the Klan used to intimidate African Americans, but then admit that they also employed violence. By the 1979 edition of *The American Pageant*, Bailey includes the excerpts of an African American man's testimony before Congress about the racial violence his community suffered.

According to *American Pageant*, Reconstruction ultimately came to an end as a result of the violence white Southerners executed against Black and white Republicans. But the larger reason for Reconstruction's failure was that Radical Republicans' vengeance went too far. Granting political rights to black people proved to be the undoing of Reconstruction. "The outcome was bad for the ex-slaves, bad for white Southerners, and bad for the Republicans. Large-scale Negro voting in the South was jeopardized, once the federal troops had withdrawn support, and within another generation the black voter had virtually disappeared" (Bailey, 1971, p. 503). By 1979, this same sentiment remains in *American*

Pageant, with Bailey and Kennedy arguing that "the Northern ideals of national unity and human freedom were largely lost sight of in an orgy of hate and corruption" (Bailey & Kennedy, 1979, p. 449).

The Civil Rights Era was marked by differing social conceptions of the status of Black civil rights. While some textbooks of this era did begin to include more multiracial voices (Jimenez, 2020), the book we reviewed, different versions of Bailey's *American Pageant*, continue the narrative of African American unreadiness for citizenship. While later editions of *American Pageant* begin to acknowledge the violent realities of white supremacy and minimally recognize Black political contributions, we do not see as strong a connection between the Civil Rights era texts and revisionist conceptions of Reconstruction as we did the Progressive Era and the Dunning School of thought. Bailey's portrayal of African Americans in *American Pageant* seems at odds with the political realities of Civil Rights-era Black grassroots activism and legal challenges that resulted in the end of legal racial segregation. This is a particularly interesting finding given that one can assume a major disconnect between what students read in that particular text versus what they were confronted with on the nightly news, or in the communities in which they lived.

The Multicultural Turn

With the advent of the multicultural turn and the move away from the Dunning School interpretation of Reconstruction, textbooks from the 1990s onward have shifted their approach to how they cover Reconstruction. Whereas previous eras focused primarily on the political events surrounding Reconstruction, Multicultural Turn Era texts portray a more expansive understanding of the goals of Reconstruction. While they still focus on the issues of how to bring the South back into the Union, rebuild the Southern economy, and determine the status of newly freed people, they emphasize that Reconstruction was a quest to create a multiracial democracy and a more equitable society. In doing so, they foreground the experiences of African Americans and their attempts to capitalize on their hard-won freedom.

Unsurprisingly, Eric Foner's textbook, *Give Me Liberty!: An American History*, goes further than the others in providing a comprehensive examination of Reconstruction. Rather than focusing his treatment of the era solely on political developments, Foner casts Reconstruction as reconfiguring the very definition of freedom. He begins the chapter with a discussion of what freedom meant to African Americans and the centrality of land ownership to their vision of freedom. He notes that "in the years following the Civil War, former slaves and their white allies, North and South, would seek to redefine the very meaning and boundaries of American freedom" (Foner, 2010, p. 586). In Foner's telling, African

Americans were not inept political tools easily manipulated by white Republicans, but rather, central actors who actively shaped the trajectory of Reconstruction. Foner is attentive to the political contributions Black officeholders made to southern society, but he also attends to the community building that African Americans engaged in, including the creation of public schools, black churches, and mutual aid societies. In other multicultural era textbooks such as *American Pageant* and *The Americans*, African Americans are not depicted as unqualified or ill-prepared for voting rights. They acknowledge that black people were active agents in seizing and safeguarding their freedom. *American Pageant* states, "For many slaves the shackles of bondage were not struck off in a single mighty blow; long-suffering blacks often had to wrench free of their chains link by link" (Kennedy & Cohen, 2013, p. 466). Collectively, the institution building that African Americans embarked on is given much more attention in multicultural turn era textbooks, than it was in textbooks from previous eras, and acknowledged as being an assertion of African Americans' freedom.

In these textbooks Radical Republicans also undergo a dramatic recharacterization. These texts foreground Republicans' desire to expand democracy and protect freedpeople. In discussing the response to Johnson's reconstruction plan, *The Americans* notes that "The Radicals were especially upset that Johnson's plan, like Lincoln's, failed to address the needs of former slaves in three areas: land, voting rights, and protection under the law" (Danzer et al., 2012, p. 378). Foner (2010) insists that the radical legislation Republicans passed was not vindictive or a ploy for political power, but instead a response to the flagrance of the Black Codes and the refusal of white Southerners to adopt free labor. Indeed, he contends that "what motivated the North's turn against Johnson's policies was not a desire to 'punish' the white South, but the inability of the South's political leaders to accept the reality of emancipation" (p. 601).

White supremacy and racial violence take on new importance and lethality in multicultural turn texts. Foner is the most direct in linking racial violence and white supremacy, to the overthrow of Reconstruction. He states "the most basic reason for the opposition to Reconstruction, however, was that most white southerners could not accept the idea of former slaves voting, holding office, and enjoying equality before the law. In order to restore white supremacy in southern public life and ensure planters a disciplined, reliable labor force, they believed, Reconstruction must be overthrown. Opponents launched a campaign of violence in an effort to end Republican rule" (Foner, 2010, p. 617). These texts also offer a new characterization of the Klan as a terrorist group. *The Americans* call the Klan a "violent terrorist organization" (Danzer, et. Al, 2012, p. 394) while *Give Me Liberty!* States that their tactics included "mass terrorism" (Foner, 2010, p. 617). *American Pageant* remains an outlier in this regard. It retains much of the language from Civil Rights era editions of the text, and still introduces the Klan by discussing the trickery they used to intimidate black people, before describing the violence and death threats they employed to usurp Republican rule.

According to Multicultural Turn textbooks, the campaign of violence that white southerners waged against African Americans is one of the primary reasons why Reconstruction ultimately came to an end. There is also consensus that the North was complicit in the failure of Reconstruction. As a result of racism and an economic depression, Northerners' support for Reconstruction and protecting the rights and lives of freedpeople in the South waned. All of the texts agree that white supremacy and racism posed a monumental obstacle to successfully reconstructing the South as a multiracial democracy. The failure of the federal government to take more extensive measures to African Americans truly free and independent citizens, such as land reform and legislation to protect freedpeople's rights, ultimately led to the failure of Reconstruction.

Taken together, textbooks of the Multicultural Turn reflect expanding conceptions of whose perspectives and narratives should be included in historical narratives. Indeed, Foner (2010) goes beyond most other textbooks in including information about feminism of the time period and the continued disenfranchisement of women. These texts' reframing of Reconstruction as the United States grappling with what it means to be a multiracial society reflect more recent cultural discussions about the need to not only secure access to the ballot and equal protection under the law, but also measures to address enduring economic inequities.

DISCUSSION

Overall, we found that there is a connection between shifts in the historiography of Reconstruction and how textbook representations of Reconstruction are framed. This is especially evident in the Progressive Era textbooks we analyzed, which reflect the Dunning School of thought. African Americans are consistently portrayed as ill-equipped for the responsibilities of citizenship and are devoid of all agency, instead serving as pawns of the Radical Republicans and white racial violence is framed as a justifiable response to the expansion of Black citizenship and institution of Republican state governments. Similarly, we see a connection between the repositioning of Reconstruction as an "unfinished revolution" that extended some rights but didn't go far enough (Foner, 1988). As curricular inclusiveness grew in whose stories could be told, history textbooks began to include content that recognized the contributions of African Americans during Reconstruction. We found that our Civil Rights Era text was out of sync with the historiographical context of its time period and did not fully reflect revisionist thinking about Reconstruction but recognize the limitation of our sample for this era. Therefore, while we can say that *American Pageant*, as a popular textbook, still aligned with many elements of the Progressive Era texts, it may not be indicative of the time.

The connection between the historiography of Reconstruction and its representation in American history textbooks cannot be taken on its own. Instead, using the lens of critical history, this finding needs to be situated within the larger social and political contexts that created the dominant discourses they fit within. We opened this chapter with Apple and Christian-Smith's (1991) quote about textbooks being a result of compromise and a reflection of dominant social discourse. When we view our findings in this light, it stresses the importance of what is acceptable to the dominant audience in terms of inclusion in the textbook.

Despite the changes to textbook representations that have occurred over time, the overarching narrative of Reconstruction has remained relatively constant. With the exception of Foner's *Give Me Liberty!*, the textbooks we analyzed skew to a fairly typical narrative about Reconstruction. To wit, chapters begin with a discussion about Lincoln's plans for Reconstruction, followed by Andrew Johnson's approach to Reconstruction, the institution of Black Codes, the advent of Radical Reconstruction and the gradual failure of Reconstruction. As textbooks have expanded and come to include more social history, there are chapter sections devoted to Black daily life and the failure of land reform. Foner's volume includes all of these benchmarks, as well, but he alone starts his chapter by focusing on Black Americans' definition of freedom and the various ways that freedom was experienced prior to delving into the politics of the era. Thus, his text is the only one we reviewed that situates Reconstruction as being primarily concerned with Black experiences of Reconstruction, as opposed to a more typical framing of Reconstruction as a primarily nation re-building endeavor that included the integration of emancipated African Americans into broader society.

Part of the consistency of this narrative is that, regardless of changes to the content, it fits a dominant social understanding of the time and the master narratives of expanding progress that U.S. history textbooks often skew towards. Zimmerman (2002), writing in the aftermath of the controversy that surrounded the creation of the first national history standards in the mid-90s, notes "Our 'history wars' have usually surrounded the issue of 'inclusion'—who gets into the national narrative, and who does not—rather than the structure of the narrative itself" (p. 214). Quoting a 1927 edition of the New York Times, he goes on to say "each 'race' gets to have its heroes sung… but no group may question the melody of peace, freedom, and economic opportunity that unites them all" (p. 214). In other words, while the characters in the story may change, the narrative largely remains the same.

Another element of the steadiness of the narrative is the fact that some textbooks have persisted over a period of 50 years or more. In *The American*

Pageant's 15th edition (it is now in its 17th edition), Kennedy and Cohen still title the Reconstruction chapter "The Ordeal of Reconstruction," a title that conveys a negative perception of the time. The chapter still includes text from much earlier editions that we analyzed, including the statement that the "The moonlight-and-magnolia Old South of ante-bellum days had gone with the wind" (Kennedy & Cohen, 2013, p. 465). Such language harkens back to earlier conceptions of Reconstruction and potentially point to some elements of those conceptions still having resonance in contemporary culture. The reality of textbook writing, as James Loewen (1995/2007) argues, is that the historians who are listed on the book do not really do the writing. Instead, it's editorial teams that go through and make changes. The result, at least in books that have undergone multiple revisions, is an additive approach to curriculum where new, in this case multicultural, information/perspectives are brought in, but the fundamental structure of the curriculum remains unchanged. (Banks, 2010). The result may very well be that students get important information about previously marginalized and curricularly underrepresented groups, but the meaning they are able to make of this information is limited by the way the content is still deployed in a disjointed way.

The textbooks we studied, predominantly written by white males and created for largely white audiences, reflect and reinforce dominant social conceptions of Reconstruction, but they are not the only books out there. While, as Werner (2000) argues, textbook depictions of the past are always partial representations, there are textbooks that provide interpretations and depictions of Reconstruction that challenge dominant white narratives in important ways. Just as DuBois was challenging the Dunning School in his own interpretation of Reconstruction (an interpretation that is now central to contemporary understandings of the time period), Black scholars/educators of the 1920s/30s were writing textbooks for predominantly Black audiences that challenged the depiction of African Americans that Black students encountered in their school texts. Such texts provided important counter-narratives that directly challenged the dominant white perspective inherent in mainstream textbooks and presented a vision of Black citizenship based, in part, on the actions of African Americans during Reconstruction (King, 2014).

IMPLICATIONS

Although textbooks are not the only source of information in a classroom and this study does not make any claims about how Reconstruction is taught by teachers or understood by students, we believe that there is much to be gained from engaging students in a more critical approach to interacting with their textbook.

While history and social studies standards have become more skill-focused with the advent of the Common Core State Standards, C3 Framework, and shifts in state-level standards documents, these skills primarily focus on source analysis, evidence evaluation and other important skills historians employ, there is still a need to engage students with history in ways that examine the power dynamics inherent in the construction of historical narratives. As Segall (2006) argues, such an engagement is disciplinary in nature, as it involves students in the work of understanding the processes through which history is created. Reconstruction, due to the revisions and reinterpretations it has gone through by historians, provides a clear entry-point for understanding the links between/among the broader socio-political context of a time period, who has the power to construct the past and how that past gets represented as official knowledge within a textbook. By providing students opportunities to interrogate the production of history, we allow them to move beyond the idea that representations of historical knowledge are objective and allow them to see the subjective work at play in the construction of the past.

REFERENCES:

Alridge, D. P. (2006). The limits of master narratives in history textbooks: An analysis of representations of Martin Luther King, Jr. *Teachers College Record, 108*(4), 662–686.

Apple, M., & Christian-Smith, L. (1991). The politics of the textbook. In M. Apple & L. Christian-Smith (Eds.), *The politics of the textbook* (pp. 1–19). Routledge.

Bailey, T. A. (1966). *The American pageant: A history of the republic* (3rd ed.). D. C. Heath and Company.

Bailey, T. A. (1971). *The American pageant: A history of the republic* (4th ed.). D. C. Heath and Company.

Bailey, T. A., & Kennedy, D. M. (1979). *The American pageant: A history of the republic* (6th ed.). D. C. Heath and Company.

Banks, J. A. (2010). Approaches to multicultural curricular reform. In J. A. Banks & C. A. McGee Banks (Eds.), *Multicultural education: Issues and perspectives, 7th edition* (pp. 233–256). Wiley.

Beard, C. A., & Bagley, W. C. (1920). *The history of the American people*. The Macmillan Company.

Beard, C. A., & Bagley, W. C. (1925). *The history of the American people: Revised edition*. The Macmillan Company.

Bowers, C. (1929). *The Tragic Era*. Riverside Press.

Brown, A. L., & Brown, K. D. (2010). Strange fruit indeed: Interrogating contemporary textbook representations of racial violence toward African Americans. *Teachers College Record, 112*(1), 31–67.

Danzer, G., Klor de Alva, J., Krieger, L. S., Wilson, L. E., & Woloch, N. (2012). *The Americans*. Holt Mcdougal.

Du Bois, W. E. B. (2017). *Black reconstruction in America: Toward a history of the part which black folk played in the attempt to reconstruct democracy in America, 1860–1880*. Routledge. (Original work published 1935).

Dunning, W. (1907). *Reconstruction: Political and economic, 1865–1877*. Harper and Brothers Publishers.
Fite, E. D. (1923). *History of the United States* (2nd ed.). Henry Holt and Company.
Foner, E. (1988). *Reconstruction: America's unfinished revolution, 1863–1877*. Harper and Row.
Foner, E. (2010). *Give me liberty!: An American history* (3rd ed.). W. W. Norton & Company.
Hart, A. B. (1920). *School history of the United States* (2nd ed.). American Book Company.
Jimenez, J. (2020). Race, language, and the passive voice: Hardship narratives in US social studies textbooks from 1860 to the present. *Journal of Social Studies Education Research, 11*(2), 1–26.
Kennedy, D. M., & Cohen, L. (2013). *The American pageant* (15th ed.). Cengage.
King, L. J. (2014). When lions write history: Black history textbooks, African-American educators, & the alternative black curriculum in social studies education, 1890–1940. *Multicultural Education, 22*(1), 2–11.
Loewen, J. W. (2007). *Lies my teacher told me: Everything your American history textbook got wrong*. The New Press. (Original work published 1995).
Montgomery, D. H. (1920). *The leading facts of American history* (7th ed.). Ginn and Company.
Schocker, J. B., & Woyshner, C. (2013). Representing African American women in U.S. history textbooks. *The Social Studies, 104*, 23–31.
Schramm-Pate, S. L. (2006). Disrupting the North/South binary: a deconstruction of two social studies textbooks' portrayal of the Reconstruction Era in America (1861–1877). *Journal of Curriculum Theorizing, 22*(2), 139–158.
Segall, A. (2006). What's the purpose of teaching the disciplines, anyway? The case of history. In A. Segall, E. E. Heilman, & C. H. Cherryholmes (Eds.), *Social studies—The next generation: Re-searching in the postmodern* (pp. 125–139). New York: Peter Lang.
Seixas, P. (2000). Schweigen! Die Kinder! Or, does postmodern history have a place in the schools. *Knowing, teaching, and learning history: National and international perspectives*, 19–37.
Werner, W. (2000). Reading authorship into texts. *Theory & Research in Social Education, 28*(2), 193–219.
Zimmerman, J. (2002). *Whose America?: Culture wars in the public schools*. Harvard University Press.

Appendix A

List of Assessed Textbooks

Title/Author(s)	Year of Publication	Publisher
The History of the American People Beard and Bagley	1920	The Macmillan Company
The History of the American People Beard and Bagley	1925	The Macmillan Company
History of the United States Fite	1923	Henry Holt and Company
School History of the United States Hart	1920	American Book Company

Title/Author(s)	Year of Publication	Publisher
The Leading Facts of American History Montgomery	1920	Ginn and Company
The American Pageant: A History of the Republic Bailey	1966	D. C. Heath and Company
The American Pageant: A History of the Republic Bailey	1971	D. C. Heath and Company
The American Pageant: A History of the Republic Bailey & Kennedy	1979	D. C. Heath and Company
Give Me Liberty!: An American History, 3rd ed. Foner	2010	W. W. Norton and Company
The American Pageant: A History of the American People Kennedy and Cohen	2013	Cengage
The Americans Danzer, Klor de Alva, Krieger, Wilson, Woloch	2012	McDougal Littell

Appendix B

	Inquiry Design Model (IDM) Blueprint™
Compelling Question	How does my textbook's author shape my understanding of the past?
Standards and Practices	National Council for the Social Studies C3 Framework D2.His.6.9-12. Analyze the ways in which the perspectives of those writing history shaped the history that they produced. D2.His.7.9-12. Explain how the perspectives of people in the present shape interpretations of the past. D2.His.8.9-12. Analyze how current interpretations of the past are limited by the extent to which available historical sources represent perspectives of people at the time. D2.His.10.9-12. Detect possible limitations in various kinds of historical evidence and differing secondary interpretations.

Inquiry Design Model (IDM) Blueprint™		
Staging the Question	Discuss the following question: What are the most trustworthy sources of information about the past? How do you know they are trustworthy sources?	
Supporting Question 1	Supporting Question 2	Supporting Question 3
What is "Representation?"	How are African Americans, Radical Republicans and Southern Whites portrayed in a 1920s textbook chapter on Reconstruction?	How are African Americans, Radical Republicans and Southern Whites portrayed in my textbook's chapter on Reconstruction?
Formative Performance Task	Formative Performance Task	Formative Performance Task
Write a narrative about what happened in class the day before. Then, share your narrative with the rest of the class. Compare your accounts. How is each one a representation of what happened as opposed to what exactly happened?	Fill out a graphic organizer highlighting how African Americans, Radical Republicans, and Southern Whites are represented in the textbook chapter.	Fill out a graphic organizer highlighting how African Americans, Radical Republicans, and Southern Whites are represented in the textbook chapter.
Featured Sources	Featured Sources	Featured Sources
Source A: Student narratives	Source A: Chapter XXIII. Reconstruction. The Rise of the New South from Beard and Bagley's (1925) *The History of the American People* (available via Google Books)	Source A: Reconstruction chapter from your course/classroom textbook

	Inquiry Design Model (IDM) Blueprint™	
Summative Performance Task	Argument	Draft an essay that compares and contrasts how African Americans, Radical Republicans and Southern Whites are represented in the two Reconstructions chapters you examined. How did these chapters change over time? Why do think these changes occurred? Address the following questions: What types of voice were used? How could textbooks representations of Reconstruction impact how people think about different groups from that time period?
	Extension	Design an interview questionnaire that focuses on what people today know about Reconstruction and how they learned it. Conduct these interviews with family members and members of your local community in order to draw comparisons between how your textbook represents Reconstruction and how the time period is popularly remembered.
Taking Informed Action	\multicolumn{2}{l	}{**Understand:** Research how an historically oppressed/marginalized group is represented throughout your textbook, paying particular attention to how they are described, if they are integrated in the main text, and if group members are quoted or named. **Assess:** Create a list of possible people, events, and/or sources that could be used to promote greater representation in your textbook. **Act:** Draft a letter to the publisher of your textbook outlining recommendations for how to expand the representation of your chosen group in the text.}

CHAPTER SEVEN

The Road to the 19th Amendment: Examining the Women's Suffrage Movement during the Reconstruction Era with Historical Empathy Pedagogies

KATHERINE PERROTTA
Mercer University Tift College of Education

Historical empathy is an important aspect of social studies and history education that is shaped through students' analyses of the historical context of documents, and how those contexts impacted the perspectives of people in the past (Endacott & Brooks, 2018; Perrotta, 2018a, 2018b; Yilmaz, 2007). A powerful reason to foster historical empathy is to highlight and include the histories of underrepresented people and groups in the social studies curriculum. Scholarship has grown on the inclusion of diverse groups and individuals in mainstream narratives of United States history; however, there continues to be a lack of representation of gender and women's histories in states' social studies and history standards. For example, the National Women's History Museum's study *Where are the Women? A Report on the Status of Women in the United States Social Studies Standards* highlights that the majority of states' K-12 social studies content standards (1) prioritized the inclusion of women of accomplishment such as Rosa Parks and Harriet Beecher Stowe, (2) overlooked the "breadth and depth" of women's history, (3) emphasized women's domestic roles (4) limited focus on women's history to certain periods of time, (5) failed to present women's histories from a woman's perspective, and (6) lacked representation of women in science, technology, engineering, and mathematics fields (Mauer, Patrick, Britto, & Millar, 2017). Such omissions of women in these standards are problematic, for they present a narrow emphasis on the complex experiences, challenges, and achievements of women with regard to suffrage, particularly during the Reconstruction Era.

In order to promote historical empathy through examination of the women's suffrage movement, teachers must emphasize that the fight for the right to vote resulted after decades of activism and agitation, particularly before and after the Civil War. Although the suffragist movement was intertwined with the antebellum abolitionist movement and subsequent ratification of the 13th and 14th amendments, many suffragists were disappointed when the 15th amendment in 1870 did not include women's right to vote, hence highlighting the limitations of the 14th amendment concerning the rights of women as citizens, and amplifying discriminatory attitudes of White suffragists towards women of color.

PURPOSE OF CHAPTER AND COMPELLING QUESTION

The purpose of this chapter is to provide pedagogical supports for social studies educators to teach about the intersections of race and gender in the debate for suffrage during the Reconstruction Era. Using the National Council for the Social Studies (NCSS) College, Career, and Civic Life (C3) Framework (2013) C3 Framework Inquiry Arc and Inquiry Design Model (Grant, Lee, & Swan, 2018), I outline how the use of primary sources that highlight various perspectives of suffragists, women of color, white women, and Black men to promote historical empathy through examination of the compelling question, *"do challenges to vote still exist?"* Documents highlighted will demonstrate how practitioners can promote historical empathy when teaching the complexities of the women's suffrage movement with regard to race during the Reconstruction Era, as well as how primary source analysis connects to student demonstration of historical empathy through deliberation of taking informed action on the historical and contemporary issue of voting rights.

HISTORICAL EMPATHY AND THE WOMEN'S SUFFRAGE MOVEMENT DURING RECONSTRUCTION

In order to promote historical empathy through examination of the women's suffrage movement, teachers must emphasize that women's fight for the right to vote did not happen in a vacuum in 1920, but as a result of decades of activism and agitation dating back to the 18th century. Linda Kerber (1998) explains that while women "have been citizens of the United States as long as the republic has existed" (p. xxi), they were not entitled to their right to vote, even after Abigail

Adams urged her husband John Adams during the Revolution to "Remember the ladies and be more generous and favorable to them than your ancestors. Do not put such unlimited power into the hands of the Husbands. Remember all Men would be tyrants if they could" (Adams, 1776). When the Declaration of Sentiments was written at the Seneca Falls Convention in 1848, attendees such as Elizabeth Cady Stanton and Lucretia Mott made legal demands for women's rights. Stanton (1848) wrote, "The history of mankind is a history of repeated injuries and usurpations on the part of man toward woman...Having deprived her of this first right of a citizen, the elective franchise, thereby leaving her without representation in the halls of legislation, he has oppressed her on all sides." Although the suffragist movement was intertwined with the antebellum abolitionist movement and subsequent ratification of the 13th and 14th amendments during Reconstruction, many women were disappointed when the ratification of the 15th amendment in 1870 did not include women's right to vote, hence highlighting the limitations of the 14th amendment concerning the rights of women as citizens.

Moreover, the shortcomings of the 14th amendment particularly amplified discriminatory attitudes of white suffragists towards women of color. According to abolitionist Sojourner Truth (1851), who spoke at the Women's Convention in Akron, Ohio:

> That man over there says that women need to be helped into carriages, and lifted over ditches, and to have the best place everywhere. Nobody ever helps me into carriages, or over mud-puddles, or gives me any best place! And ain't I a woman?

Truth's powerful speech put on national display that the issue of women's suffrage was a complex issue predating the Civil War. Views about the inferiority of people of color persisted during the Reconstruction Era. Not only were Americans debating whether Black men should vote, but also whether Black women were also considered citizens who were guaranteed the right to franchise.

Teachers can engage students in examining the complexities and intricacies of the suffrage movement during Reconstruction through the implementation of historical empathy pedagogies. The suffrage movement was not a monolith, as differing views with regard to race among suffragists, such as Susan B. Anthony and Lucy Stone, led to the formation of the National Women's Suffrage Association (NWSA) and American Women's Suffrage Association (AWSA), respectively. Once the movement splintered, debates persisted with regard to whether suffragists should support the 15th amendment for universal male suffrage, which the AWSA's stance, or oppose it until women were included, which was the NWSA's position. Although many suffragists, such as Anthony and Elizabeth Cady Stanton allied with abolitionists such as Frederick Douglass during the Civil War, rifts among white suffragists with regard to the exclusion of women's right to vote with the ratification of the 15th amendment "prompted white suffragists to differentiate themselves from Black women" (Lange, 2020, p. 7). Although Black women such as Sojourner Truth and Frances Harper "actively engaged in a grassroots political culture that valued the participation of the entire community," they were "doubly burdened by racism and sexism" as they faced unprecedented challenges not only attaining the right to vote, but facing discrimination and violence in Jim Crow America (Jones, 2020, p. 9).

HISTORICAL EMPATHY CURRICULAR AND ASSESSMENT FRAMEWORKS

In order to promote historical empathy through analysis of the women's suffrage movement during Reconstruction, teachers must explore frameworks that emphasize inquiry of historical contexts and perspectives through primary and secondary source analysis. The National Council for the Social Studies (NCSS) College, Career, and Civic Life (C3) Framework supports teaching historical empathy through implementation of its Inquiry Arc. The Inquiry Arc is organized into four dimensions that methodically outlines an inquiry-based process that can also promote historical empathy by (1) developing compelling questions, (2) applying concepts and tools to content investigations, (3) evaluating primary and secondary sources, and (4) communicating conclusions and taking informed action (NCSS, 2013, p. 18). While this model is prevalent in social studies, there are other curricular initiatives that support the promotion of historical empathy.

The National Council for History Education (NCHE) identifies in its Ten Habits that historical empathy involves perceiving "past events and issues as they might have been experienced by the people of the time." Furthermore, the Southern Poverty Law Center's (SPLC) (2016) Learning for Justice Standards includes empathy as a part of its diversity and action standards with regard to building connections with others by showing "respect and understanding regardless of... similarities or differences" (p. 10). Additionally, Facing History and Ourselves highlights four key elements for promoting historical empathy by (1) presenting "lesser known" stories to students, (2) pairing secondary sources with document to provide historical context of primary sources, (3) providing examples of children who participated in historical events and activism, and (4) engaging in role-playing activities as a means to not only help students connect with the past, but also provide them with the tools to better understand how that past has shaped the present (Mai, 2018).

Although the implementation of historical empathy pedagogies has benefits, teachers may encounter difficulties, particularly with assessing the affective aspects of historical empathy. Grading students based on their emotive responses is extremely challenging because such thoughts and feelings happen in the minds of students (Cunningham, 2009). However, developing a framework to measure academic and affective responses to content can be useful to determine student engagement in the process of historical empathy. Therefore, I adapted Lee and Shemilt's five-level framework for my research because their rubric provided a range in which to measure student demonstration of historical empathy. The five-level framework rubric includes:

> Level (1) students use stereotypes to view the past as inferior, lack of use of primary and secondary sources and does not make relevant affective connections to content
> Level (2) students use some primary and secondary sources to make generalizations about historical context and perspectives and makes vague affective connections to content
> Level (3) students use primary and secondary sources to identify historical perspectives and contexts with some explanation of how the past and present differ, and provides some relevant affective connections to content,
> Level (4) students use primary and secondary source evidence to explain how people in the past made decisions based upon the times they lived; describes how the past and present differ without a presentist lens; makes several affective connections to content
> Level (5) students demonstrate all criteria in the previous level, plus explain how they can take informed action about an issue in the present (Perrotta, 2018a, 2018b; Lee & Shemilt, 2011).

While assessing for historical empathy may not always be possible, aligning instruction to a framework to measure academic and affective responses to content can be useful to determine student engagement in the process of historical empathy over time.

ALIGNING HISTORICAL EMPATHY TO THE C3 FRAMEWORK

Promoting historical empathy in social studies is as relevant, timely and important as ever, particularly with regard to matters of voting rights, race, and gender since the 2020 presidential election. Since curricular initiatives such as the NCSS C3 Framework Inquiry Arc support curricular aims of historical empathy, teachers can use research-based frameworks that can support their design of lesson plans and instructional units that foster the cognitive and affective elements of historical empathy. The Inquiry Arc is designed in alignment with the Inquiry Design Model, which outlines unit and lesson plan formats in the following parts:

- **Asking Compelling Questions** that drive student inquiry of issues found in and across the academic disciplines that make up social studies
- **Connections to Standards** that establish the foundation of inquiry of the Compelling Question
- **Staging the Compelling Question** by introducing the main concepts, ideas, and themes that are essential to answering the Compelling Question
- **Creation of three to four Supporting Questions** that are intended to assist students with key terms, concepts, definitions, and processes that are integral to examining content and demonstrating skills during the inquiry of the Compelling Question
- **Design of Formative Performance Tasks** that serve as activities in which students practice skills necessary for demonstration of content understandings
- **Examination of Featured Sources** that are inclusive of primary and secondary sources necessary for students to become interested and engaged in the inquiry and analyze historical context and perspectives that aid in completion of formative performance tasks.
- **Design of Summative Performance Tasks and Extension Activities** at the end of instruction where students cite primary and secondary sources as evidence to form arguments that address the Compelling Question
- **Considerations to Take Informed Action** where students discuss how historical inquiry connects to broader or contemporary contexts and craft a logical plan to "act in ways that allow students to demonstrate agency in a real-world context" (Grant, Swan, Lee, 2018).[1]

When using the Inquiry Design Model to promote historical empathy through teaching the women's suffrage movement during Reconstruction, teachers provide students with robust intellectual materials that can lead students to care about the study and application of the social studies content areas (Grant, Swann, & Lee, 2018, p. 200).

The application of the Inquiry Design Model can be an effective way for teachers to engage students in analysis of how the historical contexts of the 19th and 20th centuries shaped the women's suffrage movement. A sample C3 Framework lesson aligned with the Inquiry Design Model about suffrage can be found on the C3Teachers.org website where the compelling question asked, "was the vote enough?" Supporting questions to this inquiry include "why did Americans oppose granting suffrage for women?", "Were some rights not gained in the 19th Amendment?", and "What is the Equal Rights Amendment?" Formative tasks included writing letters to an imaginary daughter about why she cannot vote, creating a T-chart comparing and contrasting the arguments of those for and against women's suffrage, and debating whether the Equal Rights Amendment would have improved equality for women. Using featured sources including brochures from the National Women's Suffrage Association and the Texas Association Opposed to Women's Suffrage, and the text of the 19th amendment, the summative task asked students to formulate an argument as an essay or poster where they answered the compelling question. With regard to taking informed action, students are asked to investigate a threat to civil rights (understand), determine the motivations for that threat (assess), and create a poster that illustrates the struggle for civil rights (act). This lesson provides a good example of how historical empathy can be implemented in a manner that is inclusive and representative of the perspectives, contexts, and relevant connections students can make between historical content and experiential knowledge.[2]

LEARNING ACTIVITIES

The following activities are designed in alignment with the Inquiry Design Model Blueprint of the C3 Framework Inquiry Arc. Teachers can implement these activities over the course of several class periods as part of a connected learning unit where students can engage in historical empathy strategies through source analysis of the women's suffrage movement during the Reconstruction Era. To set the stage for this inquiry, teachers can present the following Big Idea, Compelling Question, and Essential Understandings before engaging students in the process of historical empathy through primary and secondary source analyses:

Big Idea: Equality
Compelling Question: Do challenges to vote still exist?
Essential Understandings: Although initially aligned with the abolitionist movement, women suffragists shared differing views on the role of race when obtaining the right to vote.

Introducing students to these aforementioned components of these learning activities will serve to active prior knowledge and support students' acquisition of historical content knowledge and skills through considering their experiential knowledge concerning matters of equity, equality, and citizenship in a democratic society.

Learning Activity #1: Activating Prior Knowledge and Setting the Stage for the Compelling Question—Appendix A

After setting the stage, teachers will begin inquiry about the suffrage movement during Reconstruction by asking students to brainstorm a definition of what the term *equality* means. Next, the teacher can ask students the reflection question "how do you think the time after the Civil War impacted the suffrage movement for women's right to vote?" Students can deliberate issues such as emancipation from enslavement, the role women played in the abolitionist movement, and the limits of the 15th amendment with regard to universal male suffrage. After this discussion, the teacher can ask students what challenges they think women, particularly women of color, faced during the Reconstruction with regard to race, civil rights, and equality. Among the responses students may provide include, but are not limited to, the passing of black codes to suppress the Black vote, the violence of organizations like the Ku Klux Klan to intimidate African American enfranchisement, the role of the Freedman's Bureau with supporting Black education and employment at the conclusion of the Civil War, and ratification of the 15th amendment that excluded women from gaining the right to vote.

Learning Activity #2: Secondary Source Analysis—Appendix B

Next, students can read secondary sources to establish their understandings of the historical context of the women's suffrage movement during Reconstruction. Eric Foner's (2014) seminal work, *Reconstruction: America's unfinished revolution, 1863–1877*, can be excerpted to provide contextual background of the Reconstruction including the ratification of the 13th, 14th, and 15th amendments, Presidential and Congressional Reconstruction, the clashes between Radical Republicans and Andrew Johnson, and socio-economic conditions of freedmen and women after the war. Other tertiary sources on background information about Reconstruction that can support students' understandings of the historical contexts of the women's suffrage movement include The New York Historical Society's *Women and the American Story's* curriculum that includes a timeline of women's history from Native America through the 20th century.[3]

In addition to Foner's book, students can read excerpts from Martha S. Jones' book *Vanguard* highlights the matter of inclusion of women of color in the narratives of the women's suffrage movement. By terming the Black women in her book as the *Vanguard*, Jones (2020) writes that "they were the nation's original feminists and antiracists, and they built a movement on those core principles. They raised the bar high for all Americans and showed allies, among men and women, Black and white, how to work in coalition" (p. 11). Allison Lange's (2020) book *Picturing political power* is an in-depth analysis of how the use of images such as cartoons and photographs were used by suffragists and anti-suffragists to convey messages about their positions not only women's rights to vote, but whether Black women should be included in these debates. Moreover, Tera W. Hunter's (1997) book, *To' joy my freedom: Southern Black women's lives and labors after the Civil War* and Cathleen D. Cahill's (2020) *Recasting the vote: How women of color transformed the suffrage movement* provides a pivotal history of women's lives and challenges during Reconstruction. Teachers can provide students with a graphic organizer where students read and record pertinent information from these secondary sources to continue inquiry of the compelling question.

Learning Activity #3: Primary Source Analysis—Appendix C

Upon completion of secondary source analysis, students can examine document-based questions about women's roles and perspectives on suffrage and race to gain deeper insights into the complexities of the suffrage movement during Reconstruction. First among these documents should include perspectives of those who were against Black suffrage. For example, an 1866 cartoon in *Harper's Weekly* titled "Holy Horror Mrs. McClaffraty is in a Washington D.C Street Car" depicts a well-dressed African American woman sitting next to a stereotypical Irish immigrant woman on a streetcar. Below the image is the caption, "Mr. McClaffraty voted against Negro suffrage ("Holy horror," 1866)." According to the *Harper's Weekly* digital archive, the cartoon highlighted racist attitudes against Black suffrage. Furthermore, the cartoon in *Puck* "Well, Missy! Heah We Is!" 1913 engraving from *Puck* of three stereotypically depicted Black women holding a flag VOTES FOR COLORED LADIES startles a white woman suffragist (Glackens, 1913). Although the cartoon was published after the Reconstruction, its message connects to the time period because the aim was to criticize the efforts of the NAWSA and National Woman's Party, neither countered with positive images of African Americans because "they wanted support from officials who supported laws that disenfranchised people of color. White women wanted to be equal to white men, not to fight for equality with black women" (Lange, 2020, pp. 175–176).

Second, students can examine primary sources of white suffragists about their stance on inclusion of Black women in the suffrage movement. For instance, Thomas Nast's (1872) cartoon "Get Thee Behind Me Mrs. Satan" depicts Victoria Woodhull as a devil during her presidential campaign in which her running mate was Frederick Douglass. Woodhull's candidacy was controversial due to her age, gender, stance on marriage and feminism, as well as her support of the 15th amendment. Conversely, Susan B. Anthony's infamous quote with regard to the ratification of the 15th amendment is a prime example for analysis of opposing perspectives on Black women's suffrage through historical empathy. Anthony stated, "I will cut off this right arm of mine before I will ever work or demand the ballot for the Negro and not the woman" in response to requests from abolitionists Wendell Phillips and Theodore Tilton to abandon calls for universal suffrage for women (Harper, 1899). Although this quote has been interpreted as Anthony expressing racist views over Black enfranchisement, Brzustowicz (2018) contends that this quote is misinterpreted. Anthony also stated, "It is not a question of precedence between women & black men. Neither has a claim to precedence upon an Equal Rights platform. But the business of this association is to demand for every man black or white, & for every woman, black or white, that they shall be this instant enfranchised & admitted into the body politic with equal rights & privileges" (Harper, 1899). As a result, examination of Anthony's perspectives on race in the context of Reconstruction politics concerning Black male enfranchisement and the women's suffrage movement would be a compelling exercise in engaging students in historical empathy.

Third, documents highlighting the views of Black suffragists provides further perspectives on the complexities of Black women's enfranchisement in the suffrage movement during Reconstruction. For instance, Frances Ellen Watkins Harper was a prolific African American abolitionist, writer, and poet who was among the few free women to attend women's suffrage conferences before and after the Civil War (Alexander, 2020). She gave a speech at the National Women's Rights Convention in New York in 1866, calling out white colleagues who were against or apathetic to Black women's suffrage, stating:

> I do not believe that giving woman the ballot is immediately going to cure all the ills of life. I do not believe that white women are dew-drops just exhaled from the skies. I think that like men they may be divided into three classes, the good, the bad, and the indifferent. The good would vote according to their convictions and principles; the bad, as dictated by prejudice or malice; and the indifferent will vote on the strongest side of the question, with the winning party (Harper, 1866).

Additionally, Harper's (1872) poem, "Aunt Chloe's Politics" is another example of a document that can be examined by students from a historical empathy approach with regard to her observations concerning corruption and matters of race in politics. This excerpt states:

> Now I don't believe in looking
> Honest people in the face,
> And saying when you're doing wrong,
> That "I haven't sold my race."

From a historical empathy standpoint, students could examine these documents by analyzing the years in which they were produced, who produced the images, the intended audience for the images, and message in order to discuss how the contexts of the 19th century impacted why suffragists were split with regard to race, and how matters concerning women's rights today could be compared and contrasted with the social movements women reformers were involved in during the decades leading to the ratification of the 19th amendment. Teachers can instruct students to read these documents and complete a graphic organizer to record information that can be used as evidence to explain the contexts and perspectives of those involved in the women's suffrage movement during Reconstruction.

Learning Activity #4: Display Findings from Source Analysis—Appendix D

In order to display findings and demonstrate understandings of the context and perspectives of the suffrage movement, students will synthesize evidence from primary and secondary sources to write a document-based essay answering the following question based on the Essential Understandings and Big Idea, "how and why did women suffragists share differing views on equality with regard to the role of race when obtaining the right to vote during Reconstruction?" This essay will include discussion of multiple perspectives of those involved in the women's suffrage movement during Reconstruction in order for students to highlight the divisions and tensions among suffrage organizations with regard to race and the right to vote, particularly as voter enfranchisement connects to the Long Civil Rights Movement in the United States.

Learning Activity #5: Debrief, Inquire, and Take Informed Action—Appendix E

To conclude the historical empathy investigation of the women's suffrage movement during Reconstruction, debriefing can take place as students share their findings from their essay. To further engage students in inquiry, students can work in cooperative groups to discuss the compelling question, "do challenges to vote still exist?" as a means to deliberate on how to take informed action about matters concerning race, voting, gender rights, and social justice. Students can research contemporary issues concerning voting in the United States and propose a plan of action to address the identified issue. Among the issues students can research include, but are not limited to, the work of Stacey Abrams in Georgia during the 2020 presidential election to register voters, examination of the Supreme Court decision in 2013 that relaxed federal oversight of elections as imposed by the 1965 Voting Rights Act, analysis of the "Bloody Sunday" violence in Selma and the life of the late John Lewis, and the election of Kamala Harris as the nation's first woman of color Vice President. Depending on the issue selected for research, students can use the following outline to assist with their creation of a plan of action of potential steps to address this issue. Among the ideas for cooperative projects include, but are not limited to, creating infographic flyers, recording documentary videos, constructing informative websites, hosting podcasts, painting murals, composing songs, and writing letters to elected officials. This summative performance task not only engages students in applying what they learned about race and the women's suffrage movement during Reconstruction through engagement in historical empathy pedagogies, but encourage inquiry for future lessons concerning long civil rights and social justice in United States history.[4]

CONCLUSION

Examination of the suffrage movement in the context of the Reconstruction when teaching United States history is important in order for students to grasp that the movement did not start with Seneca Falls, halt during the Civil War, and then re-emerge at the turn of the 20th century. The struggle for women's right to vote continued as a nuanced, complex, and difficult endeavor with regard to suffragists' views of race and gender during the 19th and 20th centuries. Over a century after the ratification of the 15th amendment and 19th amendment, there is still a need for scholarship dedicated "to gender and feminist scholarship in social studies education, from a ground-up approach of exploring how these constructs are realized in actual classrooms." (Bohan, 2017, p. 246). Considering the 100th anniversary of women gaining the right to vote coincided with a contentious presidential election, a controversial Supreme Court nomination of after the passing of Ruth Bader Ginsberg, the COVID-19 pandemic, the #metoo movement, and Black Lives Matter protests, now is an opportune time to examine how teachers, scholars, and stakeholders can promote historical empathy in social studies through examination of women's histories, especially the histories of women of color, during the Reconstruction and throughout United States history.

Notes

1 See Grant, S. G., Lee, J., & Swan, K. (2018). Inquiry design model at a glance. www.C3Teachers.org. Retrieved from http://www.c3teachers.org/wp-content/uploads/2019/08/Inquiry-Design-Model-at-a-glance.pdf.
2 See C3 Teachers. Women's suffrage. Retrieved from http://www.c3teachers.org/inquiries/womens-suffrage/
3 See The New York Historical Society. (2020). Women and the American Story. Retrieved from https://wams.nyhistory.org/modernizing-america/. Content spanning the New Republic, Civil War, and late-20th and 21st centuries are forthcoming on the website.
4 See Rada Abdo. "10+ Project Based Learning Examples for Educators." *Venngage*. Retrieved from https://venngage.com/blog/project-based-learning-examples/.

REFERENCES:

Adams, A. (1776). *Letter from Abigail Adams to John Adams, 31 March 1776*. Massachusetts Historical Society. Retrieved from https://www.masshist.org/digitaladams/archive/doc?id=L177 60331aa

Alexander, K. L. (2020). Frances Ellen Watkins Harper. *National Women's History Museum*. Retrieved from https://www.womenshistory.org/education-resources/biographies/frances-ellen-watkins-harper.

Bohan, C. H. (2017). "Gender and feminist scholarship in social studies research." In M. M. Manfra, & C. M. Bolick (Eds.), *The Wiley handbook of social studies research*. John Wiley and Sons, Inc.

Brzustowicz, V. (2018). Susan B. Anthony—Still controversial after all these years. *National Susan B. Anthony Museum & House*. Retrieved from https://susanbanthonyhouse.org/blog/tag/stand-against-racism

Cahill, C. D. (2020). *Recasting the Vote: How Women of Color Transformed the Suffrage Movement*. UNC Press Books.

C3 Teachers. (2020). *Inquiries: Women's suffrage*. Retrieved from http://www.c3teachers.org/inquiries/womens-suffrage/

Cunningham, D. L. (2009). An empirical framework for understanding how teachers conceptualize and cultivate historical empathy in students. *Journal of Curriculum Studies 41*(5), 679–709. https://doi.org/10.1080/00220270902947376

Foner, E. (2014). *Reconstruction: America's unfinished revolution, 1863–1877*. Harper Collins.

Glackens, L. M. (1913). Well miss, Heah we is! *Puck Magazine*. Retrieved from https://www.loc.gov/pictures/item/2002720355/

Grant, S. G., Lee, J., & Swan, K. (2018). Inquiry design model at a glance. *C3 Teachers*. Retrieved from https://c3teachers.org/wp-content/uploads/2024/10/Inquiry-Design-Model-glance.pdf.

Harper, I. H. (1899). *The life and work of Susan B. Anthony including public addresses, her own letters and many from her contemporaries during fifty years, Volume I*. Bowen-Merrill Company. Retrieved from https://www.gutenberg.org/files/15220/15220-h/15220-h.htm

Harper, F. E. W. (1866). We are all bound up together (Speech). *Eleventh National Women's Rights Convention*. Retrieved from https://awpc.cattcenter.iastate.edu/2017/03/21/we-are-all-bound-up-together-may-1866/

Harper, F. E. W. (1872). Aunt Chloe's Politics (Excerpt). *Society History for Every Classroom Resources for Teachers*. City University of New York Graduate Center. Retrieved from https://shec.ashp.cuny.edu/items/show/762.

Holy horror Mrs. McClaffraty. (1866, February 24). *Harper's Weekly*. Retrieved from https://www.harpweek.com/09Cartoon/BrowseByDateCartoon.asp?Month=February&Date=24

Hunter, T. W. (1997). *To'joy my freedom: Southern Black women's lives and labors after the Civil War*. Harvard University Press.

Jones, M. S. (2020). *Vanguard: How Black women broke barriers, won the vote, and insisted on equality for all*. Basic Books.

Kerber, L. K. (1998). *No constitutional right to be ladies: Women and the obligations of citizenship* Hill and Wang.

Lange, A. K. (2020). *Picturing political power: Images in the women's suffrage movement*. Chicago: University of Chicago Press, 2020, 7.

Lee, P., Shemilt, D. (2011). "The concept that dares not speak its name: Should empathy come out of the closet?" *Teaching History*, 143, 39–49.

Mai, L. (2018). Use historical empathy to help students process the world today. Facing History and Ourselves. Retrieved from https://facingtoday.facinghistory.org/use-historical-empathy-to-help-students-process-the-world-today

Mauer, E., Patrick, J., Britto, L. M., & Millar, H. (2017). *Where are the women? A Report on the status of women in the United States social studies standards*. National Women's History Museum. Retrieved from https://www.womenshistory.org/sites/default/files/museum-assets/document/2018-02/NWHM_Status-of-Women-in-State-Social-Studies-Standards_2-27-18.pdf.

Nast, T. (1872). Get thee behind me, (Mrs.) Satan. *Harper's Weekly*. Retrieved from the Library of Congress https://www.loc.gov/pictures/item/95512460/

National Council for History Education. (2021). History's habits of mind. Retrieved from https://ncheteach.org/Historys-Habits-of-Mind

National Council for the Social Studies. (2013). *College, Career, and Civic Life Framework for Social Studies State Standards*. Retrieved from https://www.socialstudies.org/sites/default/files/2017/Jun/c3-framework-for-social-studies-rev0617.pdf.

Perrotta, K. A. (2018a). A study of students' social identities and a historical empathy gap in middle and secondary social studies classes with the instructional unit "The Elizabeth Jennings Project." *Curriculum and Teaching Dialogue*, 20(1&2), 53–69. https://www.proquest.com/openview/f12ec7b509a09cf117daad2bc417919c/1?pq-origsite=gscholar&cbl=29703

Perrotta, K. A. (2018b). Pedagogical conditions that promote historical empathy with "The Elizabeth Jennings Project." *Social Studies Research and Practice*, 13(2), 129–146. https://doi.org/10.1108/SSRP-11-2017-0064

Southern Poverty Law Center. (2016). Social justice standards: Teaching tolerance anti-bias framework. Retrieved from https://www.learningforjustice.org/sites/default/files/2017-06/TT_Social_Justice_Standards_0.pdf

Stanton, E. C. (1848). *Declaration of Sentiments*, Retrieved from https://www.nps.gov/wori/learn/historyculture/declaration-of-sentiments.htm

Truth, S. (1851). Speech entitled "Ain't I a Woman?" Women's National Convention, Akron, Ohio. Retrieved from https://thehermitage.com/wp-content/uploads/2016/02/Sojourner-Truth_Aint-I-a-Woman_1851.pdf

Yilmaz, K. (2007). Historical empathy and its implications for classroom practices in schools. *The History Teacher*, 40(3), 331–337. https://doi.org/10.2307/30036827

Appendix A

Learning Activity #1: Activating Prior Knowledge and Setting the Stage for the Compelling Question

Directions: In the bubbles, brainstorm at least four ideas about what you think the term "equality" means. Next, answer the reflection question based on your experiences and knowledge of social studies. Be ready to share!

EXAMINING THE WOMEN'S SUFFRAGE MOVEMENT | 149

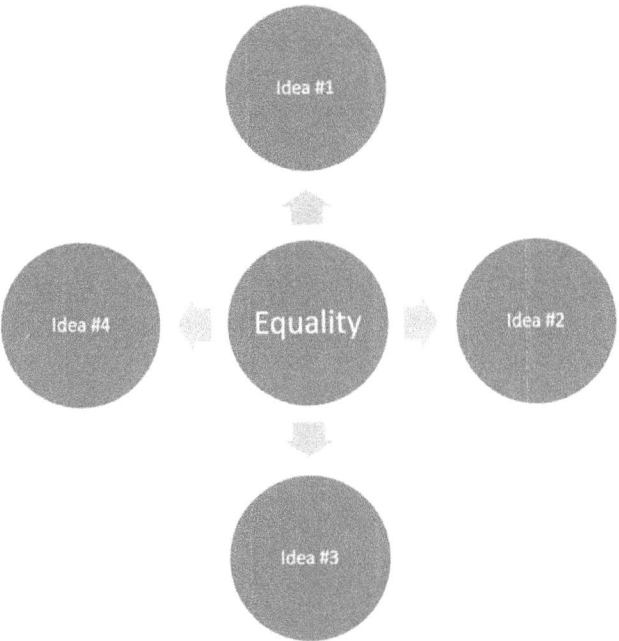

Reflection: What challenges do you think women faced during Reconstruction to gain the right to vote? Do you think there are challenges for people vote today? If so, how do you think these challenges are similar and different to those experienced during Reconstruction?

Appendix B

Learning Activity #2: Secondary Source Analysis

<u>Directions:</u> List the author, title, and date of the secondary sources reference list about Reconstruction. Read the books and complete the chart below. Answer the reflection questions in at least 1 complete sentence.

Author(s), title, date	Major Challenges during Reconstruction	Major Achievements during Reconstruction	Main People and Events	Where and When did the Events Took Place	Evidence Author(s) provide about suffrage during Reconstruction

> Reflection
>
> Directions: Answer each question in at least one complete sentence.
>
> What information from the sources provide you with insights about the historical context of the women's suffrage movement during Reconstruction?
>
> What information from the sources provide you with insights about the perspectives of the people involved with women's suffrage during Reconstruction?
>
> After reading these sources, what insights have you gained about challenges to vote in the past? Can these challenges compare to issues today? Why or why not? Explain your answer.

Appendix C

Learning Activity #3: Primary Source Analysis

Directions: Read the following documents and use the information from those sources to complete the chart below.

Document Author, Title, Date	What is the Document About?	Point of View of Author	Similarities between Perspectives of Authors	Differences between Perspectives of Authors

> Reflection
>
> Directions: Answer the following questions in at least 1 complete sentence.
>
> What information from the documents provided you with insights about the historical context of Reconstruction during the women's suffrage movement?
>
> How did you feel after reading these documents? What connections can you make to the perspectives expressed in these documents?
>
> After reading these documents, do you think challenges still exist to vote? Explain.

EXAMINING THE WOMEN'S SUFFRAGE MOVEMENT | 151

Appendix D

Learning Activity #4: Synthesizing Primary and Secondary Sources

Directions: Use evidence from the at least <u>four</u> documents in your essay, and your knowledge of social studies, to answer the question in a well-organized essay that includes an introduction, body paragraphs, and a conclusion.

Question: How and why did women suffragists share differing views on equality with regard to the role of race when obtaining the right to vote during Reconstruction?

<u>Introduction</u> <u>Paragraph (Main Idea/Thesis)</u>:
<u>Evidence from Primary Source 1:</u>
<u>Evidence from Primary Source 2:</u>
<u>Example of Evidence from Secondary Source 1:</u>
<u>Example of Evidence from Secondary Source 2:</u>
<u>Conclusion:</u>

Appendix E

Learning Activity #5: Project Proposal Template

<u>Directions:</u> With your group, identify a contemporary issue that relates to challenges to vote. Next, use the primary and secondary sources about the women's suffrage movement during Reconstruction to complete the template where the group plans a proposal for addressing this issue. Be ready to share!

Project Team Members' Names: _____ _____ _____ _____ _____ _____ ____

Title of Proposed Project	
Summary of Issue	
Type of Project	
Summary of Plan to Address Issue	
Use of Evidence to Explain the Steps to Complete this Project	
Resources Needed	
Roles of Members on the Project Team	
Plan to Obtain Feedback to Revise the Project	
Plan to Share the Project Proposal	
Reflection on the Project	
Remaining Questions for Future Projects	

CHAPTER EIGHT

Reconstruction's Accomplishment: Black Education and the Rise of the Civil Rights Movement

SCOTT L. STABLER, JUSTIN SHELDON, AND
TIMOTHY J. MCKEEBY

INTRODUCTION

The educational foundation laid during Reconstruction marks the era at least a partial success. At the beginning of the 20th century, *The Advance* newspaper best explains the period's history as, "...a 'nation' that had been 'born in a day' out of bondage and utter poverty and illiteracy, [and] was, under sanction of the National Government started forth on the new road of universal education and of everything implied in [the] term 'Americanization'" (Howard, 1906-07). The foundation laid took time to bear fruit, but if one thinks of how many people went from illiterate to educated it proves Black agency. Southern white racism caused Reconstruction to falter, but out of that period came several victories, not the least of which entailed establishing a nationwide formal education system. Though often under-funded due to Jim Crow and racial attitudes, segregated schools accomplished turning out generations of educated African Americans who only a few years before were considered property. Tracing historically Black colleges and universities (HBCUs) and their graduates from establishment to the Civil Rights Movement demonstrates a Reconstruction success (Anderson, 1988).

President Barack Obama, speaking before the graduating class of Howard University in May of 2016, had this to say about the educational efforts of the Black colleges and universities founded during Reconstruction:

> The spirit of achievement and special responsibility has defined this campus ever since the Freedmen's Bureau established Howard just four years after the emancipation proclamation. Two years after the Civil War came to an end. They created this university with a vision of uplift, a vision of America where our place would be determined not by our gender, race, or creed, but where we would be free to pursue our intellectual—individual and collective dreams. It is that spirit that has made Howard a centerpiece of African American life and a centerpiece of a larger American story. This institution has been the home of many firsts. The first Black Nobel Peace prize winner. The first Black supreme court justice. But its mission has been to ensure those firsts were not the last. Countless scholars, professionals, artists, leaders from every field received their training here. The generations of men and women who walk through this yard, helped reform our government, cure disease, grow a Black middle class, advance civil rights, shape our culture. The seeds of change for all Americans were—sowed here (Obama, 2016).

Most historians argue that Reconstruction failed as it took one hundred years for a "real" civil rights movement led by African Americans to begin the process of making "all men equal." However, consider the number of prominent African Americans that attended or worked at one of the HBCUs formed during the Reconstruction period; their connection bolsters the "success" point. Some of the more prominent graduates, but only a small sample, include Booker T. Washington (Hampton 1875, founder of Tuskegee Institute), W.E.B. DuBois (Fisk 1888, professor at Atlanta), Ida B. Wells (attended Rust and Fisk), Thurgood Marshall (Howard 1933 JD), Martin Luther King Jr. (Morehouse 1948), Toni Morrison (Howard 1953), and Medgar Evers (Alcorn 1952). Some contemporary notable figures include Jesse Jackson (North Carolina AT&T 1964), Kamala Harris (Howard 1986), Oprah Winfrey (Tennessee State 87), and Ta-Nehisi Coates (Howard attended and now professor).[1]

President Obama also gave a speech at Morehouse University laying out the importance of the HBCU's legacy in one individual.

> It was that mission—not just to educate men, but to cultivate good men, strong men, upright men—that brought community leaders together just two years after the end of the Civil War. They assembled a list of 37 men, free Blacks and freed slaves, who would make up the first prospective class of what later became Morehouse College. Dr. King was just 15 years old when he enrolled here at Morehouse. He was an unknown, undersized, unassuming young freshman who lived at home with his parents. And I think it's fair to say he wasn't the coolest kid on campus—for the suits he wore, his classmates called him "Tweed." But his education at Morehouse helped to forge the intellect, the discipline, the compassion, the soul force that would transform America. It was here that he was introduced to the writings of Gandhi and Thoreau, and the theory of civil disobedience. It was here that professors encouraged him to look past the world as it was and fight for the world as it should be (Obama, 2013).

In 2019, President Donald Trump stated, "This nation owes a profound and enduring debt of gratitude to its HBCUs," calling them "noble institutions" (Kreibaum, 2019).

Educating African Americans after Reconstruction at HBCUs led to the Civil Rights Movement. Reconstruction with its noble goals of full civil rights for freedpeople was not reality at the time. It moved freedpeople from slavery to the Senate in a few years along with suffrage and other rights. This stunned White Southerners. Reconstruction's "top-down movement" in which the federal government took on a heavy role, led to White backlash—passive and active.

When comparing affirmative action today to Reconstruction one can better understand the Era's failure. Though only modestly aiding African Americans, affirmative action draws strong vitriol and is railed against as "reverse discrimination" by its detractors. Statistically affirmative action helps White women most and impacts primarily government entities. Perceptions do not always match reality, but White resistance remains strong today as state referendums have depleted affirmative action throughout the country (Pew Research Center, https://www.pewresearch.org/fact-tank/2014/04/22/supreme-court-says-states-can-ban-affirmative-action-8-already-have/). For African Americans to go from the field to the Senate, from property to soldiers, from racial "inferiors" to lawmakers was not an actuality the vast majority of White Southerners were willing to accept, and most Northern Whites were not willing to enforce. Many White Southerners not only opposed the efforts to promote civil equality by a government that had just defeated them in a brutal war, but they also resisted ferociously. White backlash brought violence never seen before in times of "peace" in the United States. Terrorism worked and by 1877 the downturn of Reconstruction was in full swing, and the rise of Jim Crow swung inversely.

HISTORIOGRAPHY

Reconstruction has divided historians for roughly the last one hundred and forty years. Foremost among the contentious issues centers on the question of the Reconstruction policies as a tool for the victors to inflict further punishment on the White South.[2] Reconstruction historiography has gone through basically three iterations. Except for a few historians such as W.E.B. DuBois, the Dunning School primarily influenced the perception of Reconstruction until the era of the Civil Rights Movement. For much of the twentieth century the debate about Reconstruction policies surrounded the issue of racism. This came in no small measure due to the efforts of William A. Dunning, a Columbia University history professor in the early twentieth century, who influenced a whole generation of historians, for which the school-of-thought bears his name (Smith & Lowery, 2013, pp. 1–2). The Dunning School saw Reconstruction as a resounding and dismal failure due to the basic premise of African American inferiority tied to Northern interference and big government ran amok. This distorted view of Reconstruction bled into popular culture as well. Early cinematic blockbusters like *Birth of a Nation* and *Gone with the Wind* made Klansman heroes protecting the virtuous South from uncivilized African Americans and fortune-grabbing White Northerners. Scholars have referred to this effort as Redemption (Schuessler, 2015). The second phase involves a brief period during the Civil Rights Movement when historians tended to blame the federal government and Northerners for not doing more to help carry out the promise of equality for African Americans during Reconstruction. Finally, in the last thirty plus years, Reconstruction has seen a "restoration" among scholars, foremost among them Eric Foner, another Columbia University history professor, and his breakthrough 1988 book *Reconstruction: America's Unfinished Revolution*. This school holds that White Southern racism along with the violence it generated doomed Reconstruction.

FREEDMEN'S BUREAU AND EDUCATION

"The Bureau's greatest success was in education" wrote prominent African American historian John Hope Franklin (Franklin, 1994, p. 38). Yet, historians have largely ignored that legacy. A variety of entities and people, both White and Black, helped create and continue a formal school system that educated and continues to educate African Americans. After the Civil War, White southern Democrats, the KKK, White Leagues, and other oppressors reaped murder and mayhem upon the freedpeople in the South. Southern Whites eventually reestablished political control stripping African Americans of their newly won constitutional rights, but they did not eliminate their schools, particularly HBCUs. The legacy of these schools, primarily created during Reconstruction, had a profound impact on the Civil Rights Movement throughout the 20th century. The education of Black Americans serves as one of the most enduring legacies of Reconstruction.

The Southern states suffered an extreme culture shock after their defeat. Not only did the Confederacy face conquest in a war, but it also experienced military occupation and death to an economic and cultural system that served as a bedrock for most Southern Whites. This defeat also came with the intrusion of a new social welfare agency meant to primarily aid the freedpeople. The Bureau of Refugees, Freedmen, and Abandoned Lands, better known as the Freedmen's Bureau, served as the catalyst for freedpeople's education in the defeated Confederacy.

The Freedmen's Bureau held the task of integrating the formerly enslaved people into a society in which the longtime 'peculiar institution' no longer existed. The Bureau formed a new type of social welfare agency that put the federal government in direct contact with the population. A multitude of daunting tasks faced the Bureau from guaranteeing freedom to suffrage as it sought to aid freedpeople in the war-devastated South, including the task of providing education. The Bureau established 4,329 schools, primary, secondary, and college-level (Horton, 1977, p. 229). The commissioner, Major General O. O. Howard, the namesake and one-time president of Howard University, saw it as his personal mission to aid the freedpeople. Howard would say, "Proper education will fit them [freedpeople] for higher and higher positions and enable them better and better to perform the duties devolved on them by the Creator" (Howard, 1898).

Due to the lack of federal financial support, the Bureau relied on the aid of charitable organizations to support schools. The Bureau did facilitate the transportation for the teachers and in most cases distributed the funding for the school buildings. It spent a total of $5.5 million dollars on education for the freedpeople from 1865 to 1871, but it could not pay teachers (Carpenter, 1999, p. 159). From the very beginning of the Bureau's work, Howard expected his agents and officers to give assistance to the Northern philanthropic organizations and the freedpeople in establishing schools. The supporters primarily consisted of religious organizations such as the American Missionary Association (AMA) and the American Freedman's Union Commission (AFUC) (Foner, 2002, p. 145). These groups recruited teachers through advertisements and the cooperation of various church organizations and sent them south (Library of Congress, 2022). In 1869, 3,000 schools served over 150,000 pupils. A year later, 250,000 freedpeople enrolled in one of the now 4,300 schools. These numbers do not include the many evening and private schools operated by missionary societies and by Blacks themselves (Foner, 2002, p. 149). When the Bureau closed in 1873 more Black children in Washington D.C. were attending school than White. Black illiteracy overall went from 82.5% in 1865 to 70.5% in 1870 and 48.4% in 1880 and 35% in 1890 down to 26.1% by 1900 (Horton, 1977, p. 217).

The Freedmen's Bureau and the philanthropic organizations may have provided the knowledge and money for the establishment of the freedpeople's schools, but the impetus and persistence for learning originated from the freedpeople themselves. The reasons varied. Some wanted to read the *Bible*. One elderly freedman sitting beside his grandchild in a Mobile, Alabama school explained to a Northern reporter, "he wouldn't trouble the lady [teacher] much, but he must learn to read the Bible and the Testament" (Foner, 2002, p. 97). Others realized that learning to read and write could provide economic advancements. One freedperson stated, "I gets almost discouraged, but I does want to learn to cipher so I can do business" (Foner, 2002, p. 97). For others, learning to read and write served as a sign of independence, a marked change from when they were enslaved, as most states either outright banned literacy for African Americans in slavery or strongly discouraged it. After the war, urban African Americans took immediate action to set up schools, sometimes holding classes temporarily in abandoned warehouses, billiards rooms, or in New Orleans and Savannah, former slave markets (Wright, 1909, p. 14). In the case of Richmond, less than a month after the Union had occupied it in April of 1865, more than 1,000 Black children and seventy-five adults attended schools established by Richmond's Black churches and the American Missionary Association. Freedmen's Bureau officials repeatedly expressed surprise at discovering classes organized by African Americans already meeting in churches, basements, or private homes. One Bureau officer described what he called "way-side schools. A negro riding on a loaded wagon, or sitting on a hack waiting for a train, or by the cabin door, is often seen, book in hand delving after the rudiments of knowledge" (Foner, 2002, p. 97).

African American students showed a craving for learning. They routinely begged their teachers to skip recesses, to hold regular class through traditional holidays, and to continue teaching through summer vacation. William R. Hooper writing in the *Lippincott's Magazine* in 1869 remarked:

> That they [schools] should be kept open nearly under the Tropics, in all the heat of a Southern summer, seems more incredible. But that they should be kept open in summer, under a tropical climate, at the request of the boys and girls themselves, and partly at their expense, seems altogether incredible: it is not juvenile human nature. And yet it is the fact. So desirous of learning are the dark-hued scholars of our Southern States that their schools, when closed for three months of summer, that their Northern teachers may return home to recuperate, have been reopened and their old teachers either engaged to remain or new ones been employed of their own color (Butchart, 2013, p. 7).

Freedpeople financed their education too. Landless, impoverished, and surrounded by bitter, angry Southern Whites, they raised and spent two million dollars, counting only the expenditures of the schools the Bureau tracked. It is very possible that they could have doubled that amount, if one considers the value of the donated labor of those who built and maintained schoolhouses, the value of lodging and food for teachers and fuel to heat the buildings, the value of the labor of underpaid African American teachers, and the other intangible costs educators bore to assure access to education (Butchart, 2013, pp. 6–7). When in December of 1864, General William T. Sherman captured Savannah, local African American ministers established the Savannah Educational Association, which by February of 1865, before the war was even over, had raised nearly $1,000, employed fifteen African American teachers, and enrolled 600 pupils in schools. Howard noted in 1869 that "the freedmen are already doing something. Last year it is estimated that they raised for schoolhouses and the support of teachers no less than $200,000" (Wright, 1909, p. 14).

THE TEACHERS

White Northern teachers played a significant role in establishing the education system in the South. Booker T. Washington in his seminal work titled *Up From Slavery* stated, "Whenever it is written—and I hope it will be—the part that the Yankee teachers played in education of the Negroes immediately after the war will make one of the most thrilling parts of the history of this country" (Myrdal, 2009, p. 1416). However, African Americans formed the backbone of teachers in the South. Just four years after the war, in 1869, African American teachers, for the first-time, outnumbered Whites with approximately 3,000 Black educators in the South (Foner, 2002, p. 145). The teachers largely came from the first HBCUs including Atlanta, Fisk, Hampton, and Tugaloo, all initially designed to train teachers.

To African Americans, joining the Republic as equals also meant putting their education to good use, particularly when it came to political involvement. By 1868, African American men constituted a majority of registered voters in South Carolina and Mississippi, and armed with those numbers, African American men began to run for state and national office. By 1870, Republican officials in Mississippi reported that 85% of African American jurors could read and write. After the 1872 elections, African Americans held 15% of the offices in the South, a larger percentage than in 1990 (Egerton, 2015, p. 11).

HIGHER EDUCATION

As noted, the founding of universities initially served the purpose of educating African Americans to teach in Southern schools. Commissioner Howard realized that establishing grade schools for African Americans would not be enough. He succinctly sums up the equation, "It was given in this form: You cannot keep up the lower grades unless you have the higher." The commissioner followed up by stating, "In the case of the higher schools, such were capable of educating and supplying efficient teachers for a vast field" (Howard, 1907, p. 402).

Just after the turn of the 20th century, Booker T. Washington and W.E.B. DuBois, both HBCU graduates, took an active role in higher education. DuBois, a Fisk graduate, was the first African American granted a Ph.D. from Harvard University and Washington, a Hampton graduate, founded Tuskegee Institute. However, the story of Richard Robert Wright clearly demonstrates the legacy education formed out of Reconstruction. As a teenager Wright told Commissioner and General Howard to tell those in the North "We are Rising." This young student's legacy serves as a microcosm of the importance of Black education then and today. Upon breaking the shackles of slavery, Wright's mother marched him for a month nearly 200 miles from Cuthbert, Georgia to Atlanta so he could attend school (Hayre, 1999, p. 6). After meeting Howard, Wright's stepfather made him quit school, but with the help of the Bureau, he obtained a job teaching high school. He went on to graduate magna cum laude and obtained a master's degree from Atlanta University (HBCU). Later, as a trustee of his alma mater, Wright aided in the hiring of DuBois. Next, he founded Ware High School for African Americans in the same city, the first Black public high school in Georgia. He went on to become president of the Georgia State Industrial College for Colored Youth, what is now known as Savannah State University (Haynes, 1997, pp. 17/47). A Classics education advocate, Wright ran head-on into Booker T. Washington and his political patronage machine that believed Wright's promotion of teaching Greek and Latin was non-germane for African Americans. For this advocacy of the Classics, Wright was fired after thirty years as Savannah State's president (Haynes, 1997, pp. 84–92).

Wright's deep roots in education grew further. He moved to Philadelphia where he remained active in civil rights giving lectures at the University of Pennsylvania titled "The Negro Problem," which dismissed the notion of Black genetic inferiority. To make his point, Wright skillfully wove science and religion (Wright, 1911). He also wrote a short work about the foundations of Black education and its importance in Georgia (Wright, 1965, p. 19). Into his 90s, Wright continued his active promotion of civil rights when he became unofficial spokesman for African Americans at the United Nations Organization Conference in San Francisco in 1945 (Woodwell, 1985, pp. 365–366).

The Wright family's heritage proves quite stunning. Richard R. Wright Jr. graduated from Georgia State Industrial College then moved to Chicago where he matriculated from the University of Chicago Divinity School in 1904. Now-African Methodist Episcopal (A.M.E.) Bishop Wright Jr. moved to Germany where he studied for two years. He next received a PhD in sociology from the University of Pennsylvania then went on to become president of Wilberforce University in Ohio for five years beginning in 1932 (Modesto, 2004, pp. 69–89).

His daughter, Ruth Wright Hayre accomplished much as well. In high school, she was told she could not take Latin and to forget college (Wright, 1965, p. 141). Nevertheless, she obtained her bachelor's degree from the University of Pennsylvania and a master's degree at age twenty and went on to get her Ph.D. from the same university, making Ruth and her father the first African American father/daughter Ph.D. recipients from the Ivy League institution.

Hayre carried on in education. She first taught at the HBCU Arkansas State College for Negroes, today the University of Arkansas at Monticello. Longing for Philadelphia, she moved back and for over 50 years Hayre ran off a string of firsts for an African American in the Philadelphia public schools—high school teacher, assistant principal, principal, and eventually school superintendent. She retired and joined the Philadelphia Board of Education where she also became the first female chairperson. The legacy continued as Dr. Wright Hayre used her grandfather's quote to start the "Tell Them We are Rising Foundation" where in 1988 she promised 116 sixth graders if they graduated from high school, she would fund their college educations. Seventy students took advantage of the offer. In 1997, she published *Tell Them We Are Rising* that opens with abolitionist poet John Greenleaf Whittier's 1888 poem "Howard at Atlanta" that tells the story of "We Are Rising." Finally, in 2018, Richard R. Wright Sr.'s quote became the basis of a documentary about HBCUs called "We are Rising" (Drezner, 2008, pp. 151–152). African Americans had risen.

RESISTANCE

Educational efforts for freedpeople were often thwarted by violence initiated by White Southerners. According to General Howard, "They [Southern Whites] strive to perpetuate ignorance by burning school-houses, by ostracising [sic.] teachers, by a perpetual effort to establish their theory of absolute inferiority of the Negro; by the very tones of voice they address to him which deny him the right of manhood, by every species of intimidation and opposition, from malicious lying to open blows, often culminating in riot and murder" (Howard, 1865). The general believed resistance to the schools came out of fear from lower class Whites that the Bureau promoted equality (Howard, 1866). Educators of the freedpeople and of course freedpeople themselves regularly faced intimidation, flogging, harassment, and even murder. In 1865, teachers of African Americans in Alabama required military protection (Vaughn, 1974, p. 32). In January 1866, the establishment of schools in the interior of Georgia was halted due to violence. Chief Inspector of Schools J.W. Alvord considered military protection necessary almost everywhere (Vaughn, 1974, pp. 32–33). The *New Orleans Tribune* listed attacks against teachers noting, "The record of the first colored teachers in Louisiana will be one of honor and blood" (New Orleans Tribune, 1866). As late as 1868, General J. J. Reynolds told Howard not to send women, who made up 75 percent of Northern teachers, to Texas because he could not protect them against "outrage or insults" (Reynolds, 1868). Thirty-seven schools were burned in Tennessee in 1869 (Jenkins, 2002). A Northern white teacher of freedpeople in Lafayette Parish, Louisiana, reported, "Twice I have been shot at in my room. The rebels threatened to burn down the school and house in which I board yet they have not materially harmed us. The nearest military protection is 200 miles distant at New Orleans" (Loewen, 2007, p. 194). Howard hoped for congressional action to allay the violence. He wrote to Senator Henry Wilson that racism in the South hindered his abilities to protect freedpeople or carry out educational objectives, "The minds of white men have been so long enslaved by prejudice and habit, that it will require time and education to bring them to a respectable degree of enlightenment" (Howard, 1865). Just before Congress reconvened in December 1865, North Carolina Bureau agent Eliphalet Whittlesey wrote the commissioner calling for more aid to the freedpeople: "The white people…are not yet ready to treat Black men justly. I hope that the Federal Government ought to retain control. Our military force ought to be increased, not reduced. In some districts I could not even safely travel in U. S. uniform. As our troops disappear and bayonets are no longer feared, the hatred of Union men begins to break out. Without a larger military force, it will be impossible to protect our teachers from violence" (Whittlesey, 1865). Despite the violence, Black children went to school. A female missionary teacher in Raleigh wrote: "It is surprising to me to see the amount of suffering which many of the people [freedpeople] endure for the sake of sending their children to school" (Parker, 1869, p. 305).

Despite violence, Jim Crow, racism, and a variety of other hinderances, the post-Civil War education system for African Americans sustained. It was without an expiration date. The real legacy of Reconstruction that stood the test of time is not just racism, bigotry, or an abused race, but a race of people that was denied education on a grand scale for over two hundred years and once they were given a taste of what historian Eric Foner calls a "seemingly unquenchable thirst for education," their thirst could not be halted. (Foner, 2015, p. 43).

Notes

1 Our focus remains on those universities founded in the slaveholding states and the District of Columbia after the Civil War. The Reconstruction period is generally defined 1865–1877, but the founding of major HBCUs preceded the Civil War and continued into the early 20th century.
2 We use White South and White Southerners as African Americans can be Southerners.

REFERENCES:

Anderson, J. (1988). *The education of blacks in the South, 1860–1935*. University of North Carolina Press.

Butchart, R. (2013). *Schooling the freed people: Teaching, learning, and the struggle for black freedom, 1861–1876*. University of North Carolina Press.

Carpenter, J. A. (1999). *Sword and olive branch: Oliver Otis Howard*. Fordham University Press.

Dubois, W. E. B. (1935). *Black Reconstruction: An essay toward a history of the hart which the black folk played in the attempt to reconstruct democracy in America, 1860–1880*. Russell & Russell.

Drezner, N. D. (2008). Ruth Wright Hayre. In H. L. Gates, Jr. and E. B. Higginbotham (Eds.), *African American National Biography* (pp. 151–152). Oxford University Press.

Dunning, W. A. (1907). *Reconstruction, political and economic, 1865–1877*. Harper & Brothers.
Egerton, D. (2015). *The wars of Reconstruction: The brief, violent history of America's most progressive era*. Bloomsbury Press.
Foner, E. (1988). *Reconstruction: America's unfinished revolution*. Harper and Row.
Foner, E. (2002). *Reconstruction: Americas unfinished revolution, 1863–1877*. Harper Perennial.
Foner, E. (2015). *A short history of Reconstruction*. Harper Perennial Modern Classics.
Franklin, J. H. (1994). Reconstruction: After the Civil War. University of Chicago Press.
General Joseph J. Reynolds to Howard, O. O. (Personal Communication) 23 October 1868, BRFAL RG 105, Misc.
Gray, C. (1994). *The Freedmen's Bureau: A missing chapter in social welfare history*. Unpublished doctoral dissertation, New York University.
Hayre, R. W. (1999). *Tell them we are rising: A memoir of faith in education*. John Wiley & Sons, Inc.
Haynes, E. R. (1997). *Unsung heroes; The black boy of Atlanta; Negroes in domestic service in the United States*. G.K. Hall and Co.
Horton, L. E. (1977). *The development of federal social policy for blacks in Washington, D.C., after emancipation*. Unpublished doctoral dissertation, Bradeis University.
Howard, O. O. (1898). *Address before the New England Society*. O. O. Howard Collection, Lincoln Memorial University, Harrogate, TN.
Howard, O. O. (1907). *Autobiography of Oliver Otis Howard, Major general, United States Army* (Vol. II). The Baker and Taylor Company.
Howard, O. O. (n.d.). Original Manuscript—"Education of the colored man". Digital Howard at Howard University. Retrieved January 30, 2022, from https://dh.howard.edu/ooh_manuscripts/7/
Howard, O. O. to Stanton (Personal Communication) 1 November 1866, BRFAL RG 105.
Howard, O. O. *What Others Have Said*. Howard Lecture Program, season 1906-07, O. O. Howard Papers, George J. Mitchell Special Collections and Archives, Hawthorne-Longfellow Library, Bowdoin College, Brunswick, ME. Howard Papers.
Howard, O. O. to Wilson (Personal Communication) 25 November 1865, Howard Papers.
Jenkins, W. L. (2002). *Climbing up to glory: A short history of African Americans during the Civil War and Reconstruction*. Rowman & Littlefield Publishers.
Kreibaum, A. (September 11, 2019). *Trump Asserts New Win for Religious HBCUs*, Inside Higher Education, https://www.insidehighered.com/news/2019/09/11/trump-administration-acts-funding-restrictions-religious-hbcus
Library of Congress. (2022). *Civil War and Reconstruction, 1861–1877* http://www.loc.gov/teachers/classroommaterials/presentationsandactivities/presentations/timeline/civilwar/freedmen/educfree.html
Loewen, J. W. (2007). *Lies my teacher told me: Everything your American history textbook got wrong*. Atria Books.
Logan, R. W. (1969). *Howard University: The first hundred years, 1867–1967*. New York University Press.
Modesto, K. F. (2004). 'Won't be weighted down:' Richard R. Wright Jr.'s contributions to social work and social welfare. *Journal of Sociology and Social Welfare, 31*(2).
Murphy, L. G., Melton, J. G., & Ward, G. L. (Eds.). (1993). *Encyclopedia of African American Religions*. Garland Publishing, Inc.
Myrdal, G. (Ed.). (2009). *An American Dilemma* (Vol. II). Harper and Row.
New Orleans Tribune, September, 5, 1866.

Nichols, J. L., & Crogman, W. H. (1969). *Progress of race.* Arno Press and the New York Times.

Obama, B. speech at Howard University, May 07, 2016. https://obamawhitehouse.archives.gov/the-press-office/2016/05/07/remarks-president-howard-university-commencement-ceremony

Obama, B. speech at Morehouse University, May 19, 2013. https://obamawhitehouse.archives.gov/the-press-office/2013/05/19/remarks-President-Morehouse-College-Commencement-Ceremony

Parker, M. A. (1869, February 22). *The way we lived, 1,* 305.

Schuessler, J. (2015). "Take another look at the Reconstruction era". *New York Times.* https://www.nytimes.com/2015/08/25/arts/park-service-project-would-address-the-reconstruction-era.html

Smith, J. D., & Lowery, J. V. (2013). *The Dunning School: Historians, race, and the meaning of Reconstruction.* University Press of Kentucky.

Vaughn, W. P. (2014). *Schools for all: The blacks and public education in the South, 1865–1877.* University of Kentucky Press.

Whittlesey, E. to Howard, O. O. (Personal Communication) 1 December 1865, Howard Papers.

Woodwell, R. H. (1985). *John Greenleaf Whittier: A biography.* Trustees of the John Greenleaf Whittier Homestead.

Wright Jr, R. (1965). *87 Years behind the black curtain: An autobiography.* Rare Book Co.

Wright Jr, R. (1911). *The negro problem: Being extracted from two lectures on "The sociological point of view in the study of race problem," and "The negro problem; What it is not and what it is".* A. M. E. Book Concern.

Wright Jr, R. (1909). *Self-help in negro education.* Committee of Twelve.

Historically Black Colleges and Universities Lesson Plan Structured

Standards:

D1.1.6-8. Explain how a question represents key ideas in the field.

D2.His.4.6-8. Analyze multiple factors that influenced the perspectives of people during different historical eras.

D2.His.5.6-8. Explain how and why perspectives of people have changed over time.

D3.3.6-8. Identify evidence that draws information from multiple sources to support claims, noting evidentiary limitations.

D4.1.6-8. Construct arguments using claims and evidence from multiple sources, while acknowledging the strengths and limitations of the arguments.

Materials Needed:

- King in the Wilderness Interview https://m.youtube.com/watch?v=qYaGKmsCVjc (watch the first 5 minutes)
- Comparison Images https://api.time.com/wp-content/uploads/2020/06/protests-civil-rights-black-lives-matter-1960-2020.jpg
- March Graphic Novel https://www.penguinrandomhouse.com/series/1MA/march (have students read Book 1 & 2 ahead of time for homework)
- Barack Obama's HBCU Commencement speech https://www.nytimes.com/2020/05/16/us/obama-hbcu-speech-transcript.html

- State of HBCUs https://stateofhbcus.wordpress.com/tag/diane-nash/
- Student handout https://docs.google.com/document/u/0/d/1pVjHxycC9t65jMDCD0DFbQDpjuktyO5IEiHIvWNlU-M/edit

Lesson Duration:
2–3 days (depends if you want to extend the exit slip to a full short response)

After Day 1:
Students will have done:

- Warm Up
- 2 of the Stations.
- Debrief (5–10 minutes)
    - Ask students what shocked them, what made them wonder, what challenged perceived preconceived notions, etc.

After Day 2:
Students will have done:

- Last 2 Stations
- Lesson Closure (5–10 minutes)
    - You can make this exit slip a full or short response depending on if you want to provide extensions.

Lesson Instructions:

Warm Up: 10 minutes

Begin class by asking students about their future plans. Open the dialogue–use this as an opportunity to learn your students' future desires. On the third question, direct the conversation to the benefits of college:

- People want to improve themselves.
- People are exposed to all walks of life and exposed to different perspectives and different life experiences.

Station 1: 20–25 minutes

The instructor will utilize a political cartoon/visual analysis tool in order to make direct comparisons between the two images. The instructor should allow students to examine the images for about 10 minutes in silence (instructor can use this time to check for understanding at the other stations). Instructor will write down what the students see in the picture. Then using the guiding question, derive meaning from the images–drawing conclusions between similarities and differences between the two eras–focus on the signs in the background. In the final 5–7 minutes, the instructor will ask students to think about other questions they still have about these images.

After the allotted time, ask your students to rotate to the next station.

Station 2: 20–25 minutes

The instructor will check for understanding from students at the beginning of the station activity. Students will be expected to read the graphic novels featured in Materials Needed. It is recommended that students are asked to read these assignments beforehand and recap on these ideas in groups.

After the allotted time, ask your students to rotate to the next station.

Station 3: 20–25 minutes
The instructor will check for understanding from students at the beginning of station activity. Students will answer the questions using the videos and article link featured. Students are expected to collaborate with each other in order to get the answer.
After the allotted time, ask your students to rotate to the next station.

Station 4: 20–25 minutes
The instructor will check for understanding from students at the beginning of the station activity. Students will read or listen to Obama's commencement speech using the video or article featured. Students are expected to collaborate with each other in order to get the answer.
After the allotted time, ask your students to rotate to the next station.

Lesson Closure:
Instructor will then ask students to examine Reconstruction and evaluate its value in history citing specific examples from those specific stations. If your students are advanced, you may get rid of the sentence stems so the students can formulate their own arguments.

Historically Black Colleges and Universities Lesson

Purpose: Students will be able to analyze the different voices within the Reconstruction movement and evaluate the success of Reconstruction.

Warm Up: Do you want to go to college? Why or why not? How does attending higher education impact changes in perspectives?

_____
_____

Station 1: Picture Analysis (Based on Comparison Images)
https://api.time.com/wp-content/uploads/2020/06/protests-civil-rights-black-lives-matter-1960-2020.jpg

Image from the March to Washington for Jobs and Freedom on August 28, 1963 (left) and Image from the protest of George Floyd's death in Harlem, New York on May 30, 2020 (right)

Guiding Question: What are the similarities and differences between the two protests?

Observe: What do you see?	Analyze: What does what you see mean? How does it connect to the guiding question?	Questions: What are you still curious about? Construct **ONE** question per image
Left:	Left:	Left:
Right:	Right:	Right:

Station 2: March Graphic Novel Book 1 and Book 2 (https://www.penguinrandomhouse.com/series/1MA/march)
Directions: Read the following graphic novel and answer the following questions.
1. How did the role of education impact John Lewis (Book 1: pp. 35–55)?
2. Why was the older generation less enthused about the decision in *Brown v. Board of Education*? (Book 1: pp. 35–55)
3. Thinking about the warm up, how did exposure to higher education and Jim Lawson impact John Lewis and his classmates? Who were they exposed to that would be foundational to their ideals? (Book 1: pp. 71–80)
4. Why are young college students more ideal candidates for being on the front lines as agents of change than an older man or woman with a young family?
5. What triggered the divide within SNCC?
6. How did the use of technology such as the television, radio, etc. impact the movement?
7. What are other characters' vision for the movement, especially Malcolm X and the new generation of SNCC?

Station 3: State of HBCUs
Directions: Read the following article and watch the videos at the bottom of the page (https://stateofhbcus.wordpress.com/tag/diane-nash/) in order to answer the following questions.
1. Why were HBCUs great places for collaboration?
2. Who impacted Martin Luther King Jr. and his contemporaries?
3. Based on the quotes from Stokely Carmichael and Dr. King, what was the relationship between higher education and the movement? Explain using support from the article.
4. Based on the article and the graphic novel, what did these college students accomplish? Provide at least TWO specific accomplishments.

Station 4: HBCU's Commencement Speech
Directions: Read President Obama's speech in order to answer the following questions. https://www.nytimes.com/2020/05/16/us/obama-hbcu-speech-transcript.html
1. What specific inequalities does Obama highlight in his speech? Provide TWO specific examples.
2. What does Obama believe about the difference between this generation and the previous generation?
3. What are three pieces of advice Obama gives?
4. How do Obama's words of advice reflect the ideals of John Lewis' movement?
5. Based on the speech, were Reconstruction's objectives for equality achieved? Why or why not. Cite specific examples from Obama's speech.

Exit Slip:
Based on the information from modern history and the information from Reconstruction, was the Reconstruction era a success or failure? Cite **TWO** specific examples to support your answer.

Reconstruction was a success/failure because…

_____

For example,

_____

This is significant because it demonstrates...

_____

Furthermore,

_____

This is significant because it demonstrates...

_____

Inquiry Design Model (IDM) Blueprint™		
Compelling Question	How should Reconstruction be viewed, as a success or failure?	
Standards and Practices	D1.1.6-8. Explain how a question represents key ideas in the field. D2.His.4.6-8. Analyze multiple factors that influenced the perspectives of people during different historical eras. D2.His.5.6-8. Explain how and why perspectives of people have changed over time. D3.3.6-8. Identify evidence that draws information from multiple sources to support claims, noting evidentiary limitations. D4.1.6-8. Construct arguments using claims and evidence from multiple sources, while acknowledging the strengths and limitations of the arguments.	
Staging the Question	After the Civil War, America entered a difficult era. The period of Reconstruction saw the end of slavery in America and the beginning of freedoms for people of color. Along with the 13th, 14th, and 15th Amendments, the rise of Freedpeople's education and Historical Black Colleges and Universities (HBCUs) highlight the positive notes of Reconstruction. The Ku Klux Klan, Black Codes/Jim Crow Laws, and the legacy of oppression African Americans endured stained Reconstruction.	
Supporting Question 1	Supporting Question 2	Supporting Question 3
How did access to higher education impact the movement?	What evidence supports the claim that Reconstruction succeeded?	What evidence supports the claim that Reconstruction failed?
Formative Performance Task	Formative Performance Task	Formative Performance Task
Station work including reading a graphic novel and answering questions	Station work analyzing a political cartoon.	After completing station work, using a mind map in order to articulate the successes and failures of the movement.

RECONSTRUCTION'S ACCOMPLISHMENT | 169

Inquiry Design Model (IDM) Blueprint™		
Featured Sources	**Featured Sources**	**Featured Sources**
Look at featured lesson plan	Look at featured lesson plan	Look at featured lesson plan
Summative Performance Task	Argument	Construct a short response arguing the success or failure of Reconstruction
	Extension	Have a syncretic seminar on the movement: How did the differing ideas among black leaders in Reconstruction lead to fracturing within the movement? • March Chapter 3 Graphic Novel • King in the Wilderness Interview https://m.youtube.com/watch?v=qYaGKmsCVjc (watch the first 5 minutes)
Taking Informed Action	Students would gain an understanding about the long-lasting empowerment of Black education and HBCUs that started during Reconstruction and is still continuing to this day.	

Inquiry Design Model (IDM) Blueprint™	
Compelling Question	How should Reconstruction be viewed? As a success or failure?
Standards and Practices	D1.1.6-8. Explain how a question represents key ideas in the field. D2.His.4.6-8. Analyze multiple factors that influenced the perspectives of people during different historical eras. D2.His.5.6-8. Explain how and why perspectives of people have changed over time. D3.3.6-8. Identify evidence that draws information from multiple sources to support claims, noting evidentiary limitations. D4.1.6-8. Construct arguments using claims and evidence from multiple sources, while acknowledging the strengths and limitations of the arguments.

Inquiry Design Model (IDM) Blueprint™		
Staging the Question	After the Civil War, America entered a difficult era. The period of Reconstruction saw the end of slavery in America and the beginning of freedoms for people of color. Along with the 13th, 14th, and 15th Amendments, the rise of Freedpeople's education and Historical Black Colleges and Universities (HBCUs) highlight the positive notes of Reconstruction. The Ku Klux Klan, Black Codes/Jim Crow Laws, and the legacy of oppression African Americans endured and endure stained Reconstruction.	
Supporting Question 1	**Supporting Question 2**	**Supporting Question 3**
What events occurred during the Reconstruction Era?	What evidence supports the claim that Reconstruction failed?	What evidence supports the claim that Reconstruction succeeded?
Formative Performance Task	**Formative Performance Task**	**Formative Performance Task**
Multi-flow Map about the cause and effects of Reconstruction	Bubble map about the failures of Reconstruction	Bubble map about the successes of Reconstruction
Featured Sources	**Featured Sources**	**Featured Sources**
CBS Sunday Morning "The Story of Reconstruction" https://www.youtube.com/watch?v=CjetWrsQb-E	History News Network "Understanding a Political Cartoon: Nast & Reconstruction" https://historynewsnetwork.org/article/179588	PBS "Schools and Education During Reconstruction" https://www.pbs.org/wgbh/americanexperience/features/reconstruction-schools-and-education-during-reconstruction/

RECONSTRUCTION'S ACCOMPLISHMENT | 171

Inquiry Design Model (IDM) Blueprint™		
Summative Performance Task	Argument	Fishbowl discussion supporting if Reconstruction was a failure or a success.
	Extension	Activity: Concentric circles about how the effects of Reconstruction are still relevant today. Additional Resources: Time Magazine "How Reconstruction Still Shapes American Racism" https://time.com/5562869/reconstruction-history/ Facing History and Ourselves "Using Reconstruction to Understand Today's Racial Tension" https://facingtoday.facinghistory.org/using-reconstruction-to-understand-todays-racial-tensions
Taking Informed Action	Students would gain an understanding about the long-lasting empowerment of Black Education and HBCUs that started during Reconstruction and is still continuing to this day.	
Additional Resources	Link to a Google Doc that explains the multi-flow map, the bubble maps, instructions for the fishbowl discussion, and the guidelines for the concentric circles. https://docs.google.com/ document/d/e/2PACX-1vQTCXkkmCPr6wcE v5Lnon7MtGAQKI-3jwFAUOvBXtAZM7 paPYRQZYT8p6BIBk2Y3uk3M zdrNmm0xurs/pub	

CHAPTER NINE

"There Is No Redemption from Our History": Reconstruction, Memorialization, and Public Memory

MARK PEARCY
Rider University

On the 75th anniversary of World War II, the president of Germany, Frank-Walter Steinmeier, invoked the importance of collective memory in German cultural life: "there is no end to remembering…There is no redemption from our history" (Tharoor, 2020). This idea—that history lives with us—means that it is the product (and subject) of ongoing debate, especially in our classrooms. While Germany continues a public reckoning with its actions in World War II and the Holocaust even today, the United States may be just beginning down a similar path, in collectively accounting for our nation's sins, omissions, and crimes—especially slavery. In our public memory, the Civil War is the singular event that reunited a fractious country and moved us away from the threat of violent secession. In truth, however, it was the failure of Reconstruction, following the war, which has kept the U.S. from meaningfully reconciling its past with our ideals.

Part of this failure is present today, in our public memory. Two different nations, America and Germany, have taken different paths to memorializing their separate histories, and their respective "memory cultures" represent distinct acts of collective historicization. Teachers can benefit from an understanding of these cultures, as well as how we can employ make use of memorials teach about reconciliation after the Civil War and Reconstruction, and more notably, our failure to fully achieve it.

MEMORIALS, MONUMENTS, AND MEMORY

There are markers scattered across America, in nearly every town, city, and state. These represent what Doss (2011) described as the process of "how, and why, cultural memory is created, and how it shapes local and national authority" (p. 27). For teachers, monuments "provide opportunities for student learning and engagement," the type of which is difficult to replicate inside a comparatively sterile classroom (Marcus & Levine, 2010, p. 131). And, too, monuments represent a particular value beyond other historically or socially relevant sites—they are generally free to visit (p. 132).

There is also a significant artistic element which other historical sites—e.g., a battlefield—can't or don't generally present. For instance, in 2018, the city of Chattanooga, Tennessee, selected an artist named Jerome Meadows to create a work of public art memorializing the victims of lynching in the American South—specifically, a Black man named Ed Johnson who was hanged from Chattanooga's Walnut Street Bridge by a mob in 1906. Meadows' work represents Johnson and his two attorneys, Noah Parden and Styles Hutchins (Moody, 2021). See https://www.edjohnsonproject.com.

The memorial shows Johnson stepping out of a noose placed on the ground; the figures themselves have distended, almost unnatural physical dimensions, meant to represent, according to Meadows, the three themes of grace, courage, and compassion. Meadows describes his artistic choices by stating:

> I prefer artwork that is more poetic than prose, that engages you to draw from yourself, but forms that challenge you to think, *what is that supposed to be?* Ed's arms are a bit exaggerated because he was a laborer. Noah [Parden]…is standing like a warrior. He's looking at the bridge so his vision is fixed. Noah is courage. Styles [Hutchins] is compassion. He's reaching, except for the fact that he couldn't hold on to Ed (Moody, 2021).

These aesthetic elements present students and teachers with a rare opportunity—to analyze not just the geographic presence of a historically relevant event, but an artistic interpretation of that event and its importance. In this, memorials and monuments are unique, and intrinsically interdisciplinary (Uhrmacher & Tinkler, 2007, para. 2).

It is worth considering exactly what we mean with these terms, *monument* and *memorial*. Though they may seem synonymous, there are distinctions that are important to keep in mind, when examining them. Savage (2007) describes the process of commemoration which produces them, the marking of "an event or a person or a group by a ceremony or an observance or a monument of some kind" (p. 2). Johnson (2001) considers a monument to aspire to be "eternal and unchanging…[standing] for that which made all things possible," like the Washington Monument in the nation's capital; while a "memorial" like the national shrine to Abraham Lincoln is a depiction of a "martyr" which is meant to "inspire awe," in spite of its "palpable aura of death" (p. 4).

Other descriptions are less lyrical—the Southern Poverty Law Center describes a monument simply as a "stone object that cannot be easily removed" (SPLC, 2019). Monument Lab (2021), a nonprofit art and history studio working in collaboration with the Andrew W. Mellon Foundation, produced a *National Monument Audit* that categorizes the number and variety of public markers in the U.S., describes a "monument" as "statues or monoliths constructed with stone or metal, installed or maintained in a public space with the authority of a government agency or institution—as well as nonconventional monument objects like buildings, bridges, streets, historical markers, and place names" (p. 9). More powerfully and evocatively, the *Audit* describes a monument in a manner that illustrates its outsized role in public memory—it is a "statement of power and presence in public" (p. 4).

It is the stolidity of these monuments that present a challenge to teachers who wish to utilize them as pedagogical resources. Savage (1999) points out that the presence of a monument in a public space can create around it a sense that history is settled, and that any debate around it has receded: "public monuments…instill a sense of historical closure," a "process of condensing the moral lessons of history and fixing them in place for all time" (p. 1). Beyond the imposing structure of many classically-defined markers, it is this sense that can lead to a collective passivity in considering whether or not they still represent history—and whose.

In the recent past, there has been an accelerating movement towards the reconsideration of memorials and monuments in public space, as well as their removal. Statues of Confederate icons like Stonewall Jackson, Robert E. Lee, and Jefferson Davis have been taken down in a number of southern states ("Recent Confederate Monument Removals," 2020). This has created the opportunity for teachers to engage in critical and timely debate with their students about the fate of these markers; but also, it should require a deeper exploration of how these monuments were proposed, designed, and installed, and whose narratives were privileged before their eventual dislocation. This means that teachers need to help students investigate the proliferation of memorials across the United States in the years after the Civil War, as well as the agenda of those supporting that proliferation. Their presence, and ubiquity, points to a distressing element of the era of Reconstruction—the embedding of a "memory culture" dedicated to oppression, racial supremacy, and the consolidation of white political power.

CONFEDERATE MEMORIALS IN THE UNITED STATES

In the years after the Civil War, there were comparatively few markers posted in remembrance of the conflict and its casualties. It wasn't until the end of

Reconstruction, in 1877, that Southern states—newly "freed" from government oversight and governed by "Redeemers" intent on erasing postwar changes—began to see a massive expansion of pro-Confederate memorials. These memorials, endorsed and funded by groups like the United Daughters of the Confederacy, whose primary goal was to "achieve vindication for its Confederate ancestors, men and women, whom UDC members believed had defended a 'just' cause, namely states' rights and white supremacy, during the Civil War" (Cox, 1997, pp. 1–2). These memorials represent a revisionist view of the war and the Reconstruction era, as well as an act of collective public memory.

In fact, it is jarring how the very presence of these memorials across the U.S. indicates a general willingness to accept the historical legitimacy of the Confederacy, a short-lived political entity that was explicitly dedicated to the institution of slavery. Frederick Douglass, in 1871, decried the efforts of those who would ask Americans, "in the name of patriotism to forget the merits" of the Civil War, "and to remember with equal admiration those who struck at the nation's life, and those who struck to save it—those who fought for slavery and those who fought for liberty and justice" (Blight, 2018, p. 521).

The United Daughters of the Confederacy were widely successful in their efforts—in the first two decades of the 20th century, over 400 monuments were erected to Confederate leaders, soldiers, and at Civil War battlefields (particularly Southern victories). This first wave of memorialization was implicitly dedicated to the overall revisionist view of the South as a bucolic and largely peaceful domain, whose traditional ways of life were disrupted by rapacious Northern invaders.

Consider, for example, the "Silent Sam" statue at the University of North Carolina. The statue was bequeathed by the UDC and erected in 1913, dedicated to "the sons of the University who died for their beloved Southland, 1861-1865" ("Confederate Monument," 2004). The statue earned its nickname because the soldier, as depicted, isn't carrying an ammunition belt. See https://museum.unc.edu/exhibits/show/civilwar/silent-sam. Though defenders of such memorials may argue (and frequently do) that the markers represent a blend of regional pride and mythic nostalgia, it is impossible to deny what they generally meant at the time of their construction. At the dedication of "Silent Sam" in 1913, a speech was given by a member of the University Board of Trustees, Julian Carr, who reminisced fondly about the exploits of Confederate soldiers in defending "the welfare of the Anglo-Saxon race," as well as the "pleasing duty" he had performed on the UNC campus after his own return from war—the whipping of a "negro wench until her skirts hung in shreds because she had maligned and insulted a Southern lady [.]" (Carr, 1913, p. 9). The statue's dedication, in effect, was a paean to both white supremacy and racial violence.

The "Silent Sam" statue at the University of North Carolina was one of the first memorials to be the subject of the current wave of activism—in 2018, protesters gathered around the marker's base and pulled the statue down, and ultimately the university removed the base, as well, which had featured a commemorative plaque dedicated to UNC students who fought for the Confederacy (Thomason, 2018; Jacobs, 2019; Svrluga, 2019). At the time, such incidents were comparatively rare, and singular in nature—a fact which distorted the reality of pro-Confederate memorialization across the U.S. South after the Civil War. Between 1920 and 1940, there was a second wave of monument-building, again spurred and advocated by groups like the UDC. Rather than trying to memorialize the "Lost Cause" ethos, this effort was meant to undercut the increasing calls for the restoration and defense of Black Americans' civil rights. To that point, a considerable number of these statues and markers were erected, ominously, on the grounds of local courthouses (Judt, 2019, para. 1). Federal installations, too, were named after Confederate icons—ten military bases, specifically (Thompson, 2015; Petraeus, 2020). According to the Southern Poverty Law Center, as of 2019 there were almost 800 memorials or monuments to the Confederacy in the United States (SPLC, 2019). According to Monument Lab's national audit (2021), there are at present almost 60 monuments dedicated to Robert E. Lee, placing him just behind figures like Abraham Lincoln, George Washington, and Martin Luther King, Jr. (p. 12).

The proliferation of these monuments from the late 1860s to the 1940s represents a willful assembling of a "memory culture," one dedicated to a racial hierarchy and the suppression of political/cultural/legal efforts to achieve equality of opportunity for Black Americans. Though there have been multiple examples in recent years of such markers being reconsidered or relocated, their continued presence throughout the U.S.—and the often ferocious resistance to their removal on the part of their defenders—signals that this "culture" will be difficult to completely dislodge.

GERMANY AND *ERINNERUNGSKULTUR*

In contrast, post-World War II Germany underwent its own form of public memorialization. The German concept of *erinnerungskultur* ("memory culture") is built on the premise that contentious history must be central in German public life, to ensure a steady and effective reckoning with the events that inspired memorialization. See https://www.visitberlin.de/en/kaiser-wilhelm-memorial-church. The Kaiser Wilhelm Memorial Church in western Berlin is known by its nickname: *der hohle Zahn*, "the hollow tooth." It was badly damaged in an Allied bombing raid in 1943, and after the war, was never repaired. Its continued presence in Germany today is a reminder of the brutality and widespread destruction of World War II, and it is also representative of a conceptual distinction between types of memorials in German culture.

There are essentially two different types of memorials—*denkmals* and *mahnmals*. The former is from the German word *denken*, "to think," and refers to memorials that are meant to evoke remembrance of a particular event or person—essentially, "a testament to something on which we have a duty to reflect" (Russell, 2013, para. 4). A *denkmal* is meant to "justify" a historical event (even a traumatizing one) in order to "redeem it historically," if possible (Young, 1999, p. 2). *Mahnmals* (taken from the word *mahnen*, "to admonish"), on the other hand, are warnings, against action that resulted in shameful conduct, wrongdoing, or crimes—taking the idea of "never again," according to Russell (2013), and "[giving] it shape" (para. 5).

"The hollow tooth," in effect, is both a *denkmal* and a *mahnmal*—a remembrance of a historical event on which we are meant to reflect, but also a warning about the actions of the Nazi regime which precipitated the war's devastation. In postwar Germany, the presence of *mahnmals*, and their role in German "memory culture," is the element that is conspicuously missing from post-Reconstruction American history.

Every year in Berlin, residents take part in something called the "Annual Day of the Open Monument" (*Tag des offenen Denkmals*), part of European Heritage Days ("Open Monument Day," 2021). On this day, the second Sunday in September, more than 7,500 historical monuments, parks and archaeological sites open their doors to visitors. The event has been held since 1993 and is coordinated nationwide by the German Foundation for Monument Protection, under the auspices of the federal government ("Tag des Offenen Denkmals," 2021). The idea behind this event—that memory culture is a collective act, one which requires a mass commitment—is certainly derived from the traumatic history of Germany through the 20th century and the continued national dialogue about how to remember—and to atone—for the nation's actions.

What has resulted, in Germany, is the proliferation of memorials which are unique, and for an American audience, incongruous. Consider, for instance, the *Monument Onbekende Deserteurs Duitse Wehrmacht*, (the "Memorial to Unknown Deserters of the German Wehrmacht") in Erfurt, Germany. See https://www.petersberg-erfurt.de/en/places-of-interest/interactive-map. The sculpture depicts eight pillars, seven of which are identical—one is turned slightly, representing a soldier who breaks formation and refuses what, in the artist's eyes, was an immoral act. The main inscription of the piece reads: To the unknown Wehrmacht deserter. To the victims of Nazi military justice. To all those who refused to serve the Nazi regime." This is accompanied by a quotation from the author Gunter Eich: "be the sand, not the oil in the works of the world" (Welch, 2012, p. 393).

The idea of a memorial to deserters—to soldiers who broke their oaths and pledges of loyalty to the nation, refusing to submit to moral outrages—is difficult to imagine in the U.S. This is particularly so when teachers and students consider the differences between German and American memory culture. For Germany, the act of memorialization was also an act of national contrition, after the horrors of World War II and the genocide of the Holocaust. It was also an act of reconciliation, as postwar generations tried publicly to reconcile the nation's identity with its collective guilt.

It is interesting to contrast German memorials from World War I with their post-1945 equivalents. Wheatcroft (2014) points out that monuments from that earlier conflict were "not so much mournful as defiant," some listing the names of war dead and concluding "not one too many died for the Fatherland." The memorial to students of the University of Berlin who died in combat carries the inscription "*Invictis Victi Victuri*," which oracular and ambiguous words could possibly be taken to mean, "To the unconquered from the conquered, who will themselves conquer" (Wheatcroft, 2014). This approach to memorialization was radically different from the post-World War II approach, and bears, in fact, a great deal of similarity to America's historical attempts to reconcile our myth with our history after the Civil War. The *erinnerungskultur* of the United States has been built on a geographic division, between North and South. During and after Reconstruction, Southerners could use war memorials as objects of pride, while Northerners could view them as a necessary evil, a way to allow former enemies to salve their pride and rejoin the Union (Arellano-Fryer, 2017).

TEACHING ABOUT (AND WITH) MEMORIALS

It would understandable if teachers resisted this line of inquiry, given how political pressure, in recent years, has increased around the country, as some states have enacted new limitations as to what can be taught, and when (Gross, 2022; Schwartz, 2021). The political environment is currently tumultuous for social studies educators—however, as every veteran teacher knows, what actually goes on in the classroom is entirely the purview of the individual educator in the room, and justifiably so (Thornton, 1991). What teachers need, then, is not just a mindset aimed at, for lack of a better word, subverting political agendas that try to limit our choices; they also need pedagogical strategies to accomplish that subversion (Mitsakos & Ackerman, 2009).

Teachers can make ready use of memorials as resources and as pedagogical tools. Essentially, any analysis of a monument, as the result of the process of memorialization, revolves around these central questions:

(1) Whose stories are told?
(2) Whose stories are privileged (which group's story is justified or vindicated by the memorial), and whose are minimized?

(3) To what purpose or for what reason?
(4) What does the process of memorialization, in this case, indicate about the society that produced it?

The final question, in referencing the "process of memorialization," refers to how we make use of public spaces as a form of shared memory. Marcus and Levine (2010) see such questions as part of a general inquiry into "who [we are] as Americans…what aspects of our heritage are important to remember, celebrate, and memorialize?" (p. 131) This inquiry is especially vital in the U.S. where the legacy of institutionalized discrimination is still felt, and where it is equally important for teachers to "commit to confronting racism and equipping our students to do the same" (Hawley & Jordan, 2017).

Below I outline two pedagogical approaches that teachers can employ in teaching about memorialization: **referent/design/reception** and the process of **reconciliation**.

REFERENT/DESIGN/RECEPTION

Uhrmacher and Tinkler (2007) recommend a three-stage framework in which students consider the following questions (para. 12–14):

- **Referent** (whose story does the monument tell?)
- **Design** (how does the memorial tell its story?)
- **Reception** (how does it affect us?)

What is most useful about this framework is that it encourages students to move beyond a straightforward critical appraisal of the memorial and its message. It also allows students to critique the aesthetic choices of the designer, as well as the degree to which those choices impact the viewer—to see, in other words, how "artistic representations characterize a particular interpretation of that person or event" (Uhrmacher & Tinkler, 2007, para. 14).

Students can consider, for instance, the Confederate memorial at Stone Mountain, Georgia. See https://www.atlantahistorycenter.com/monument/. The sculpture of three Confederate military figures—Robert E. Lee, Thomas J. "Stonewall" Jackson, and Jefferson Davis—was first proposed in 1914, but was not finished until 1954, when Marvin Griffin, a gubernatorial candidate, picked up the cause as a protest to the recent Supreme Court ruling in *Brown v. Board of Education* and the order to desegregate schools (Pratt & Rojas, 2021). That the memorial was meant to be central to Southern iconography is clear; the park even officially opened on April 14, 1965, one hundred years to the day after the assassination of Abraham Lincoln (McKinney, 2018).

Students can consider the memorial using the three-stage framework described above. For *referent,*, it is clear whose story is being told—that of white Southerners, especially advocates of the "Lost Cause" myth around Confederate valor and self-defense (McKinney, 2018). From a *design* standpoint, the depiction of Lee, Jackson, and Davis, represents the largest bas-relief sculpture in the world, and the mere scale of the monument infers the artist's perception of his subject. Finally, students can debate *reception*—how does this monument affect us? Whether or not a memorial is "effective" is, of course, not the same thing as "good"—but a veteran teacher will surely steer the analysis towards the deeper question of whether or not a given monument is reflective of the society we want to have, moving forward.

RECONCILIATION

A second process teachers can adopt in analyzing monuments is that of *reconciliation*—asking students, in effect, to reconcile the monument as a public work with our contemporary beliefs and historical fact. The process of truth and reconciliation has been practiced by nations in the wake of mass trauma, such as Uganda and South Africa (Asghar et al., 2013); after the murder of George Floyd in Minnesota in 2020, a national commission was proposed to "examine the effects of slavery, institutional racism, and discrimination against people of color, and how our history impacts laws and policies today" (Lee, 2020). In effect, all such initiatives are derived from the idea that a full accounting of crimes, mistakes, and wrongdoing is essential for a society to fully heal itself.

Students can emulate this process with memorials and monuments, investigating why they were built, to whose benefit (and whose detriment), and what should be done with them, if anything. Any such investigation can result in one of the four conclusions below (Asghar et al., 2013, p. 4):

- **Removal**: the monument is permanently moved from public view.
- **Retention**: the monument stays in place, unaffected or unchanged.
- **Reformulation**: the monument is changed or reconceptualized, to present a different perspective or to rectify a historic wrong

For many students, removal may seem like the most effective and desirable option. Probably the most infamous of these memorials, The Robert E. Lee statue in Charlottesville, Virginia, was commissioned in 1917 and erected seven years later (see Figure 7) See https://www.nytimes.com/2017/08/13/us/charlottesville-rally-protest-statue.html.

When the statue was dedicated in 1924, speakers praised Lee as the embodiment of "the moral greatness of the Old South," and a proponent of reconciliation with the Union, while the Civil War was characterized as a battle over divergent views of the Constitution and "ideals of democracy," rather than a war over slavery (Appelbaum, 2017, para. 7; Woodley, 2017, para. 9). In 2017, those divergent views were on display in a more horrifying manner—the white nationalist "Unite the Right" rally was held in Charlottesville to protest the proposed removal of the statue (Forten, 2017). What resulted was violence, rioting, and the death of a pedestrian, when a white nationalist intentionally drove his car into a crowd of protesters (Heim, 2017).

Given the circumstances of the Lee statue's creation, and the violence associated with it in more recent years, it would be expected for students to conclude that removal is the only acceptable option. And, in fact, that is what happened—in the summer of 2021, the statue was removed. The city's mayor, Nikuyah Walker, commemorated the event by stating that "taking down this statue is one small step closer to the goal of helping Charlottesville, Virginia, and America, grapple with the sin of being willing to destroy Black people for economic gain" (Paviour, 2021). Similarly, the larger statue of Robert E. Lee was removed from Richmond, Virginia's Monument Avenue, in September 2021 (Schneider & Vozzella, 2021). However, teachers can ask students to consider more diverse cases and options. Consider, for instance, the Confederate Soldier Memorial in Denton, Texas (Davis, 2015; Martinez, 2015). Erected in 1918, and displayed in front of the county courthouse, the statue was vandalized in 2015 with the words "this is racist". See https://www.dallasnews.com/news/crime/2015/07/21/video-shows-pair-vandalizing-confederate-monument-in-denton/.

Given the anger that this memorial clearly engendered, it might seem obvious to students that it simply has to go. However, teachers can then present students with the decision ultimately agreed upon by the citizens of Denton—rather than being destroyed, the statue was moved to a museum adjacent to the courthouse and put under the control of the Texas Historical Commission. Additionally, historical context was to be added to the display—about the history of American slavery, its role as the primary cause of the Civil War, and a description of the African-American experience at the time of the monument's construction (Harper, 2021).

Is this the right decision? Certainly, the examples of the two Lee statues show that removal has the support of many in contemporary society—according to the Southern Poverty Law Center, over 160 Confederate symbols and markers were removed in 2020, more than in the previous four years combined (Vigdor & Victor, 2021). According to the same report, however, there are still more than 2100 Confederate symbols (including 704 monuments) still standing throughout the U.S., a seemingly permanent reminder of the failures of Reconstruction to establish a lasting racial reconciliation in the United States (SPLC, 2019).

This reality is also evident in the lingering misapprehensions about the Civil War, its causes and aftereffects. A 2019 national poll showed that just over half

(52%) of respondents thought slavery was the main cause of the war, while 42% thought it was "another reason." According to the same poll, though, 67% of the public said the legacy of slavery was still affecting American society today (Gaskin, Clement, & Heim, 2019). This is, oddly, encouraging, in that it means the opportunity exists to cement that knowledge with our students—the fact that the legacy of the war, and that of Reconstruction, remain to be dealt with.

It is interesting to hear critics of these efforts bemoan what they characterize as efforts to "erase" history (Allison, 2020; Morris, 2020), when, by correcting a faulty historical narrative, it's fair to say that, as a nation, we are in the process of "making" history (Perry, 2017). And the U.S. has a long history of reconsidering memorials and statues and whether or not they should remain standing—most notably, after World War II, when the Allied powers issued the "Denazification Directive 30" (Dessem, 2017). Directive 30 prohibited the creation or display of any marker "which tends to preserve and keep alive the German military tradition, to revive militarism or to commemorate the Nazi Party." The directive also commanded that "every existing monument, poster, statue, edifice, street, or highway name marker, emblem, tablet or insignia" that commemorated Nazism "must be completely destroyed and liquidated," along with all military museums and exhibitions (Office of Military Government for Germany, 1948, p. 30).

There may validity to the notion that this directive, and others like it, paved the way for postwar Germany to assemble a new version of *erinnerungskultur,* one which was built around reconciliation and remonstrance. Still, just as the U.S. deals with historical revisionism and denial about Reconstruction, Germans contend today with right-wing nationalism and Holocaust denialism (Courbet, 2020), as well as a rejection of what younger people consider a culture of "German angst and pessimism" about their past (Marinic, 2018). To combat this, one state legislator, Sawsan Chebli, proposed a law that would make visits to Nazi concentration camps mandatory for all citizens. Her argument represented the essential idea of a "memory culture"—"this is about who we are as a country... We need to make our history relevant for everyone: Germans who no longer feel a connection to the past and immigrants who feel excluded from the present" (Bennhold, 2018).

A similar spirit among Americans is present in the National Memorial for Peace and Justice, in Montgomery, Alabama, a powerful monument to one of the least-explored examples of racial violence in the U.S.—lynching. See https://legacysites.eji.org/about/memorial/ or https://www.nytimes.com/2018/04/25/us/lynching-memorial-alabama.html.

The main structure of the memorial is long, with a sloped floor, where 816 steel slabs hang from the ceiling, each one representing an African-American lynching victim. The floor inclines farther down as visitors move through the building, until eventually the slabs are suspended at head level. This powerful reminder of the horror of racial violence is also rooted in a kind of "memory culture"—as the Equal Justice Initiative (the organization behind the memorial) describes it, "A history of racial injustice must be acknowledged, and mass atrocities and abuse must be recognized and remembered, before a society can recover from mass violence. Public commemoration plays a significant role in prompting community-wide reconciliation" (EJI, 2018).

What is singularly shocking about the failure of Reconstruction to help create this sense of national reconciliation is the frequency of lynching during the postwar era—rather than being used as a tool of vigilante justice, lynching was used almost exclusively as a tool of racial terror and subjugation. According to the EJI's report, *Lynching in America* (2015), the ratio of African-American lynching victims to white lynching victims "was 4 to 1 from 1882 to 1889; increased to more than 6 to 1 between 1890 and 1900; and soared to more than 17 to 1 after 1900."

Teachers have a singular role in promoting an active "memory culture" in their classrooms, particularly with regard to how we, as a nation, have largely failed to reconcile our past with the present. Even addressing memorials with a seemingly benign origin can provide opportunities to develop this understanding. The Freedmen's Memorial in Washington, D.C., for instance, was erected in 1876 and was meant to commemorate Abraham Lincoln's signing of the Emancipation Proclamation (Kavi, 2020). Though the money for the memorial was raised by former enslaved persons, they had no input on the memorial's design, which ultimately featured a newly freed slave kneeling at the feet of Lincoln. See https://www.nps.gov/places/000/emancipation-memorial.htm.

Though certainly the motivation behind this memorial was benign, it was controversial even in its own day—Frederick Douglass criticized it, saying "What I want to see before I die is a monument representing the Negro, not couchant [submissive on the ground] on his knees like a 4-footed animal, but erect on his feet like a man" (White & Sandage, 2020). Today, many African-Americans reject the design out of hand—one man said, "When I look at that statue, I'm reminded my freedom and my liberation is only dictated by white peoples' terms" (Kavi, 2020).

CONCLUSION: "A STEADY RESTORATION OF THE NATION'S HUMANITY"

In 1869, Robert E. Lee urged Americans to move past the war, if possible: "I think it wiser, moreover, not to keep open the sores of war but to follow the examples of those nations who endeavored to obliterate the marks of civil strife, to commit to oblivion the feelings engendered" (Desjardins, 2017). This quotation, which has been used regularly by Lee's defenders to argue for his role as a conciliator, instead points to the abiding flaw in America's memorialization of war, reconstruction, and history—our failure to fully reckon with what led to the Civil War, and how we had failed to address those causes in the postwar era.

Marcus and Levine (2010) ask the question at the heart of every national memorial or monument: "who are we as Americans? What aspects of our heritage are important to remember, celebrate, and memorialize?" (p. 131).The failures of Reconstruction were political, economic, and social, and still with us today. Teachers can help confront these failures in their classroom through the process of monument reconciliation. In so doing, we risk uncovering painful stories, events, and trauma, but with the possibility of what Nelson Mandela described after the fall of apartheid in South Africa: "If the pain has often been unbearable and the revelations shocking to all of us, it is because they indeed bring us the beginnings of a common understanding of what happened and a steady restoration of the nation's humanity" ("Statement by Nelson Mandela on receiving Truth and Reconciliation Commission Report," 1998).

REFERENCES:

Allison, N. (2020, July 9). Capitol Commission approves moving Nathan Bedford Forrest bust to Tennessee State Museum. *The Tennessean*. Retrieved from https://www.tennessean.com/story/news/politics/2020/07/09/tennessee-capitol-commission-votes-remove-nathan-bedford-forrest-bust/5380243002/

Appelbaum, Y. (2017). Take the statues down. *The Atlantic Monthly*. Retrieved from https://www.theatlantic.com/politics/archive/2017/08/take-the-statues-down/536727/

Arellano-Fryer, L. (2017). The north's role in supplying the south with Confederate monuments. Retrieved from https://hyperallergic.com/384776/the-norths-role-in-supplying-the-south-with-confederate-monuments/

Asghar, F., Ghimire, S., von Hatzfeldt, S., Jakubowska, K., King, F., Krasniewski, M., and Maib, E. (2013). Transitional justice—Reconciliation talks: A simulation for use in youth and adult education. *Humanity in Action*. Retrieved from https://www.humanityinaction.org/

Banks, J. A. (2010). Approaches to multicultural curricular reform. In J. A. Banks & C. A. McGee Banks (Eds.), *Multicultural education: Issues and perspectives, 7th edition* (pp. 233-256). Wiley.

Bennhold, K. (2018, March 11). "Never again": Fighting hate in a changing Germany with tours of Nazi camps. *The New York Times*, March 11, 2018. Retrieved from https://www.nytimes.com/2018/03/11/world/europe/germany-anti-semitism.html?smprod=nytcore-ipad&smid=nytcore-ipad-share

Blight, D. (2018). *Frederick Douglass: Prophet of freedom*. New York: Simon & Schuster.

Carr, J. (1913, June 2). Unveiling of Confederate monument at university, June 2, 1913. Retrieved from https://exhibits.lib.unc.edu/files/original/c1160e4341b86794b7e842cb042fb414.pdf

"Confederate Monument" (Silent Sam). (2004). The Graduate School at the University of North Carolina. Retrieved from https://gradschool.unc.edu/funding/gradschool/weiss/interesting_place/landmarks/sam.html

Courbet, D. (2020). "Visitors are questioning the truth": Germany's Holocaust memorial sites fight new threat from far-right. Retrieved from https://www.thelocal.de/20200414/visitors-are-questioning-the-truth-holocaust-memorial-sites-fight-new-threat-from-far-right

Cox, K. L. (1997). Women, the lost cause, and the new south: The United Daughters of the Confederacy and the transmission of Confederate culture, 1894–1919. (Unpublished doctoral dissertation). University of Southern Mississippi, Hattiesburg, MS.

Davis, T. L. (2015). Denton Confederate memorial vandalized overnight. *NBCDFW.* Retrieved from https://www.nbcdfw.com/news/local/denton-confederate-monument-vandalized-overnight/1983826/

Desjardins, L. (2017). Robert E. Lee opposed Confederate memorials. *PBS NewsHour.* Retrieved from https://www.pbs.org/newshour/nation/robert-e-lee-opposed-confederate-monuments

Dessem, M. (2017). How did we treat monuments to white supremacists when they weren't *our* white supremacists? *Slate.* Retrieved from https://slate.com/culture/2017/08/read-the-allied-order-to-destroy-nazi-monuments-in-germany.html

Doss, E. L. (2011). Remembering 9/11: Memorials and cultural memory. *OAH Magazine of History, 25* (3), 27–30.

Downs, G. & Masur, K. (2015). *The world the Civil War made.* University of North Carolina Press.

Equal Justice Initiative. (EJI) (2015). *Lynching in America: Confronting the legacy of racial terror.* Retrieved from https://legacysites.eji.org/about/memorial/

Equal Justice Initiative. (EJI) (2018). The National Memorial for Peace and Justice. Retrieved from https://museumandmemorial.eji.org/memorial

Fortin, J. (2017, August 13). The statue at the center of Charlottesville's storm. *The New York Times.* Retrieved from https://www.nytimes.com/2017/08/13/us/charlottesville-rally-protest-statue.html

Gaskin, E., Clement, S., & Heim, J. (2019, August 28). Americans show spotty knowledge about the history of slavery but acknowledge its enduring effects. *The Washington Post.* Retrieved from https://www.washingtonpost.com/education/2019/08/28/americans-show-spotty-knowledge-about-history-slavery-acknowledge-its-enduring-effects/

Gross, T. (2022). From slavery to socialism, new legislation restricts what teachers can discuss. National Public Radio. Retrieved from https://www.npr.org/2022/02/03/1077878538/legislation-restricts-what-teachers-can-discuss

Harper, D. (2021). Denton County courthouse Confederate monument moving inside to Town Square Museum. *NBCDFW.* Retrieved from https://www.nbcdfw.com/news/local/denton-county-courthouse-confederate-monument-moving-inside-to-town-square-museum/2607739/

Hawley, T. S., & Jordan, A. W. (2017). Discussing "Dixie"—A teachable moment. *The Bitter Southerner.* Retrieved from http://bittersoutherner.com/from-the-southern-perspective/education/discussing-dixie-a-teachable-moment

Heim, J. (2017, August 14). Recounting a day of rage, hate, violence and death. *The Washington Post.* Retrieved from https://www.washingtonpost.com/graphics/2017/local/charlottesville-timeline/?utm_term=.9e32125def80

Jacobs, J. (2019, January 15). U.N.C. chancellor to leave early after ordering removal of "Silent Sam" statue's base. *The New York Times.* Retrieved from https://www.nytimes.com/2019/01/15/us/silent-sam-statue-removal-unc.html

Johnson, S. (2001). Political not patriotic: Democracy, civic space, and the American memorial/monument complex. *Theory & Event*, 5(2). DOI: 10.1353/tae.2001.0012.

Judt, D. (2019). Atlanta's Civil War monument, minus the pro-Confederate bunkum. *The Atlantic*. Retrieved from https://www.theatlantic.com/ideas/archive/2019/03/how-atlanta-cyclorama-lost-its-confederate-overtone/584938/

Kavi, A. (2020, June 27). Activists push for removal of statue of freed slave kneeling before Lincoln. *The New York Times*, June 27, 2020. Retrieved from https://www.nytimes.com/2020/06/27/us/politics/lincoln-slave-statue-emancipation.html

Lee, B. (2020). *In the wake of COVID-19 and murder of George Floyd, Congresswoman Barbara Lee calls for formation of Truth, Racial Healing, and Transformation Commission* [Press release]. Retrieved from https://lee.house.gov/news/press-releases/in-the-wake-of-covid-19-and-murder-of-george-floyd-congresswoman-barbara-lee-calls-for-formation-of-truth-racial-healing-and-transformation-commission

Marcus, A. S., & Levine, T. H. (2010). Remember the Alamo? Learning history with monuments and memorials. *Social Education*, 74(3), 131–134.

Marinic, J. (2018, November 13). Germany's real political divide is generational. *The New York Times*. Retrieved from https://www.nytimes.com/2018/11/13/opinion/germany-baby-boomers-young-voters.html

Martinez, K. (2015). Confederate memorial in Denton vandalized. *KERA News*. Retrieved from https://www.keranews.org/news/2015-07-20/confederate-memorial-in-denton-vandalized

McKinney, D. (2018). Stone Mountain: A monumental dilemma. *Intelligence Report* (Southern Poverty Law Center), Spring 2018.

Mitsakos, C. L., & Ackerman, A. T. (2009). Teaching social studies as a subversive activity. *Social Education*, 73(1), 40–42.

Monument Lab. (2021). *National monument audit*. Andrew W. Mellon Foundation. Retrieved from https://monumentlab.com/audit

Moody, C. (2021, September 17). Some asked, "Does Chattanooga Need a lynching memorial?" *The New York Times*, September 17, 2021. Retrieved from https://www.nytimes.com/2021/09/17/arts/design/meadows-chattanooga-lynching-memorial.html?referringSource=articleShare

Morris, P. (2020). As monuments fall, how does the world reckon with a racist past? *National Geographic*. Retrieved from https://www.nationalgeographic.com/history/2020/06/confederate-monuments-fall-question-how-rewrite-history/

Office of Military Government for Germany. (1948). Report of the military governor. Denazification, cumulative review. Report, 1 April 1947-30 April 1948. Retrieved from http://digital.library.wisc.edu/1711.dl/History.Denazi

"Open Monument Day." (2021). Retrieved from https://www.iamexpat.de/lifestyle/expat-events-festivals/open-monument-day

Paviour, B. (2021). Charlottesville removes Robert E. Lee statue that sparked a deadly rally. National Public Radio. Retrieved from https://www.npr.org/2021/07/10/1014926659/charlottesville-removes-robert-e-lee-statue-that-sparked-a-deadly-rally

Perry, A. (2017). Removing racist monuments is about making history, not erasing it. *The Hechinger Report*. Retrieved from https://hechingerreport.org/removing-racist-monuments-making-history-not-erasing/

Petraeus, D. (2020). Take the confederate names off our army bases. *The Atlantic Monthly*. Retrieved from https://www.theatlantic.com/ideas/archive/2020/06/take-confederate-names-off-our-army-bases/612832/

Pratt, T., & Rojas, R. (2021, May 24). Giant Confederate monument will remain at Stone Mountain. *New York Times*. Retrieved from https://www.nytimes.com/2021/05/24/us/stone-mountain-confederate-monument-georgia.html?referringSource=articleShare

"Recent Confederate Monument Removals." (2020). Retrieved from http://cwmemory.com/recent-confederate-monument-removals/

Russell, F. (2013). "Places of Remembrance." Retrieved from https://themillions.com/2013/09/places-of-remembrance.html

Savage, K. (1999). The past in the present. *Harvard Design Magazine, 9*. Retrieved from http://www.harvarddesignmagazine.org/issues/9/the-past-in-the-present

Savage, K. (2007). History, memory, and monuments: An overview of the scholarly literature on commemoration. National Park Service. Retrieved from https://www.nps.gov/parkhistory/resedu/savage.htm

Schneider, G. S., & Vozzella, L. (2021, September 8). Robert E. Lee statue is removed in Richmond, ex-capital of Confederacy, after months of protests and legal resistance. *The Washington Post*, September 8, 2021. Retrieved from https://www.washingtonpost.com/local/virginia-politics/robert-e-lee-statue-removal/2021/09/08/1d9564ee-103d-11ec-9cb6-bf9351a25799_story.html

Schwartz, S. (2021). Four states have placed limits on how teachers can discuss race. More my follow. Education Week. Retrieved from https://www.edweek.org/policy-politics/four-states-have-placed-legal-limits-on-how-teachers-can-discuss-race-more-may-follow/2021/05

Southern Poverty Law Center (SPLC). (2019). *Whose heritage? Public symbols of the Confederacy.* Retrieved from https://www.splcenter.org/sites/default/files/2018-whose_heritage-community_action_guide.pdf

Statement by Nelson Mandela on receiving Truth and Reconciliation Commission Report. (1998). Retrieved from http://www.mandela.gov.za/mandela_speeches/1998/981029_trcreport.htm

Svrluga, S. (2019, January 15). UNC chancellor says Confederate monument Silent Sam must go — and so will she. *Washington Post*. Retrieved from https://www.washingtonpost.com/education/2019/01/15/unc-chancellor-says-confederate-monument-silent-sam-must-go-so-will-she/?utm_term=.6c28a883e03c

"Tag des Offenen Denkmals." (2021). Retrieved from https://www.tag-des-offenen-denkmals.de/

Tharoor, I. (2020, May 11). The shadow of World War II hangs over the pandemic. *The Washington Post*, May 11, 2020. Retrieved from https://www.washingtonpost.com/world/2020/05/11/shadow-world-war-ii-hangs-over-coronavirus-age/

Thomason, A. (2018, August 20). Protestors tear down Chapel Hill's divisive Confederate monument. *The Chronicle of Higher Education*. Retrieved from https://www.chronicle.com/article/Protesters-Tear-Down-Chapel/244318?cid=cp220

Thompson, M. (2015). U.S. flag waves over 10 army bases proudly named for confederate officers. *Time*. Retrieved from https://time.com/3932914/army-bases-confederate/?referringSource=articleShare

Thornton, S. (1991). Teacher as curricular-instructional gatekeeper in social studies. In J. Shaver (Ed.), *Handbook of Research on Social Studies Teaching and Learning* (pp. 237–248). Macmillan.

Uhrmacher, P. B., & Tinkler, B. (2007). A monumental curriculum. *Educational Leadership, 64* (9). Retrieved from http://www.ascd.org/publications/educational-leadership/summer07/vol64/num09/A-Monumental-Curriculum.aspx

Vigdor, N., & Victor, D. (2021, February 23). Over 160 confederate symbols were removed in 2020, group says. *The New York Times*, February 23, 2021. Retrieved from https://www.nytimes.com/2021/02/23/us/confederate-monuments-george-floyd-protests.html?referringSource=articleShare

Welch, S.R. (2012). Commemorating "heroes of a special kind": Deserter monuments in Germany. *Journal of Contemporary History, 47*(2), 370–401.

Wheatcroft, G. (2014, December 9). The myth of the good war. *The Guardian*. Retrieved from http://www.theguardian.com/news/2014/dec/09/-sp-myth-of-the-good-war?CMP=twt_gu

White, J. W., & Sandage, S. (2020). What Frederick Douglass had to say about monuments. *Smithsonian Magazine*. Retrieved from https://www.smithsonianmag.com/history/what-frederick-douglass-had-say-about-monuments-180975225/

Woodley, J. (2017). Charlottesville, Virginia: The history of the statue at the centre of violent unrest. *The Conversation*. Retrieved from http://theconversation.com/charlottesville-virginia-the-history-of-the-statue-at-the-centre-of-violent-unrest-82476

Young, J. E. (1999). Memory and counter-memory: The end of the monument in Germany. *Harvard Design Magazine, 9*, 1–10.

CHAPTER TEN

Reconstruction Resources

JENICE L. VIEW, CAROLINE R. PRYOR, AND AMY WILKINSON

Prior to the 150th anniversary of Reconstruction Amendments and laws, there were few available teacher- or classroom-friendly resources for learning about this historical era. Among the reasons was the fact that the historical significance and interpretation of the Reconstruction Era were contested, long before the contemporary climate of avoiding and outlawing historical material that is considered challenging or divisive. The Reconstruction Era was indeed challenging and divisive, as it intended to remake the U.S. Constitution, state laws, and the U.S. economy from a nation founded on the enslavement of millions of African descended people to a nation of free and wage-earning citizens, regardless of skin color and the conditions of their birth.

This book is one of the few compilations for providing classroom teachers with a breadth of useful instructional resources on the era. The resources in this chapter are arranged in the following five sections: *Background reading and resources for teachers*; *Reconstruction teaching activities and lesson plans*; *Teaching the 13th, 14th, and 15th Amendments to the US Constitution* (primary sources; websites and other media; books and articles); *Local histories of Reconstruction*; and *Children's and young adult fiction and nonfiction*.

BACKGROUND READING AND RESOURCES FOR TEACHERS

Blight, D. (2015, April 27). The first Decoration Day. *Newark Star Ledger.*

In this article, Yale historian David Blight documents the first commemoration of war dead, called Decoration Day, that was initiated by 10,000 Black people in Charleston, SC in 1865, at the beginning of the Reconstruction Era. Decoration Day later became a national holiday in 1868 known as Memorial Day. Retrieved from

http://www.davidwblight.com/public-history/2015/4/27/the-first-decoration-day-newark-star-ledger?rq=first%20decoration

Downs, G.P. & Masur, K. (2017). *The Era of Reconstruction, 1861-1900.*

Prepared for the U.S. National Park Service, this study on the history of the Reconstruction Era offers six major themes for a deep exploration of the period. It is available as a free download from http://www.npshistory.com/publications/nhl/theme-studies/reconstruction-era.pdf

DuBois, W. E. B. (1935). Foner, E. & Gates, H.L. (Eds.). (2021). *Black Reconstruction in America.*

Originally published in 1935, Du Bois' *Black Reconstruction* was the first book to challenge the prevailing racist historical narrative of the era, telling the story of the Civil War and Reconstruction from the perspective of African Americans. It was written specifically to challenge the Encyclopedia Britannica and influential historians of the period whose ideas and emphases had disfigured the historical record of the Reconstruction era.

Foner, E. (2015). *A Short History of Reconstruction, Updated Edition.*

In this "people's history" view of the Reconstruction era, Foner chronicles the way in which Blacks and whites responded to the unprecedented changes unleashed by the Civil War and the end of chattel slavery, including the quest of freedpeople searching for economic autonomy and equal citizenship; the remodeling of Southern society; the evolution of racial attitudes and patterns of race relations; and the emergence of a national ideas concerning the principle of equal rights for all Americans.

Rosen, H. (2017, March). Teaching race and Reconstruction. *The Journal of the Civil War Era,* 7(1), pp. 67–95.

In this accessible academic article, Rosen argues for the historical importance and contemporary relevance of teaching the Reconstruction Era. More importantly, she argues that it must be taught well at the time of its sesquicentennial and in a new era of racial reckoning.

Van der Valk, A. (2018, Summer) Be your own historian. *Learning for Justice 59*.

In this article, Harvard historian Dr. Timothy McCarthy talks through the history of Reconstruction and why it is important to get it right, particularly considering contemporary racial justice campaigns.

Wolfe-Rocca, U. (2022, Winter). How state standards misteach the meaning of one of the United States' most important eras. *Rethinking Schools, 36*(2).

This article shares the results of the first-ever comprehensive review of state standards on Reconstruction, noting that Zinn Education Project researchers found that the standards fail to define the era or outline its crucial themes. The article also offers what the Zinn Education Project proposes for state and district standards (see below, Rosada, Cohn-Postar, & Eisen).

RECONSTRUCTION TEACHING ACTIVITIES AND LESSON PLANS

American Social History Project (1996). *Freedom's unfinished revolution: An inquiry Into the Civil War and Reconstruction.*

With a foreword by Eric Foner, this teaching guide provides primary historical documents, including letters, speeches, and excerpts from novels and newspapers, to offer students a firsthand look at the aftermath of the Civil War and the struggle to rebuild the South and construct a new society. Photographs, engravings, art, and political cartoons are included, as well as pre-reading and discussion questions, critical thinking exercises, timelines, and a glossary.

Bigelow, B. *Reconstructing the South: A Role Play.* (n.d.)

This role play activity engages students in thinking about what freedpeople needed to achieve—and sustain—real freedom following the Civil War. Textbooks and curricula tend to emphasize what was done to or for newly freed people. Instead, this activity asks students to imagine themselves as people who were formerly enslaved and to wrestle with several issues about what they needed to ensure their own freedom, including ownership and uses of land; the fate of Confederate leaders; voting rights; self-defense; and the conditions placed on the former Confederate states prior to being allowed to return to the Union. It is followed by a chapter from the book *Freedom's Unfinished Revolution* (see above). The website also includes testimonials from classroom teachers that have used the activity. Available by download from https://www.zinnedproject.org/materials/reconstructing-south-role-play/

Center for History and New Media. (n.d.). https://chnm.gmu.edu/acpstah/units/lessons.pdf

> The downloadable pdf provides six lessons on Reconstruction that examine the events that took place as the Civil War ended. Each lesson contains links to primary sources to support student inquiry. Students will identify the problems facing the nation at this time and evaluate different plans for dealing with these challenges.

Facing History and Ourselves (2015). *The Reconstruction Era and the fragility of democracy.*

> This teaching guide includes a collection of readings, lessons, videos, and primary sources to teach about Reconstruction. The guide also includes a set of writing strategies that supplement the unit on the Reconstruction era and help educators to guide students through the process of organizing their ideas and crafting a thesis in response to the writing prompts. These strategies also offer tips for students while writing and editing drafts, sharing their essays, and reflecting on the writing process. Both the unit and the writing strategies are downloadable for free from the Facing History and Ourselves website https://www.facinghistory.org/reconstruction-era/unit.

Green, H. N. (2017, October 6). Teaching Reconstruction: Some strategies that work. *The Journal of the Civil War Era.* Retrieved from *https://www.journalofthecivilwarera.org/2017/10/teaching-reconstruction-strategies-work/*

> Written by a university professor for a college student audience, this article nevertheless offers strategies and dispositions that are useful to K-12 classroom instructors who are teaching about Reconstruction.

Jump Back in Time—Reconstruction (1866–1877) https://www.americaslibrary.gov/jb/recon/jb_recon_subj.html?&loclr=reclnk

> Jump Back in Time from the America's Library website from the Library of Congress provides thirty-three short stories for the Reconstruction Era. The short stories highlight people or events during the reconstruction era containing secondary information and primary sources to inspire curiosity into the past.

Reconstruction and Its Aftermath—The African American Odyssey: A Quest for Full Citizenship https://www.loc.gov/exhibits/african-american-odyssey/reconstruction.html?&loclr=reclnk

> *The African American Odyssey: A Quest for Full Citizenship* is a companion website to a 1998 exhibit at the Library of Congress that explores the Reconstruction and its aftermath. There are wood engravings by Thomas Nast, a German-born

American editorial cartoonist, drawings and prints by Harper's Weekly, plat maps, portraits, broadsides, an account book, newspaper clippings, songs and sheet music for which African Americans participated in relation to government, employment, education and land ownership.

Rosado A., Cohn-Postar, G., & Eisen, M. (2022). *Erasing the Black Freedom Struggle: How state standards fail to teach the truth about Reconstruction.* Retrieved from https://www.teachreconstructionreport.org

This is a report and a website that consider what Reconstruction was, why people in the United States often struggle to remember it, and why it remains so relevant today. It asks four fundamental questions:

- Do state social studies educational standards for K–12 schools recommend or require students to learn about Reconstruction?
- Is the content that state standards recommend or require on Reconstruction historically accurate and reflective of modern scholarship?
- What would an ideal set of historically accurate state standards on Reconstruction look like?
- What are some efforts underway to give the Reconstruction era the time and perspective it deserves?

Sanchez, A., & Mthethwa, N. (n.d.). *When the impossible suddenly became possible: A Reconstruction mixer.*

This mixer role play explores the connections among the different social movements during Reconstruction, and features the likes of Abram Colby, Augusta Lewis, Benjamin Montgomery, Charlotte "Lottie" Rollins, Elizabeth Cady Stanton, Frances Ellen Watkins Harper, Frederick Douglass, Henry Highland Garnet, Ira Steward, Isaac Myers, John Roy Lynch, Kate Mullany, Lucy Stone, Lydia Maria Child, Newton Knight, P. B. S. Pinchback, Susan B. Anthony, W. J. Whipper, Walter Moses Burton, Wendell Phillips, and William Sylvis. Downloadable from the Zinn Education Project website, https://www.zinnedproject.org/materials/the-impossible-became-possible-reconstruction-mixer/

Zetts, A. (2018). Focus on Reconstruction: New Teaching Activities.

Written by a high school history teacher, this blogpost describes the uses of specific primary sources from the National Archives to deepen his instruction of the Reconstruction era. Retrieved from The National Archives Education Updates, https://education.blogs.archives.gov/2018/02/27/reconstruction-zetts/

TEACHING THE 13TH, 14TH, AND 15TH AMENDMENTS TO THE US CONSTITUTION

The 13th Amendment Abolition of Slavery

Primary Sources
13th Amendment to the U.S. Constitution: Primary Documents in American History—Research Guide https://guides.loc.gov/13th-amendment

> The *13th Amendment to the U.S. Constitution: Primary Documents in American History* is a research guide from the Library of Congress that introduces the 13th Amendment and provides links to digitized primary sources including debates, bills, laws, journals, pamphlets, speeches, a telegram from John G. Nicolay reporting passage of the 13th Amendment by Congress, the 13th Amendment to the States signed by Abraham Lincoln, and historic newspaper articles announcing the Adoption of the Constitutional Amendment. Beyond linking to Digital Collections, the research guide links to Related Online Resources like presentations and exhibits and External Websites related to the 13th Amendment to the U.S. Constitution.

U.S. History Primary Source Timeline: The Freedmen https://www.loc.gov/classroom-materials/united-states-history-primary-source-timeline/civil-war-and-reconstruction-1861-1877/freedmen/

> The presentation, *U.S. History Primary Source Timeline: The Freedmen* from the Library of Congress, highlights primary sources such as publications and letters from the *African American Pamphlet and Daniel Murray Pamphlet Collection* related to freedmen and the Freedmen's Bureau after the Emancipation Proclamation and Thirteenth Amendment.

Websites
American Battlefield Trust https://www.battlefields.org/learn/articles/slavery-united-states?ms=googlegrant&ms=googlegrant&gclid=Cj0KCQjw-daUBhCIARIsALbkjSbsgKLOrUPansJYoJUE6qmzeTZzvd9vg65fmBZ94ZYEeH3mn4MOdH4aAh9MEALw_wcB

> This website provides a brief overview to the "root cause" of the American Civil War, and events that led to the passing of the 13th Amendment of the Constitution. This site includes Civil War curriculum, virtual tours, lesson plans and links to primary sources. A link to share in Google classroom is provided.

National Constitution Center .https://constitutioncenter.org/interactive-constitution/big-question/13-amendment

This website provides videos (e.g., YouTube) interpretations, and a media library on the 13th Amendment: This site includes a section on Finding Family after slavery. Interactive website. http://informationwanted.org

Books and Articles

Crofts, D. W. (2016). *Lincoln and the Politics of Slavery: The Other Thirteenth Amendment and the Struggle to Save the Union.* The University of North Carolina Press, Chapel Hill.

As backdrop for his investigation of an 1861 prospective 13th amendment, the author provides historical interpretation emanating from national and congressional philosophy and legal debates on emancipation. Ensuing discussions serve to deeply illuminate topics such as how the South's political leaders regarded the political environment in the South, after Lincoln's 1860 election. The focus of this book is twofold: the ideas centered on a potential enactment of the other (1861) Thirteenth Amendment, inquiry into (accuracy) of historical remembrance. Both topics as well as the debates can be useful in high school curricula.

Vorenberg, M. (2004). *Final Freedom: The Civil War, the Abolition of Slavery and the Thirteenth Amendment.* Cambridge University Press, UK.

This book provides an overview to topics foundational to the composition of the 13th amendment. As background to the development of the amendment, the author provides insight on the topics of race, slavery, secession, and legal theory as a basis for the drafting and codification of emancipation. Book chapters include topics often less noted such as the divisiveness on emancipation among political parties in the election of 1864, the campaign for constitutional emancipation, and the ensuing ratification of the amendment.

Wolford, D. (2013). Spielberg's Lincoln fulfills the President's emancipation legacy. *Social Education*, (1), January/February, 44–48(5). National Council for the Social Studies.

This article provides a review of Spielberg's portrayal of Lincoln and the passage of the 13th Amendment. The characterization of slavery and Lincoln's leadership in his final days are reviewed as the article is a resource that can be used to augment teachers' use of the film with students.

The 14th Amendment: Citizenship and Equal Civil and Legal Rights

Primary Sources
14th Amendment to the U.S. Constitution: Primary Documents in American History—Research Guide https://guides.loc.gov/14th-amendment

The *14th Amendment to the U.S. Constitution: Primary Documents in American History* is a research guide from the Library of Congress that introduces the 14th Amendment and provides links to digitized primary sources such as debates, bills, laws, journals, newspaper articles, and rare books, and to online presentations related to the 14th Amendment. Beyond linking to Digital Collections, the research guide links to Related Online Resources like presentations and exhibits and External Websites related to the 14th Amendment to the U.S. Constitution.

Websites

The Annenberg Classroom https://www.annenbergclassroom.org/teaching-the-constitution/the-amendments-and-landmark-cases/amendment-14-due-process-equal-protection-discrimination/

> This website provides a range of resources including a discussion of the 14th amendment and resources for teaching about due process, equal protection, and discrimination. Example links include teaching the Constitution, critical thinking, and lesson plans. Timelines, videos with Supreme Court Justices' discussions and handouts are provided.

The 15th Amendment: The Right to Vote.

Primary Sources

Library of Congress Research Guides **https://www.loc.gov/**

> The Research Guides of the Library of Congress (LOC) provides 81 subject topic guides of areas collated by the LOC. Search efforts may easily begin by using the topic header links such as African American Studies, American History or Historic American Law.

Library of Congress Research Guide: 15th Amendment to the U.S. Constitution: Primary Document in American History

> This area within the LOC Research Guides provides a range of material useable for teaching the 15th Amendment. Materials such as digital collections, related online resources, external website and print resources are all collated in this research guide.

15th Amendment to the U.S. Constitution: Primary Documents in American History—Research Guide https://guides.loc.gov/15th-amendment

> The *15th Amendment to the U.S. Constitution: Primary Documents in American History* is a research guide from the Library of Congress that introduces

the 15th Amendment and provides links to digitized primary sources such as bills, laws, journals, newspaper articles, pamphlets, broadsides, and Ulysses S. Grant's special message to Congress regarding the ratification of the 15th Amendment in 1870. In addition to digitized collections, there are links to primary sources from the Library of Congress' exhibitions and Prints and the Photographs Division highlighting celebrations and commemorations related to the 15th Amendment. Beyond linking to Digital Collections, the research guide links to Related Online Resources like presentations and exhibits and External Websites related to the 15th Amendment to the U.S. Constitution.

Websites and Films

Deane, E. & Graham. D. (2004). Reconstruction: The Second Civil War. Documentary film.

In this PBS documentary, historians and actors dramatize the stories of ordinary citizens to paint a picture of the Reconstruction era that is broader than most textbook accounts. At three hours in length, the film contains short segments suitable for the classroom, including the congressional battles, the multiracial legislatures in the South, and the various massacres attempting to reestablish white supremacy. In particular, the segments on Tunis Campbell and the separatist democracy he helped build in the Georgia Sea Islands demonstrate both the promise and disappointments of land distribution and economic independence for freedpeople during Reconstruction

Last Seen: Finding Family After Slavery https://informationwanted.org

A joint project of Villanova University, the National Archives, and the Pennsylvania Historical Society, Last Seen is an interactive research website that is recovering stories of families separated in the domestic slave trade. Formerly enslaved people placed these ads hoping to reconnect with family and loved ones for decades following emancipation. The ads serve as testaments to their enduring hope and determination to regain what was taken from them. Visitors to the website are encouraged to use the resources to search for personal family connections to formerly enslaved people.

Ponzi, J. A., & Baker, M. (2019). Lesson 1: The battle over Reconstruction: The aftermath of war. EDSITEment! National Endowment for the Humanities website. Retrieved from https://edsitement.neh.gov/lesson-plans/lesson-1-battle-over-reconstruction-aftermath-war

Aimed at secondary classroom teachers, the resources on this website include lessons plans, worksheets, teacher's guide, and primary sources. Some of the functionality (such as the interactive map) is limited since Adobe Player is no longer supported.

In addition, EDSITEment co-created a Smithsonian Institution Learning Lab collection on Reconstruction that includes multimedia resources, access to newspapers from the era, and artifacts from Smithsonian collections. The Lab also features resources that were used for the 2020 National History Day competition that included a focus on Reconstruction. https://learninglab.si.edu/collections/national-history-day-reconstruction/x2fUUfXUpm4Jsmqy

Roudané, M. C. (n.d.). Roudanez: History and legacy. Digital collection. https://roudanez.com

Created by a retired elementary teacher who is the descendent of Dr. Louis Charles Roudanez, this website documents the work of the founder of the first Black daily newspaper in the U.S., the *New Orleans Tribune*, with articles, excerpts, videos, photos, a virtual tour of historic sites, and a timeline. An additional resource is Roudané's October, 2015 article in *The Atlantic*, Grappling with the memory of New Orleans: A family's story traces the roots of the eclectic city, the country's first Black daily newspaper, and the evolution of racial injustice, retrievable from https://www.theatlantic.com/politics/archive/2015/10/new-orleans-black-newspaper/411973/

Seizing Freedom. https://www.npr.org/podcasts/948170667/seizing-freedom

This National Public Broadcasting (NPR) podcast tells the story of the post-Civil War Black Americans' fight for the framing of freedom –its vision and stories. The podcast includes interviews and stories of Black people's quest for liberation and progress in America. See podcasts that reframe the traditional narrative of Jim Crow, including the stories of courage in face of the forces at work against to keep freedom from them. Another example podcast "The Land of Milk and Honey" describes the late 19th and early 20th century migration from the South, and the unmet expectations of this journey.

Smithsonian: National Museum of African American History and Culture

Make Good the Promises: Reconstruction and Its Legacies
https://www.si.edu/exhibitions/make-good-promises-reconstruction-and-its-legacies:event-exhib-6538.

This exhibit features a multitude of objects, images and media programs portraying the Reconstruction era as seen through an African American lens. The theme of the exhibit is to connect today's efforts to implement the promises of the US Constitution. The exhibit also addresses the failure of the era—in which agencies of support were allowed to languish or fail.

Holman, K., & Gardullo, P. (2021). *Make good the promises: Reclaiming reconstruction and its legacies*. Smithsonian, D.C.

> A companion book to the Smithsonian exhibit *Make Good the Promises*, this volume provides a foreword by Eric Foner and historian Spencer Crew. The book portrays the legacy of the post-Civil War era with an overview to the story of Black Americans' hard-won effort for human rights. The overview narrative describes the unfilled promises of the nation of freedom, citizenship and justice for African American equality and status as citizens.

Turner, H. M. (1868, September 3). Eligibility of Colored members to seats in the Georgia legislature. Film clip. https://vimeo.com/1388488

> After organizing the first U.S. Colored Troops during the Civil War, Henry McNeal Turner (1834–1915) later joined them as Chaplain. He then became a delegate to the state constitutional convention in Atlanta, Georgia. In 1868 Turner was elected as a representative to the Georgia state legislature. Soon after, he was among twenty-four legislators expelled for the "crime" of being Black. This video clip is part of the Voices of a People's History and is read by Danny Glover. The full text of Turner's speech, "I claim the rights of a man," can be found at BlackPast.org, https://www.blackpast.org/african-american-history/1868-reverend-henry-mcneal-turner-i-claim-rights-man/

The Zinn Education Project https://www.zinnedproject.org/materials/teach-the-15-amendment

> This website provides a wide range of teaching resources. The site provides a search engine to identify historical theme, grade level and type of media. Books by reading grade level, along with links and films and film clips s are a highlight of this site. For example, one book link—regards Oscar Dunn and Reconstruction Louisiana- notes the book's time period and theme and reading grade level. Another resource type regards a 2012 film titled "Slavery by Another Name" which portrays forces in the South that enabled a neo-slavery in the Emancipation era.

The Zinn Education Project; Reconstruction: The Right to Vote https://www.zinnedproject.org/themes/reconstruction/

> This link on the Zinn Project website includes a range of resource types. Notable is a Film Clip titled "Eligibility of Colored Members to Seats in the Georgia Legislature" (H. N. Turner)—which is read by Danny Glover. Another example resource is a Teaching Guide entitled "The Reconstruction Era and the Fragility of Democracy". This guide includes lessons, videos, and primary

sources. Other links on this section of the Zinn website regards the topic of the right to vote, see https://www.zinnedproject.org/materials/teaching-voting-rights-struggle/. This link contains lessons on voting rights, and a history of the struggle to vote.

Books and Articles

Gidlow, L. (2018). The Sequel: The Fifteenth Amendment, The Nineteenth Amendment, and Southern Black Women's Struggle to Vote. *The Journal of the Gilded Age and Progressive Era, 17*(3), 433–449. doi:10.1017/S1537781418000051. Online:

https://www.cambridge.org/core/journals/journal-of-the-gilded-age-and-progressive-era/article/sequel-the-fifteenth-amendment-the-nineteenth-amendment-and-southern-black-women's-struggle-to-vote/9EDB826096C0353E6FE12E3E345FC5CF.

This article examines both the woman and African American experience to ensure voting rights. The article focus-between 1870 and 1920, investigates s the impact of the Fifteenth Amendment on this era's struggle. Among the article references are African American suffragists Mary Church Terrell and Adella Hunt Logan, who along with others called for the enforcement of the Fourteen and Fifteenth Amendments and the enfranchisement of Black women.

Hay, J. (2009). *Amendment XV: Race and the right to vote.* Greenhaven Press, Farmington Hills, MI.

This book provides historical background about the Fifteen Amendment. This text describes challenges to ensuring voting rights and efforts to ensure the affirmation of the amendment.

Mathews, J. M. (2001). *Legislative and judicial history of the fifteenth amendment.* John Hopkins University, Baltimore.

This book offers an in-depth analysis of the formation and content of the Fifteenth Amendment. Chapter topics include a preliminary discussion of the proposition for the amendment and its ensuring formation. Also discussed is an interpretation of contemporary issues, enforcement, and judicial interpretations.

Swinney, E. (1962). Enforcing the Fifteenth Amendment, 1870–1877. *The Journal of Southern History, 28*(2), 202–218.

The article –published in 1962—provides an overview to federal Enforcement Acts, as these acts challenged the Southern policies to Reconstruction.

Although published in an era preceding the Voting Right Act of 1965, the article portrays issues and challenges foundational to ensuing civil rights legislation, Several citations within the article support this portrayal of challenge and response in the Reconstruction era.

Local Histories of Reconstruction

Dier, C. (2017). *The 1868 St. Bernard Parish Massacre: Blood in the Cane Fields.* History Press.

Written by a White Louisiana high school history teacher, this book documents the 1868 St. Bernard Parish Massacre in his hometown. Intending to thwart the freed Black men from voting in the upcoming presidential election, armed mobs of white Democrats murdered 35–135 Black people. An essay version of the history is told in Unraveling a forgotten massacre in my Louisiana hometown: A history teacher discovers a racially driven rampage that still haunts his students' lives. Retrieved from Zócalo Public Square: https://www.zocalopublicsquare.org/2018/02/07/unraveling-forgotten-massacre-louisiana-hometown/ideas/essay/

Reconstruction 360. https://reconstruction360.org/lesson-plans.html

Reconstruction 360 offers students and teachers an immersive, interactive approach to studying history, with a focus on the state of South Carolina. The website includes historical photographs, documentary media, primary sources, Core American Documents (for free, otherwise available for a fee from Teaching American History), and some of the other lessons and resources available in this chapter. These standards-based lesson plans, written in conjunction with South Carolina ETV's Education Department, are intended to extend the use of Reconstruction 360 into classroom activities.

Children's and Young Adult Fiction and Nonfiction

Barton, C. (author) & Tate, D. (illustrator) (2015). *The amazing age of John Roy Lynch.*

This picture book is an in-depth look at the Reconstruction period through the life of one of the first African Americans to serve in the U.S. Congress. Due to the graphic portrayal of violence, the book is best for middle- to upper-elementary students.

Fast, H. (1944). *Freedom Road.*

This book of historical fiction, first published in 1944 with a forward by W.E.B. DuBois, has been reissued with a new introduction by Eric Foner. It tells the story of the politics and economics of the experiences of people freed from slavery after the Civil War and during Reconstruction told through historical fiction, drawing on primary source documents from the period.

Gillem Robinet, H. (1998). *Forty acres and maybe a mule.*

This historical fiction features 12-year-old Pascal, 8-year-old Nellie, and their older brother Gideon, a Union Army aide, as they claim and farm the land promised to them during Reconstruction.

Parker Rhodes, J. (2013). *Sugar.*

This historical fiction describes Reconstruction-era Louisiana through the eyes of a young girl who bridges the divide between the long-time plantation workers and the Chinese indentured servants.

Starling Lyons, K. (2012). *Ellen's Broom.*

This picture book tells the story of a young girl during Reconstruction whose parents are finally able to have a legal marriage while honoring a family wedding tradition.

Wright, B. (2012). *Crow*

This historical fiction is about a Reconstruction-era African American community violently robbed of its freedom and democracy at turn of the century North Carolina.

Contributor Biographies

Kristen Brill, Ph.D.
Kristen is a Senior Lecturer in American History at Keele University (UK). She is the author of *The Weaker Sex in War: Gender and Nationalism in Civil War Virginia* (University of Virginia Press, 2022). She is the editor of *Elite Confederate Women in the American Civil War: Lived Experiences in the Nineteenth Century* (Routledge, 2021) and *The Diary of a Civil War Bride: Lucy Wood Butler of Virginia* (Louisiana State University Press, 2017).

Matthew R. Campbell, Ed.D.
Matt is the K-12 Social Studies Coordinator in Conroe ISD. Prior to his current position, he was a Secondary Social Studies Curriculum Coach in Cypress Fairbanks ISD following several years as a dual credit and AP U.S. History teacher. He received his doctorate in social education from the University of Houston, where he also received a masters' degrees in history and public history. In 2015, he received the Humanities Texas Outstanding Early-Career Teacher Award for the State of Texas. He now spends the majority of his time writing curriculum, leading professional development, and growing the capacity of social studies teachers. In addition to working in the public-school system, Matt is an adjunct in the Urban Education department at the University of Houston—Downtown where he teaches graduate and undergraduate courses in social studies methods.

Kent A. McConnell, Ph.D.
For much of his professional career, Kent A. McConnell has explored subjects related to questions of ethics and warfare. A historian of nineteenth-century America, his research of the Civil War Era seeks to understand how violence perpetrated on the human body shaped the psychophysical experience of Americans, their rituals, and systems of belief in the aftermath of war. He currently serves as chair of the department of history at Phillips Exeter Academy. Dr. McConnell has spent for more than two decades in the classroom, dividing his career between institutions of higher and secondary education.

Timothy J. McKeeby
Timothy teaches Middle School Geography and US History at Fruitport Middle School in Fruitport, Michigan. Along with being an outstanding educator, he is a successful coach, a sports fanatic, and a typical millennial dog-dad.

Mark Pearcy, Ph.D.
Mark is an Associate Professor of Social Studies Education at Rider University in Lawrenceville, New Jersey. He teaches undergraduate methods courses and is a student teacher supervisor. Prior to this, he taught high school social studies classes for 19 years and earned National Board Certification. His research interests include American history education, civic literacy, racial residential segregation, and the "just war" doctrine.

Katherine Perrotta, Ph.D.
Katherine is a former middle school social studies teacher in the New York City Department of education, and is currently an Assistant Professor of Middle Grades and Secondary Education at Mercer University Tift College of Education. Her research on historical empathy, social studies teaching methods, and pre-service and in-service social studies teacher professional development have been published in leading journals such as *The Journal of Social Studies Research, Social Studies Research and Practice, Social Education, Middle Level Learning, The Social Studies, Curriculum and Teaching Dialogue, Educational Studies,* and *The American Educational History Journal.*

Caroline R. Pryor, Ed.D.
Caroline R. Pryor is Professor of Secondary Education and Curriculum at Southern Illinois University Edwardsville. Pryor is Editor of the 15 volume book series *Teaching Critical Themes in American History* and *Learning for Democracy: An International Journal of Thought and Practice.* Dr. Pryor is editor with Stephen L. Hansen of *Teaching Lincoln: Legacies and Classroom Strategies.* She received six National Endowment for the Humanities awards for her workshop for school teachers on

Abraham Lincoln. Pryor is chair of the Democratic Citizenship in Education Special Interest Group of the American Educational Research Association, and is a Wye Fellow of the Aspen Institute.

Adam J. Schmitt, Ph.D.
Adam is an Assistant Professor in Teacher Education and History at the University of Southern Maine. His research interests include the relationship between elements of social studies' teachers' identities and own memories of schooling and their curricular and pedagogical decision-making, as well as the relationship between collective memory and history in how teachers and students make sense of the past, present, and future.

Justin Sheldon, M.A.
Justin is a Professor of Multi-Cultural Diversity in the USA at Grand Valley State University. Justin graduated with a B.A. in History at GVSU in 2015 and a M.A. in American History at Central Michigan University in 2017. Justin's area of focus in American history is Antebellum South through Reconstruction.

Shannon M. Smith, Ph.D.
Shannon is an Associate Professor of History at the College of Saint Benedict and Saint John's University in Minnesota, where she teaches courses on the Civil War and Reconstruction in American culture, gender and race in US history, and protest and rebellion. She holds a PhD from Indiana University and an MA from the University of Nevada, Reno. She has published articles in works such as *The American Historian*, *Civil War America: A Social and Cultural History*, and *Freedoms Gained and Lost: Reconstruction and Its Meanings 150 Years Later*, as well as pieces for *The Conversation*.

Scott L. Stabler, Ph.D.
Scott teaches history at Grand Valley State University, Allendale, Michigan. His publications include: "'No More Auction Block for Me': The Fight for Freedom by the United States Colored Troops at the Battle of Nashville"; "Nuanced History: Westward Expansion in the Context of the Civil War and After"; "O.O. Howard" in *Soldiers West*; "Atlantic Slavery: Lost in Trans-lation." Dr. Stabler was a Fulbright Scholar to Ghana (2011).

Ashley Towle, Ph.D.
Ashley is an Assistant Professor in the History Department at the University of Southern Maine. She earned her PhD in History from the University of Maryland. She is the author of the chapter "Randolph Cemetery and the Politics of Death in the Post-Civil War South" in *Cultures of Memory in the Nineteenth*

Century: Consuming Commemoration, edited by Katherine Haldane Grenier and Amanda R. Mushal. She is currently at work on a book manuscript that examines how African Americans in the post-Civil War South used death to stake claims to citizenship, equality, and justice.

Jenice L. View, Ph.D.
Jenice is Associate Professor Emerita at George Mason University. Her 15-year academic career follows 20 years in the non-governmental sector, and a stint as a middle school humanities teacher. Publications include peer-reviewed journals and books including *Putting the movement back into civil rights teaching* (2004/2020) and *Antiracist Professional Development for In-Service Teachers* (2020). Research includes oral histories of Black mathematics teachers, the impact of oral history collection on students' understanding of historical content, and teachers' experiences of teaching Black history. She won the 2020 Faculty Excellence in Social Impact Earle C. Williams Presidential Medal, George Mason University.

Amy Wilkinson, M.Ed.
Amy is the Director of the Teaching with Primary Sources Project (Library of Congress, www.loc.gov) at Southern Illinois University Edwardsville and a former classroom teacher and social worker. The project's outreach has served over 2000 K-12 teachers and college education faculty in the greater Saint Louis area through a variety of professional development events and courses. In addition to working with educators locally, she collaborates with Teaching with Primary Source project directors across the region and the United States to present and deliver professional development to K-12 educators.

Tim Dorsch
He attended Bloomsburg University in Pennsylvania for his undergraduate, earning majors in Secondary Education, History, and German. After graduation he taught high school history at a public school in Florida. Tim studied at the University of Central Florida, receiving my Master's in History. His thesis focused on the role political cartoons played in the creation of popularly held images for groups like immigrants, women, and African Americans in the 1860s-1880s. Currently, he teaches high school history in Pennsylvania.

Index

A

13th Amendment Abolition of Slavery, The, 196–7
14th Amendment: Citizenship and Equal Civil and Legal Rights, The, 197–8
15th Amendment: the Right to Vote, The, 198–204
abolitionist movement, 142
Achilles heel, 37
African Americans, 93–110
Age of fracture, 31–3
Age of Lincoln, The, 40
American Freedman's Union Commission (AFUC), 157
American Missionary Association (AMA), 157, 158
American Pageant, 120
American political system, 98
American society today, 183
America's interracial democratic project, 35
America's memorialization of wa, 185
Anderson, Jourdan, 9–10
Appomattox and Fort Pillow, 56
Arendt, Hannah, 54
assessment, 26–7
asymmetrical justice, 52–4

B

bad faith, 51
Bailey, Thomas, 120
Battle of Fort Pillow, The, 54
Bell, Linda, 48
Black Codes, 11–2, 127
Black education
 and employment, 142
 higher education, 159–61
 reconstruction's accomplishment, 153–62
Black Ministers, 8–9
Black Testimony 1871, 13–4
Blair, William A., 51–2

bonds of affection, 36, 62
Brown, John, 52
bureaucracy, 54–6
Burt, John, 38

C

C3 Framework, 129
Camp Dixie, 59
Camp Fiske, 59
Camp Shiloh, 59
cartoonish depictions, 99
Chicago Tribune, The (1866), 61
Civil Rights Act of 1866, 42
Civil Rights Act of 1875, 107
Civil Rights Era, 122–4
Civil Rights Era (1960s/70s), The, 120
civil rights movement, 153
Civil Rights Movement, 117
  rise of, 153–62
Colored Conventions Project, 10
Common Core State Standards, 129
community against systems, 4
community-wide reconciliation, 184
Confederate forces, 56
confederate memorials
  at Stone Mountain, 180
  in United States, 175–7
confederate sympathies, 101
conflict management, 44
Congressional investigation, 55
content analysis of textbooks, 117
Contraband camps, 59
cranial proportions and ridiculous clothing choices, 99

D

Daily Argus, 60
Davis, Jefferson, 43, 52, 101
De Jure Belli ac Pacis, 41
design, 180–1

de Vattel, Emer, 41
Dunning School, 3

E

economic and social belonging, 10
economics of system of slavery, 69
educational efforts for freedpeople, 161
educational foundation, 153
egalitarian principles, 37
egalitarian state
  and demands transitional justice, 39
Escott, Paul, 42
ethical system, 47
explanatory theories, 39

F

Fort Pillow Massacre, 53, 55
Fort Sumter, 3
Frank Leslie's Illustrated Newspaper, 99
Frazier, Garrison, 8–9
Freedmen's Bureau and education, 156–8

G

German Foundation for Monument Protection, 178
German memorials
  and *erinnerungskultur,* 177–9
Gooch, Daniel W., 55
good faith, 50–1
Google Books, 120

H

Halleck, Henry, 51
Harrisburg Patriot and Union, 36
Hesseltine, William B., 32, 42, 52
historical context, 21–2

historical empathy pedagogies
  C3 framework, 139–41
  curricular and assessment frameworks, 138–9
  social studies curriculum, 135
  women's suffrage movement, 135–46
historical memory of the Lost Cause, 1–2
historically Black colleges and universities (HBCUs), 70, 153, 155, 159, 167
historiography, 21–2, 118–9, 155–6
Howard, Jacob Merritt, 57
human choice, 48
human rights at expense of private property rights, 38
humanitarian concerns and principles of equality, 63

I

Inquiry Arc, 14–5
Inquiry Design Model (IDM) Blueprint, 17–9, 112–4, 131–3, 141, 168–71
Instructions for the Government of Armies of the United States in the Field, 40
International Law; or Rules Regulating the Intercourse of States in Peace and War in 1861, 40

J

Jefferson, Thomas, 32
Johnson, Andrew, 51, 59
Joint Committee on Reconstruction, 57
Joint Select Committee on the Conduct of the War, 39
Journal of the Gilded Age and Progressive Era, The, 2
jus post bellum, 33, 35, 36, 38, 41–3, 45, 46, 47, 49, 61–4
Just war theory, 34–43, 47
justice against leading Confederates, 43

K

K-12 social studies content standards, 135
Ku Klux Klan, 12–3
Kyvig, David E., 38

L

Law of Nations, The, 41
Lee, Robert E., 43–52
legal formalism, 38
legal positioning, 50
literary analysis, textbook samples, 120
Loewen, James, 128

M

Macnaghten, Edward, 53
Mandela, Nelson, 185
Martin Luther King, Jr., 117
Massacre at Fort Pillow, 54–6
May, Larry, 38, 39, 46
McDermott, John J., 52
memorialization, 173–85
memorials, 174–5
memory, 174–5
Memphis riot, 56–62
Memphis Riots of 1866, 53
Montana Post, The, 61
monuments, 174–5
moral dilemmas, reconstruction, 34–43
moral faculties of white Southerners, 37
multicultural turn, 124–6
Multicultural Turn Era (1990s-present), 120
Murphy, Colleen, 46

N

Nast, Thomas, 100–10
  cartoons, 100–10

Nation, The, 52–3
National Council for the Social Studies (NCSS)
   C3 framework, 8
   College, Career, and Civic Life (C3) Framework, 136
   Standards, 71–2
National Women's History Museum's study, 135
negro massacre, 62
Negro Republican Party, 10
Negro rule, 59
North American Review, 52–3
Norton, Charles Eliot, 52–3

O

obfuscation, 54–6
objective' systems of governmental control, 44
Ordeal of Reconstruction, The 128

P

passionate ethics, 45, 49
periodization, 34
Perry, Benjamin F., 59
Pew Research Center survey, 32
plantations, management, 21–2
political and civic powers, 41
political and economic events, 73–4, 87–90
political cartoons, 5, 93–110
   analysis, 94, 95
   in classroom, 94–8
   negative images of African Americans, 98–9
   pre-analysis, 94, 95
   and social opinions, 98
   source usage and perspectives, 96–8
political conciliation, 56
political, economic, and social forces, 5
political persuasions, 60

politicization, 54–6
postbellum politics, 59
post-reconstruction timeline, 87–90
practical freedom, 10–11
pre-reconstruction timeline, 73–4
process of memorialization, 173–85
Progressive Era (1920s), The, 120
Progressive Era textbooks, 120–2
Prostrate State (1874)., *The*, 97
public and political roles, 9
public memory, 173, 175, 176

Q

Quashee's Dream of Emancipation (1863), 99
Queen of Industry or, the New South, 105

R

racial brutality, 61
racial division and hierarchy in South, 39
racial progress
   and hope, 8–11
   teaching emancipation, 7–15
racial stereotype jokes, 100
racism, expressions, 61
racist progress
   reconstruction violence, 7–15
   and violence, 11–5
radical reconstruction, 58
Radical Republicans, 3, 52
reception, 180–1
reconciliation, 181–4
Reconstruction Amendments and laws, 191
Reconstruction: America's Unfinished Revolution, 1863–1877, 119
reconstruction era
   African Americans, 93–110
   timeline, political and economic events, 75–87

reconstruction teaching activities and lesson plans, 193–5
referent, 180–1
representations of reconstruction, 115–29
Resolution of Impeachment, A, 52
resources for teachers, 192–3
River Queen, 37
Robertson, Geoffrey, 41
Rodgers, Daniel T., 31, 32

S

Sandel, Michael J., 35
Scarlett O'Hara archetype, 17–26
Schweitzer, Albert, 34
Sectional Debate, 69–70
sectional systems of justice, 45
Sherman, William T., 8–9, 158
slavery and resisted emancipation, 17–26
sleeping giants, 38
Smith, Edward, 49
social anarchy, 60
social policy, 38
social realities, 45
social signaling, 44
social transformations, 115–29
social welfare agency, 157
Southern Poverty Law Center, 182
Stanton, Edwin M., 50, 55
Stephens, Alexander H., 43
Stoneman, George. Jr., 60
Susan Cornwall unpublished diary, 24–6
Swain, David Lowry, 40

T

Teitel, Ruti G., 42, 53
textbook representations of the, 115–29
 critical history and textbooks, 116–8
 findings, 120–6
 historiography of reconstruction, 118–9
 methodology, 119–20
"The hollow tooth," 178
Thomas, George H., 58
timeline tactics, 69–90
transitional justice, 41
transitional peace, 38
Tyler, John, 23–4
Tyler, Julia Gardiner, 23–4

U

Underwood, John C., 50
Union and Confederate war effort, 40
Union forces, 58
Union prisoners, 44
U.S. Colored Heavily Artillery, 60
Usher, John P., 55

V

voting rights, 10–11

W

Wade, Benjamin F., 55
Walzer, Michael, 33
Washington, Booker T., 159
White League, 103
White Women, slaveholding, 17–26
Whittlesey, Eliphalet, 162
women's suffrage movement
 debrief, inquire, and take informed action, 145–6, 152
 display findings from source analysis, 145, 151
 historical empathy pedagogies, 135–46
 primary source analysis, 143–5, 150
 secondary source analysis, 142–3, 149–50

Y

Young Men's Lyceum of Springfield, 37

Z

Zion's Herald and Wesleyan Journal, 58

Caroline R. Pryor, Erik B. Alexander, James M. Mitchell,
Whitney Blankenship, and
Michael E. Karpyn, and Jenice L. View
General Editors

In the United States, the Common Core Standards, the C3 Framework for Social Studies Standards (NCSS), and the 10 themes of the National Curriculum Standards (NCS/NCSS) each pose challenges for teachers preparing to teach skills, content, and critical issues of American history. The problem for many middle and secondary teachers is that textbooks do not contain sufficient primary source documents and varied secondary literature linked to these standards. The volumes in the Teaching Critical Themes in American History series fill this need by providing teachers with history content, pedagogical strategies, and teaching resources. The series is organized around key problems/issues in American history so that teachers can select which critical topics upon which they might want to concentrate.

Middle and Secondary pre- and in-service educators will find the books in this series essential for developing and implementing American history and social studies curriculum in diverse and complex classrooms. Teachers will find the books in this series valuable as they search for methodologies and material that will help them address the Common Core Standards in the social sciences and history. Community College history instructors can also find the books in this series helpful as supplementary texts in their U.S. history survey courses. The practical—not to mention exciting—implementation of perspectives offered in each title is a key feature of this series.

This series will address topics such as the formation of the American Republic, the problem of slavery in America, causes of the Civil War, emancipation and reconstruction, America's response to industrialization, the New Deal, the fight for Civil Rights, and more. The series editors invite proposals for edited volumes in American history and social studies, along with articles and lesson plans for both the topics above, and other topics of the series.

For additional information about this series or for the submission of manuscripts, please contact the following series editors:

Caroline R. Pryor capryor@siue.edu
James M. Mitchell james.mitchell@csueastbay.edu

To order other books in this series, please contact our Customer Service Department: peterlang@presswarehouse.com (within the U.S.) or orders@peterlang.com (outside the U.S.). You may also browse online by series at www.peterlang.com.

www.ingramcontent.com/pod-product-compliance
Lightning Source LLC
Chambersburg PA
CBHW061712300426
44115CB00014B/2658